Praise for *Key Coac*

CW00664699

'The most complete, impactful and practical coaching book written yet – Highly recommended!'

ROB BROUWER, CEO, JOBRAPIDO

'A well-structured guide packed with powerful, practical tips that really work in the real world. A great book for leaders or coaches alike.'

DEREK MCMANUS, COO, O2 UK

'A simple, yet sophisticated, coaching toolkit that cuts through coaching theory to give practical advice to coaches, leaders and managers. In today's complex world, coaching is a key activity essential for business and personal success – whether you are new to coaching or wish to extend your skills, this book is a gift.'

LIZ JEWER, HR DIRECTOR, TMP UK LIMITED

'A powerful source of inspiration with many unique, insightful and practical coaching models to enhance your personal and professional development.'

ANDREA BERTONE, EUROPEAN PRESIDENT, MONSTER.COM

'Whether you are a professional coach wanting to further develop your abilities, or a leader who needs to get the very best from his team, this is a first-rate toolkit from one of the world's top coaches.'

PHILIP ROWLEY, CHIEF FINANCIAL OFFICER,
SONY PICTURE ENTERTAINMENT

'Now you can have your own 24/7 personal coach full of practical hints, tips and wise advice.'

LYNN BROWN, EXECUTIVE DIRECTOR OF FINANCIAL SERVICES,
GLASGOW CITY COUNCIL

Key Coaching Models

PEARSON

At Pearson, we believe in learning – all kinds of learning for all kinds of people. Whether it's at home, in the classroom or in the workplace, learning is the key to improving our life chances.

That's why we're working with leading authors to bring you the latest thinking and best practices, so you can get better at the things that are important to you. You can learn on the page or on the move, and with content that's always crafted to help you understand quickly and apply what you've learned.

If you want to upgrade your personal skills or accelerate your career, become a more effective leader or more powerful communicator, discover new opportunities or simply find more inspiration, we can help you make progress in your work and life.

Every day our work helps learning flourish, and wherever learning flourishes, so do people.

To learn more, please visit us at www.pearson.com/uk

The Financial Times

With a worldwide network of highly respected journalists, *The Financial Times* provides global business news, insightful opinion and expert analysis of business, finance and politics. With over 500 journalists reporting from 50 countries worldwide, our in-depth coverage of international news is objectively reported and analysed from an independent, global perspective.

To find out more, visit www.ft.com

[STEPHEN GRIBBEN]

Key Coaching Models

The 70+ models every manager
and coach needs to know

PEARSON

Harlow, England • London • New York • Boston • San Francisco • Toronto • Sydney
Auckland • Singapore • Hong Kong • Tokyo • Seoul • Taipei • New Delhi
Cape Town • São Paulo • Mexico City • Madrid • Amsterdam • Munich • Paris • Milan

PEARSON EDUCATION LIMITED
Edinburgh Gate
Harlow CM20 2JE
United Kingdom
Tel: +44 (0)1279 623623
Web: www.pearson.com/uk

First edition published 2016 (print and electronic)

© Pearson Education Limited 2016 (print and electronic)

The right of Stephen Gribben to be identified as author of this work has been asserted by him in accordance with the Copyright, Designs and Patents Act 1988.

The print publication is protected by copyright. Prior to any prohibited reproduction, storage in a retrieval system, distribution or transmission in any form or by any means, electronic, mechanical, recording or otherwise, permission should be obtained from the publisher or, where applicable, a licence permitting restricted copying in the United Kingdom should be obtained from the Copyright Licensing Agency Ltd, Barnard's Inn, 86 Fetter Lane, London EC4A 1EN.

The ePublication is protected by copyright and must not be copied, reproduced, transferred, distributed, leased, licensed or publicly performed or used in any way except as specifically permitted in writing by the publisher, as allowed under the terms and conditions under which it was purchased, or as strictly permitted by applicable copyright law. Any unauthorised distribution or use of this text may be a direct infringement of the author's and the publisher's rights and those responsible may be liable in law accordingly.

Pearson Education is not responsible for the content of third-party internet sites.

ISBN: 978-1-292-15190-8 (print)
        978-1-292-15191-5 (PDF)
        978-1-292-15192-2 (ePub)

British Library Cataloguing-in-Publication Data
A catalogue record for the print edition is available from the British Library

Library of Congress Cataloging-in-Publication Data
A catalog record for the print edition is available from the Library of Congress

10 9 8 7 6 5 4 3 2 1
20 19 18 17 16

Print edition typeset in 9.25 pt, Helvetica Neue LT W1G font by SPi Global
Printed in Great Britain by Ashford Colour Press Ltd., Gosport, Hampshire

NOTE THAT ANY PAGE CROSS REFERENCES REFER TO THE PRINT EDITION

Contents

About the author

This book is not a collection of theory, neither is it just commentary on a topic that is written from the sidelines of a distant keyboard. Since 1998 I have been a dedicated and professional executive coach delivering more than 25,000 hours of coaching sessions around the world; the hours, the travel and the number of clients and new content continue to extend each day. Professional coaching is what I do.

Although I remain fascinated by all things 'coaching', this has never been just a hobby or topic of interest for me; it has always been about building a successful business and career that required me to focus on and deliver results with a genuine passion and drive.

As an executive coach I have worked with CEOs and senior executives from some of the largest and most successful companies across many industries and sectors, establishing long-term relationships and a strong reputation based upon impact and results. This approach has been the catalyst for me to create practical models, tools and techniques that enable my clients to achieve great results, and for me to research and adapt for coaching the very best concepts and methods from the world of development, performance and business growth.

As with all my clients, I have presented this book as a means of making the science and psychology of coaching practical and accessible so that their benefits can be quickly and easily attained. This proven selection of 72 coaching models enables you to coach, manage and lead individuals, teams and organisations to achieve greater results and outcomes in whichever situation they wish to apply.

Contact me or find out more at:

http://www.stephengribben.co.uk

Introduction

There is no other approach to personal or professional development that produces greater and more sustainable benefits and results than coaching. For any coach, leader or manager, this book presents a unique collection of original and adapted models, tools and techniques that have enhanced the growth, performance and delivery of individuals, teams and organisations around the world. This easy-to-use, practical and high-impact selection provides you with the toolkit to develop and realise the potential in yourself, in those around you and in every situation you deal with.

Why coaching?

The very best leaders and managers in today's complex and competitive world continue to build and develop strategies and behaviours to ensure that success always remains an option; this is where coaching comes in. To be able to coach is to be able to help individuals, teams and organisations to realise and fulfil their potential and reach their desired goals.

Professional coaching brings many valuable benefits: fresh perspectives, enhanced decision-making skills, greater interpersonal effectiveness, and increased confidence. The results from individuals, teams and organisations being coached are many and varied, but are appreciated most in terms of improvements in productivity, satisfaction and the attainment of relevant goals.

Independent studies conducted by PricewaterhouseCoopers (2013 ICF Organisational Study) confirmed that improvements in work performance (70 per cent), business management (61 per cent), time management (57 per cent) and team effectiveness (51 per cent) could be directly attributed to the impact of professional coaching.

The same research conducted for the International Coaching Federation also attributed improvements in self-confidence (80 per cent), relationships (73 per cent), communication (72 per cent) and work/life balance (67 per cent) to professional coaching.

This research also discovered that professional coaching had become a highly valued approach to growth and development in terms of individuals, teams and organisations with scores collated on positive return on investment (86 per cent), overall satisfaction (99 per cent) and continuation of process (96 per cent).

Why you?

Whether you are a manager, leader or coach, this book provides you with a proven toolkit and a step-by-step guide to becoming the coach that you can be and making a sustained difference. With the practical and illustrated models you will have the confidence and conviction to influence performance with the individuals, teams and organisations you engage with.

This collection of proven methods and approaches will enable you to develop your ability to coach and integrate this into your role as a manager or leader.

You will find that most, if not all, concepts in this book will immediately resonate with you and will help you connect with your inner coach that has always encouraged you to ask the right questions, listen attentively and provide relevant direction.

Why now?

As a manager or a leader, you are expected to be able to coach to a professional standard. Coaching is now an essential part of your toolkit and it is seen as an important activity for business and career success. The days of telling people to do things are no longer relevant; the days of seeing training as the only solution have diminished as people have become better informed.

Whether competing for talent or operating in turbulent markets and conditions, retaining your best people and clients, or aiming to build the teams, products and services that will give you clear competitive advantage, your success will largely depend on your ability to coach.

And, for your own growth, development, learning and satisfaction, this is something you can benefit from right now. I can wholeheartedly vouch for it.

Structure of the book

This book is designed to cover the *six competencies of success* to be developed through coaching so that you can select the specific competency that has the greatest impact and opportunity for your client.

In each of these sections you are introduced to the *24 specific development areas* that sit within each competency of success so that you can focus on a particular behaviour, approach or capability for your client to work on.

For each specific area of development you are then offered *three proven coaching models* with a *step-by-step guide* that can be applied individually or collectively in your coaching sessions and conversations with your client. These models are each illustrated to accelerate learning and to make sharing and communication with your client easier and more effective.

Effectively, as a reference book or coaching toolkit, this book will give you 72 proven, easy-to-use and categorised coaching models designed to enhance and improve the performance of individuals, teams and organisations. In addition, there are not only helpful quotes and lists included for each model, but also *coaching tips* based upon more than 25,000 hours of professional coaching experience. This comprehensive set of coaching models is organised and presented in six key development areas:

- Part One: Developing the management core
- Part Two: Developing the leadership core

- Part Three: Results-driven coaching
- Part Four: Coaching for greater influence
- Part Five: Leadership coaching
- Part Six: High-performance coaching

PART ONE

Developing the management core

Awareness: The ability to recognise and understand personal moods, emotions and drives, and their effect on others.

Awareness is the first of the six key areas of development for individuals, teams and organisations. Individuals with high awareness are able to manage and channel energies and emotions with confidence and assurance so that successful results can be achieved. Teams with strong self-awareness work to their strengths and stay focused on their purpose; these teams stay strong through adversity, remain committed to their cause and have a collective resilience that delivers exceptional results. Self-aware organisations know how to get the most out of who they are and what they do. These organisations have a clarity and confidence in their products, services and people that guide their strategies and plans beyond just market trends.

Awareness, and self-awareness, are described in the Daniel Goleman model of emotional intelligence as the first trait, and are understood by many as being the core building block for the next four components of emotional intelligence: self-regulation, internal motivation, empathy and social skills. Daniel Goleman is an internationally renowned psychologist, science journalist and author of the bestseller *Emotional Intelligence*. This understanding is built upon the premise that when you are more aware you will manage and motivate better, and manage relationships better. This would explain why awareness, and self-awareness, are considered to be the foundation for all the key development areas that follow.

As a coach, to develop greater awareness and self-awareness in individuals, teams and organisations is to help establish and maintain the cornerstone upon which their success will be built. This is also true for the coach, as a highly aware, and self-aware coach will be able to understand how to get the best out of people and situations. We cannot communicate with others to a higher level than we communicate within ourselves; we cannot understand others to a higher level than we understand ourselves; we cannot connect with others to a higher level than we are connected within ourselves. To communicate, understand and connect with others, we must first develop the level of awareness and self-awareness that enables us to be clear on what is possible for any individual.

In this part we present awareness as the combination of these three key elements:

This selection of coaching models has been specifically designed to help develop a higher level of awareness.

Emotional management (emotional awareness)

1

[
Emotional awareness: Knowing when feelings are present and being able to label these feelings with specific feeling words, and at the highest level being able to predict and influence emotions in advance.
]

Coaching and developing greater emotional awareness in individuals enables and empowers them to have the opportunity to manage, channel and ultimately master their emotional energy towards the outcomes that they desire most. With high emotional awareness, the full power of emotion can be managed, selected and driven towards the achievement of results and goals.

People with low emotional awareness will find most of their energy used up in trying to fight, suppress or deny their emotions and will often be labelled as 'over-emotional' or 'immature', or as someone who struggles with pressure.

These benefits extend into the coaching and development of teams where the power of emotions can clearly inspire high performance or pull people apart very quickly. Teams with high emotional awareness develop an understanding and context for why people feel such emotions and respond accordingly to keep the focus on significant and common goals. High-performing teams do not have the emotions of others as a barrier to success; they channel these emotions as a driver for achieving great things.

A team that lacks emotional awareness, however, will fail to predict the emotional responses of others and will be caught up in the judgement of how people do, or should, feel. Their inability to adapt their message to influence emotion means that they will either drive powerful but conflicting emotions across their team, or encourage the suppression of emotions that do not immediately appear helpful.

Furthermore, the impact of high emotional awareness on the success of an organisation can be significant in terms of the culture and ethos of that organisation and its ability to encourage innovation, creativity and ambition. Organisations with low emotional awareness are more likely to suffer from avoidable conflict, silos and attrition.

As a coach, emotional awareness is one of the three fundamental areas of development along with accurate assessment and confidence. With a higher level of emotional awareness, an individual, team or organisation can develop the ability to manage their emotion so that their intelligence can take the lead. By doing so, they can then supercharge what they want to do with the support and drive of all their emotional power. With lower emotional awareness, that same power will only lead their thoughts and actions towards emotional outcomes, with the power of their intelligence rationalising why they are entitled to feel how they feel. There is nothing more empowering than having a great sense of emotional awareness to realise all that you are truly capable of, as a coach, as an individual, as a team or as an organisation.

Model 1. The EI model

The big picture

EI (Emotional Intelligence) is the oil in the engine of personal, professional and organisational development. This cornerstone of behaviour affects how individuals, teams and organisations manage and channel their feelings to think, communicate, react, behave and perform. If they are not able to drive their emotions with their intelligence, they will be emotionally driven and lose their sense of intelligent perspective and logical thought. EI can be learned and developed, and, with a high level of EI, they will be empowered to achieve their genuinely desired outcomes.

The EI model illustrates the importance of being able to choose the *right* emotion, to the *right* degree, to enable an individual, team or organisation to deal with any situation in a way that takes them to the outcome they desire. In doing so, they will then influence others to go there too. This model makes clear the crucial relationship between the scale of their emotions and their outcomes so that managing their emotions becomes clearer and simpler.

This model was inspired and designed in response to the book *Emotional Intelligence,* by Daniel Goleman. EI is one of the most common and valuable attributes of those who can be considered to be truly successful in all that they do.

Figure 1.1 The EI model

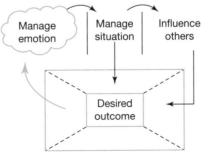

Developing a higher level of EI where there is greater emotional self-awareness opens up a world of opportunity to achieve all that an individual, team or organisation really wants to be, to have or to do.

When applied to various scenarios, the EI model as a coaching tool is a genuine game changer in terms of viewing, managing and transforming situations through greater emotional self-awareness.

When to use it

- As a powerful model for when emotions are, or could be, running high.
- As a management model for forthcoming situations where emotions are likely to run high.
- As a leadership model to influence specific situations beyond the existing emotional state to achieve a more productive and optimal outcome.

How to use it

EI has long been hailed as 'the best predictor of success in life' (*Time Magazine,* 2 October 1995) and it is widely accepted, even by sceptics, as a skill that helps predict and achieve important life outcomes. Emotional intelligence is the ability to identify and manage emotion in ourselves, and then in others, to get to a desired outcome. It can be learned and developed – and it is something that everyone already has.

Understanding how the brain works helps develop greater EI as the emotions kick in a split second before the intelligence arrives, so how someone feels (excited, scared, confident, nervous) will come in first, and then their intelligence will arrive to explain and justify why they feel the way they feel. EI is the ability to hold the initial emotional reaction for that split second so that the intelligence can get in there first to make a considered decision or choice, and then be driven and supported by the emotions (drive, passion, determination, resilience, calmness). This is how emotionally intelligent decisions and choices are made to get to desired outcomes.

The first stage of EI is the ability to *manage emotions.* This is not to attempt to suppress or reduce the emotion, but to manage it by selecting the right emotion, to the right degree, that is appropriate for the situation, to get the desired outcome. Thus, in an emergency situation, an individual, team or organisation may choose to remain calm to get to the outcome they really want, otherwise they may just panic or freeze through fear. This is also not to deny or resist their emotions, as these feelings are what bring them to life and give meaning to what they do; managing their emotions enables them to choose the emotion that they believe will work best for them and to channel it towards the result they want most.

The next stage is to *manage situations* by applying the emotion(s) they have selected to the degree that they believe is best for that situation to get to the outcome they desire. In an emergency situation, they may choose to be calm, but only to the degree that there is still a sense of urgency and purpose to get to the outcome they really want rather than being so calm that they become too relaxed or complacent.

The next stage of the process is to *influence others* and this is a natural consequence of how well they have managed their own emotions and how well they have managed the situation. If they have remained calm but focused, then those around them will have been influenced to do the same. If, however, they have panicked, others will also be influenced by this and be more likely to panic also. Importantly, if they have managed the situation towards a clear and specific outcome, they will have influenced others to aim for that same result.

Having *clear and desired outcomes* is a key component in EI. Firstly, knowing the result they really want to achieve gives individuals, teams and organisations focus, a sense of direction, something to aim for. Secondly, a clear outcome to achieve offers them a healthy perspective for their emotions and gives them the chance to manage emotions effectively. The comparison between emotions and the desired outcome is genuinely a case where size matters, because, when the outcome they want to achieve is much bigger than the emotions they bring to the situation, they will then remain objective and considered in their thinking. However, when the outcome is smaller than the amount of emotions they bring, they will be emotional and irrational in their approach. This is why they can appear to 'sweat the small stuff' but are 'strong in a crisis'.

For ongoing success and development it is important to *create the bigger picture view* for their desired outcomes, because, over time, what used to be a big achievement will become their norm. When this happens, the size of their outcome gets smaller and thus they run the risk of their emotions becoming more dominant. The approach here is not to try and pretend that the outcome is bigger than they know it now is, but to see the outcome for the size that it is and also within the bigger picture or in the context of a longer term view.

An *emotionally intelligent business* is able to manage all the highs and lows, success and learning, great results and valuable experiences in a way that drives everyone towards achieving great outcomes. These businesses do not panic or get over-excited; they do not get too anxious and they are never complacent because they have a big picture view that is greater than any situation or milestone on their journey.

Coaching tips

The EI model is a fantastic cornerstone for coaching. It is a great model to introduce first, as you will be able to refer back to it in almost every scenario and conversation from then on. Your credibility as a coach depends a lot on being able to demonstrate that you also take on the concepts you are sharing, so putting this model into practice is key, and of course beneficial.

In most coaching situations, emotions are initially seen as something to be suppressed or avoided, mainly because they are perceived as getting in the way. It is true that there are many emotions that are not helpful at times, or are too much or too little for what needs to be delivered or reached. However, emotions are hugely important, and are vital in achieving outcomes of value when they are the right emotions, to the right degree, to get the desired result. Managing them is not about suppressing them, and it is important always to make this clear. The suppression of emotion is a high-cost strategy. In the short term, these emotions will spill into areas that are inappropriate. In the long term, suppressed emotions become destructive internally and externally. Emotions are vital; they just need to be managed. (See **Model 10: The five steps to manage emotions model.**)

> *Emotional intelligence, more than any other factor, more than IQ or expertise, accounts for 85 per cent to 90 per cent of success at work . . . IQ is a threshold competence. You need it, but it doesn't make you a star. Emotional intelligence can.*
>
> *Warren Bennis*

Top 10 reasons why people with high emotional intelligence succeed

1   They have more energy.

2   They have greater focus.

3   They know how to channel their creativity.

4   They want to solve problems and issues.

5   They are happy to take risks.

6   They multitask really well.

7   They do not give up easily.

8   They are energised by support and encouragement.

9   They are sensitive and they care.

10   They enjoy what they do and have fun doing it!

Model 2. The feel–think–react model

The big picture

The highest levels of emotional management can only be achieved with a strong understanding and appreciation of how emotions can drive, influence and impact on behaviours and reactions. It is a common failing to over-estimate the value in being *right* on a thinking level and, in doing so, under-estimate the power and influence of the emotions and feelings that are then created. Yet, it will be the feelings that determine what is believed or understood, and these perceptions will then result in driving a particular reaction. (See **Model 1: The EI model.**)

Successful results are achieved by being able to influence desired outcomes. Understanding and being aware of how emotions impact on thoughts and then influence actions and reactions enable an individual, team or organisation to remain in control, with choice, and with the opportunity to influence those outcomes positively.

The feel–think–react model illustrates clearly the process and order of how feelings impact on what is thought to be happening, or has been said or done, and then on the reactions that follow as a result. Everyone *feels* first, then they *think* and then they *react* accordingly. To get the ideal reaction, individuals, teams and organisations must consider the feelings and emotions that would be necessary to take on board what is being said or done in a way that would allow their ideal reaction to occur. Their feelings will be the biggest driver of their actions and reactions; if their feelings are aligned to their ideal reaction, then they will respond and act accordingly. If their feelings are not aligned to their ideal reaction, they will respond otherwise.

This model was developed in response to the many coaching scenarios that arose from a negative, disruptive or unexpected reaction to feedback, a proposition or a situation. This was almost always due to the message being conveyed without an understanding and appreciation of the feelings that were generated, or already in place. This model empowers individuals, teams and organisations to manage how they are feeling so that they can react in the best possible way to any feedback, proposition or situation. Furthermore, the model enables them to develop their communication to influence and support others so that personal feelings are aligned with providing the best possible reaction to what they are saying or proposing.

The most common approach to an unexpected reaction is to repeat the 'what' and 'why' something has been said or proposed. Applying this model, whether with an individual, a team or across an organisation, shows that the value and drive of the reaction has less to do with the thinking and rationale, and more to do with the 'how' people have been made to feel in the process. Everyone will eventually get their heads around what has happened and eventually settle upon a 'why' something has happened; but the 'how' something has been said or done will always linger longest, whether positive or negative. (See also **Model 50: The what, why and how model.**)

As a coach, you will find that when someone feels confident, secure, respected and valued, they will see criticism and feedback as a valuable opportunity to learn, improve and grow; their reaction can then be positive and constructive. You will also find that when someone is feeling low on confidence, insecure, under-valued and ignored, they will see the same criticism and feedback as being unfair, as a personal attack and as another reminder that they are not good enough; their reaction can then be negative and destructive. Understanding the feel–think–react model enables

Figure 1.2 The feel–think–react model

you to coach with care, compassion and responsibility, and without compromise or avoidance.

When to use it

- To make sense of reactions and responses.
- As a management approach to anticipate, and be ready to deal with, the likely reactions and responses of others.
- As a leadership model to determine the ideal reaction that is desired, and then work your way back to how the audience needs to feel in order to give the optimal response.

How to use it

Emotional awareness is a key component of success as this enables individuals, teams and organisations to understand their emotional reactions, and the reactions of others, to achieve greater results and outcomes. The first stage is to understand the order of how emotions work. Feelings arrive first and, depending on those feelings, thoughts will form in accordance with those feelings. The result is that there will be a reaction to what is thought to have happened or has been said, and this will be driven by those initial feelings. If someone is feeling confident, they are more likely to think that a situation is an opportunity and then react accordingly. However, if they are feeling under threat, they are more likely to think that the same situation actually represents something to be concerned about, and again they will react accordingly.

As *feelings* are the drivers of thoughts and then the subsequent reactions, it is important to be aware of how those feelings can work for and not against the desired results. At this stage of the process it is necessary to understand how those feelings about *oneself* (more than the feelings about a *situation*) form the basis of thoughts and actions. Being aware and honest about those feelings allows the thoughts and actions to be put into context and understood. (See also **Model 10: The five steps to manage emotions model.**)

Thoughts are a symptom of how an individual, team or organisation feels, because when they feel positive they will see things more positively; however, if they are feeling a bit down they will naturally view the world more negatively. Emotional awareness enables people to go beyond the inner concerns and criticisms of their negative thoughts as their thoughts have been perfectly designed by how they feel about themselves. If they want those thoughts to improve, then all they need to do is to feel better about themselves. Their feelings are the cause; their thoughts are a symptom. If they fight the symptom but do not deal with the cause, the symptoms will only reappear. It is better to deal with the cause so that the symptoms change for good. (See also **Model 7: The confidence v self-confidence model.**)

Reactions are ultimately the consequence of how an individual, team or organisation feels about themselves as these emotions have driven their thoughts and view of the world to which they are now reacting. Emotional awareness enables them to make sense of their thoughts and reactions so that they do not need to remain concerned or confused by them. They are only reacting to what they think has happened or has been said, and this has been affected by how they feel about themselves. If they want to react in a way that works better for them and helps them achieve successful outcomes, they should go back to how they feel and put in the work there to feel better first; their improved thoughts and reactions will then follow.

Success will be achieved when they begin with the end in mind (see also **Model 31: The end in mind thinking model**), so here we look at how to achieve *ideal results*. There are three stages: define the 'ideal' reaction; identify the influential emotions; and impact on others.

Firstly, define what the ideal reaction would be and do not settle for anything less – this is about getting the *ideal* reaction. By defining what the ideal looks like, there is now something to focus on and this alone will set them ahead of most others in terms of achieving successful outcomes.

Secondly, look to *influence emotions* by considering how someone would need to feel to be able to deliver that ideal reaction. So if the ideal reaction were to 'commit' or 'engage' or 'go for it', or 'be grateful' for the opportunity, how would they need to feel to be able to react in this way? It may be that they would need to feel secure, confident, appreciated, strong, cared for, listened to, or it may be that they would need to feel considered, part of something, supported or recognised. Emotions can be influenced by connecting with all the things that someone has within and around them that can reinforce the feelings that they will now need to deliver this ideal reaction: the things that give them feelings of security, confidence and strength; the things that remind them that they are appreciated, cared for, listened to, etc.

Being able to have an *impact on others* is a significant amplifier of success as the greatest results are rarely achieved in isolation. People's reactions are driven by how they think and view their world, and how they think is designed by how they feel about themselves. To obtain great outcomes from others, individuals, teams and organisations must first know what their ideal reaction from others would be. (It is important not to sell the other person short here. We are all capable of amazing things!) With a clear definition of 'ideal', they need to consider how a person would need to feel to be able to give them that ideal reaction. Consider how the other person would need to feel, not how they themselves would need to feel, or how they think others *should* need to feel, and connect with how that person *would* need to feel. The same principles apply when they are looking to influence groups and larger audiences.

For maximum *business* impact it is important to be clear about the ideal reaction organisations are looking for from their clients, employees, colleagues, investors, partners, etc. Thus, they will know what they want their message to be, but the driver of getting what they want will come from meeting the emotional needs of that audience so that others can then react as desired. If the communication makes their audience feel engaged, important, valued, listened to and capable, they will be better equipped to meet the highest expectations.

Coaching tips

Your credibility as a coach relies heavily on your ability to demonstrate that you personally understand the tools and techniques you use and share. It is important therefore that, as the coach, you are clear on the ideal reaction you are looking for – clear on what you want to communicate and clear on how you need to communicate to ensure that your clients feel how they need to feel to give the desired reaction.

You will also have to consider that although most people will want to feel mainly *positive* about themselves, such as being confident, secure or cared for, to react in the way you desire, other people may at times require more *negative* feelings, such as being at risk, or being left behind or even under threat, to get the desired reaction. Always remember, however, that you are aiming for positive feelings and only need to sprinkle a negative emotion when you are sure it is required.

Top 10 positive emotions and feelings

1 **Praised.**
2 **Appreciated.**
3 **Considered.**
4 **Respected.**
5 **Believed in.**
6 **Interested in.**
7 **Loved/cared for.**
8 **Acknowledged.**
9 **Listened to.**
10 **Part of something.**

The more we witness our emotional reactions and understand how they work, the easier it is to refrain.

Pema Chodron

Model 3. The men v women model

The big picture

The most effective strategies of emotional management differ from women to men in respect of their individual emotional drivers. Although each gender has a range of issues that will cause them to become 'emotional', there is a primary emotional driver that accounts for their highest levels of emotion and is the cause of their

Figure 1.3 The men v women model

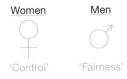

emotionally driven behaviour. When the primary emotional driver is understood, it can be managed effectively, to ensure a more logical response and thought process.

This model is designed to make clear the primary emotional driver for each gender and provide insight into the most effective ways to manage, connect, communicate and influence the men and women you coach or work with.

The model was developed in response to the many coaching scenarios where the emotional reaction of men when they saw something as being 'unfair' affected their thoughts and reactions, as did the emotional reaction of women when they believed that their control and choice was being taken from them. In this heightened emotional state, intelligence was swamped and their perspective, consideration and composure was lost, causing further emotional reaction and reducing the chances of achieving a positive outcome. This model illustrates these drivers as part of a natural process and, in doing so, allows a more objective view of the primary emotional drivers of men and women to be obtained. From this, strategies and approaches can be created to ensure that men and women can manage these emotions and allow their intelligence to drive their desired outcomes. The instructions on how to use this model make clear the importance to men that there is a fair process and that women respond best when they get to make decisions.

Often when there is an emotionally negative reaction from someone, it is assumed that this is centred on the 'what' and the 'why'. This model explains that this kind of reaction is driven more by the 'how' as this will determine whether men believe that something is fair or not, and whether women feel in more, or less, control. (See also **Model 50: The what, why and how model.**)

As a coach, you will learn never to back men into a corner and to ensure that you always leave space for women to make up their own mind so that they engage with you on a more intelligent than emotional level. With this ability you will be able to connect, communicate and influence to a level that is of great value regardless of gender. Of course, you will also develop a deeper understanding and appreciation of what you need in terms of either fairness or control.

When to use it

- To gain or to provide context for emotional reactions.
- To manage communication and avoid the emotional pitfalls.
- To influence the ideal response through inclusive, emotionally intelligent communication.

All individuals have a range of *emotional drivers* that cause them to think and view their world in a way that leads them to react accordingly. Although each individual will have a number of drivers, these drivers are not all equal. Everyone will have one emotional driver that dominates; one that is more than 50 per cent of their emotional drive; one that needs to be satisfied if they are to remain logical and rational in their approach. This driver is key to their level of emotional intelligence because, when it is not satisfied, it causes their emotions to spiral up or swamp their intelligence, and only when they have the time to calm down and their emotion subsides will their intelligence get to the front of their thinking. Understanding the dominant emotional drivers enables them to better manage their emotions and the emotions of others. (See also **Model 2: The feel–think–react model.**)

Teams and organisations are likely to be made up of a mix of genders, so an inclusive approach that covers both fairness and control needs to be applied for the best results.

The dominant driver of *emotional men* is 'fairness and justice'. This is not the only emotional driver of men, but it is dominant. It is clearly played out when men talk back or confront, on the basis of 'That's not fair!' A man will go along with a decision that he did not want, as long as there has been a fair process to get there, whereas he will feel discomfort in getting the decision he wanted if he feels it was achieved unfairly. When a man feels that something is unfair, his emotions spiral and he becomes emotional and irrational; only when he has calmed down, or found fairness or justification, will his emotions subside to allow intelligence to kick back in.

The dominant driver of *emotional women* is control. This is not the only emotional driver that women have, but it is dominant. It is clearly played out when women talk back or confront. Rather than on the basis of 'That's not fair', it will be on the basis of 'How come you get to decide?' A woman will go against what she wanted to happen if she feels that she was not in control of the decision and she will sometimes change her mind because she can, in order to feel more in control. When a woman does not feel in sufficient control, her emotions spiral above her intelligence and she becomes emotional and irrational; only when she has calmed down, or found sufficient control, will her emotions subside to allow intelligence to kick back in.

Knowing yourself in terms of your emotional drivers allows you to understand yourself and others better, to influence and communicate better to achieve greater results. If you are female, your dominant emotional driver is control; if you are male, it is about fairness. These emotional drivers are best accepted and worked with, rather than fought against or denied if you want to achieve success. When women feel in sufficient control and are focused on the elements and components that they are in control of, and when men feel that the process, conditions or outcomes are fair, then both are at their most intelligent, most considered and most likely to achieve the results they really want.

To apply these principles to foster *successful relationships*, consider the range of permutations between men and women:

- Men with men leads to successful and positive relationships when they both respect fairness and learn to do 'deals' with each other.

- Men with women lead to productive and rewarding relationships for both when men believe it is fair for the women to feel in control as long as they are happy.
- Women with women tend to have to work a little harder and longer to develop good relationships, because initially they may compete with each other for complete control before they work out the elements that are most important to them and the ones that they are happy not to be in control of.
- To create a successful male relationship that is built upon intelligent consideration it is important to explain and demonstrate fairness. The worst thing you can do is to back a man into a corner.
- To create a successful female relationship that is built upon intelligent consideration it is important to emphasise and make clear that the woman is in control of her own choices. The worst thing you can do is to take away a woman's choice.

To ensure the delivery of *inclusive communication* to groups or mixed company it is important to emphasise both fairness and control as this combination will allow the audience to satisfy its dominant emotional driver and so be able to listen, consider and engage with the message with greater intelligence and less emotional distraction.

Coaching tips

The concept of primary emotional drivers is fundamental to the coaching relationship and immediately provides a baseline for connection and empathy; the primary emotional driver will always remain. With this level of understanding you will appreciate how best to position and communicate positively and effectively.

While men are typically comfortable with their primary emotional driver of fairness, you will find that women may resist when told what their primary emotional driver is, which only serves as confirmation, but it is best to hand it over and ask that they consider it and make up their own mind.

Signs to look for

- When in a negative emotional spiral, men (fairness) will respond either by lashing out unfairly in the belief that 'it has been done to me, so it is now fair that I retaliate', or by going to the other extreme and become 'bullied'.
- When in a negative emotional spiral, women (control) will respond either by trying to control everything, or by handing over all control and becoming a 'victim'. Some women will change their minds just to show that they can, or even withdraw completely to regain a feeling of control.

The emotional awareness scale

1 Physical sensations.
2 Action tendencies.
3 Single emotions.
4 Blends of emotion.
5 Blends of blends of emotion.

Take control of your consistent emotions to consciously and deliberately reshape your daily experience of life.

Anthony Robbins

2 Individual management (accurate assessment)

[
Accurate assessment: Recognising what someone is good at, what they could be better at; their areas of unique value and their limitations.
]

Coaching and developing greater individual management in individuals provides them with an increased ability to get the very best out of themselves by understanding who they are and what they are really capable of. With strong personal management in terms of strengths, attributes and key drivers, optimal outcomes can be achieved in a way that works best with, and for, the individual.

People with a low or inaccurate assessment will find that they are expending energy in ways and areas that work against more than for them, and even when they force success in this way, their outcomes and results can be limited, unsustainable and unfulfilling.

The benefits of accurate assessment are as relevant when coaching teams in that teams can build confidence and play to their strengths rather than be restricted by their weaknesses or use energy into developing areas for the sake of doing so. Teams with an accurate assessment are able to build strategies and plans that get the best out of all the talent and resources they have available; they know how to compete and win.

Teams that lack an accurate assessment focus more on their perceived 'gaps' and 'weaknesses', getting caught up in reacting to situations and events as they try to do, and be, all the things that everyone else can; they lack identity and strategy.

Furthermore, when an organisation develops an accurate assessment it is far more aware of how best to navigate the key decisions, choices and strategies when aiming to grow and succeed, since these will be based upon its deeper understanding of what works best for the organisation and not upon what seems to work for others.

As a coach, having an accurate assessment is fundamental to your own development; it is vital for your credibility and authority to coach others. From that solid base you can help to develop individuals, teams and organisations to a level of accurate assessment that opens up their ability to achieve all that they want to achieve while remaining true to who they are. Through this process, they will also be quicker and more ready to identify, engage and collaborate with those individuals, teams and organisations who can add their complementary value and resources.

Model 4. The happiness model

The big picture

For many people the pursuit of happiness is about chasing outcomes that are external: the house, the car, the money, the security, the lifestyle, the time, etc. In this area of individual management we look at happiness in terms of the journey, not just in terms of the destination. Many coaches learn to appreciate that when good results and outcomes are achieved in a way that makes people happy throughout the process, they will be inspired and motivated to go on and achieve even more. However, when the journey is negative it can diminish the value of the achievement and pose a significant block to going again.

This model is designed to offer an objective view of what makes people happy, stressed or bored to varying degrees, and the role that confidence and challenge play. The model illustrates the concept of being happy beyond reliance upon other things happening, or other people doing things, and that happiness comes as part of a gift that is given or found. This shows that happiness is internal – it can be built, and it can be managed.

The model was developed and adapted for use in coaching as a response to the many scenarios that involved stress, boredom or the search to be happier. As with all the most effective coaching models, this model allows us to understand the component parts of being happy and the relationship between them. Illustrating happiness in this way enables a more objective view of what is for most people an emotional and intangible topic. In terms of individual management, this concept enables you to create the dynamic of confidence and challenge that works best for each individual, each team and each organisation. This freedom empowers you to move from what *should* make you happy to what *does* make you happy.

Too often happiness is perceived as an externally driven feeling, yet using this as a development model we can look to coach happiness by increasing confidence and creating the appropriate level of challenge for individuals. When it is understood how to achieve happiness, there can be far greater individual management.

For individuals, this helps them to avoid or manage their levels of stress by increasing their levels of confidence. This can also help them to avoid feeling bored or stale by creating and developing an increased level of challenge and value in what they do. The healthy perspective of getting the right balance between confidence and challenge enables people to make the adjustments required to be happy, and happy people always achieve more! Without happiness, they will continue to battle against periods of boredom and the effects of stress.

Figure 2.1 The happiness model

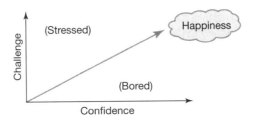

For teams and organisations, they can work to create optimal environments for all projects, initiatives and endeavours so that all those involved will be happy to achieve more. Without this appreciation of what creates happiness, they are more likely to suffer the consequences of highly stressed teams or the apathy of bored teams that lack energy or creativity.

As a coach, you will learn to achieve an optimal balance of confidence and challenge in your coaching so that you enjoy, appreciate and value your work to the full. From this position you will be able to support, challenge and influence individuals, teams and organisations to create the optimal dynamics of confidence and challenge that constitute happiness, drive, creativity and enhanced performance.

When to use it

- To gain or to provide a specific context for happiness, stress or boredom.
- To manage or adjust the specific levels of confidence and challenge required to achieve happiness.
- To influence and develop the levels of confidence and meaning in order that higher levels of happiness can be realised.

How to use it

The first component of happiness is *confidence* – the measure of how well an individual, team or organisation understands and believes in what they are good at, what they can be counted on to do and the contribution they can make. This also impacts on the strength of their connection to who they are, their values and their core beliefs. (See also **Model 7: The confidence v self-confidence model** and **Model 14: The identity decisions model.**)

The second component of happiness is *challenge* – the measure of satisfaction, meaning and sense of achievement they gain from what they are doing.

Happiness comes from the ability to *get the right balance* between their level of confidence and challenge. When their confidence is high, they will need an equal measure of challenge to be happy. When they are being highly challenged, their confidence will need to be just as great for them to be happy.

If the level of challenge they face is greater than their level of confidence, they will suffer from stress. *Avoid the stress* by encouraging them to look at ways to make things easier or simpler (reducing the level of challenge) or by reminding them about what they are good at (increasing their level of confidence).

If the level of challenge they face is less than their level of confidence, they will suffer from boredom. *Avoid the boredom* by encouraging them to look at different ways of doing what they do, so as to increase the level of challenge. This could be by testing themselves to do things better, faster, smarter, or by adding additional components to their tasks, etc.

Sustained happiness requires an individual, team or organisation to *protect their confidence* at all times. When their level of challenge is low, do not encourage them to reduce their level of confidence to match; it is always more constructive to look at ways of increasing the challenge!

Coaching tips

It is likely that you will work with as many stressed and anxious people as you will with those who are bored or fed up. It is important that you are able to focus on both the need to develop greater self-confidence and the ability to create greater meaning in what needs to be done, or could be done.

Your focus as a coach to help develop the concept of 'happiness' could be on any one, or any combination, of the following:

- *The what:* This means exploring what would help to improve their confidence, or what would increase the challenge in what they currently do. It also means that they would explore changing what they do to align better with what they are more confident at or enjoy more (always linked).

- *The why:* This means exploring why they do what they currently do and if this can be aligned to a bigger outcome or develop a greater meaning and value. It also means looking at why doing what they do demonstrates their capabilities, strengths and impact in a way that reconnects them with the abilities that they now take for granted, and so increases their confidence.

- *The how:* This means exploring how they do what they do in a way that would increase the challenge and meaning, and shows what they are capable of in order to improve their self-confidence.

Points to consider

- Some people have been stressed or bored for so long a time that this is now their current comfort zone, thus being unhappy is a state that they have become accustomed to. Be patient, considerate and compassionate, but remain determined for them.

- Some people mix their happiness and contentment together to create a state that they can live with. Although not mutually exclusive, there are two distinct places to be in: these people need not be in competition with each other; neither does there need to be a trade-off. This model is designed to help assess and develop the level of happiness. The best question to distinguish between contentment and happiness is to ask, 'How would you feel about this in another 10 years?'

The four levels of happiness

1 **Pleasure (immediate).**
2 **Achievement (short term).**
3 **Contribution (long term).**
4 **Ultimate good (enduring).**

Be happy . . . not because everything is good, but because you can see the good in everything.

Anon

Model 5. The three legs of the stool model

The big picture

Individual management is about assessing which ways work best for an individual, team or organisation and then applying this as a strategy for success. In practical terms this involves knowing what the strengths are and then building on them. The role of a coach is to help individuals, teams and organisations determine what their strengths are and the best order in which they should be applied to achieve optimal outcomes. Although many will show great appetite to focus on and develop continually the areas where they are weakest, the most consistently successful understand that by starting from a position of strength they will be able to do the things in which they normally do not excel.

This model was designed to illustrate the order, process and interdependence of three key areas of development, namely physical, emotional and psychological. The concept explains what can be achieved in all three of these areas when the process begins with the area that is considered to be the strongest. However, if the focus is on the area of weakness it is more likely to become a struggle and risks neglecting the legs of the stool that are depended upon.

The model was developed for coaching in the many scenarios where people were focusing so much on their perceived 'gaps' and weaknesses that they missed the opportunity to build on and develop their strengths. Over time, they ended up sitting on an unstable stool with a constant fear of the stool collapsing. It is also the case that some people are not aware that they actually have three legs to their stool and each can be tightened and developed further rather than trying to get by on just one or two after giving up on the others. With the understanding that there are three legs to support them, each area can be made stronger and, by tightening up their area of strength first, they will then be able to influence the other two legs to improve and develop the confidence to reach higher levels physically, emotionally and psychologically.

There will always be one leg of the stool stronger than the others, one that is weakest and one that sits somewhere in between. Each individual, team and organisation will have an area of strength that they will be most confident in, an area that is of most concern to them and then one somewhere in between. The concept behind this model is about defining the areas of 'strongest' and 'weakest' in physical, emotional and psychological terms so that they can set be in the optimal order, starting with the strongest area first. This will then begin a systematic process where the strongest leg begins to tighten the next leg and finally the weakest leg.

Once established, this optimal order and process will lead to the confidence, assurance and stability that comes from developing a key strength, which begins to tighten the next leg, which then in turn improves the strength of the weakest leg. Without this optimal order, prioritisation of the areas of weakness will serve only to imbue the areas of strength with insecurity, fear and concern.

As a coach, you are developing a level of specific management that allows individuals, teams and organisations to create an environment and order of focus that raises their level of performance and results.

When to use it

- To gain or provide context for the benefits of playing to your strengths when greater performance is required.
- To establish and stick to an optimal order for greater performance and results by starting each time with the strongest leg of the stool.
- To develop a strategy of continuous performance improvement for significant and sustained growth.

Figure 2.2 The three legs of the stool model

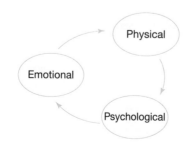

How to use it

The first step in this process to is to invite the individual, team or organisation to imagine their position as a stool with three legs. When each leg is tight and stable, they can confidently and securely sit on this stool knowing that they are well balanced and supported through all that is offered to them. However, if a leg begins to slacken or becomes unstable, they will become insecure and appear unstable on the slightest pressure, feeling vulnerable and concerned with every wobble. This process enables them to keep it tight, keep it strong, and give them a strong foundation for all that they have to deal with, even through the most volatile of times. (See also **Model 57: The accelerated learning model.**)

One of the legs of the stool is *the psychological leg,* which is where they will think things through to determine whatever is going on. When strong, this leg supports them in making sense of what is going on and gives them a degree of understanding as a platform. When loose, however, this leg will cause their thinking to unravel and lead to thoughts that are unhelpful and/or negative.

Another leg of the stool is *the emotional leg,* which is where they are aware of how they are feeling about whatever is going on. When strong, this leg supports them in selecting the most appropriate emotion(s) for the situation and outcome they really want. When loose, this leg will cause them to become over-emotional and irrational and work against what they want to achieve.

The stool is completed by *the physical leg,* which concerns the actions that they take, the things that they do to deal with whatever situation they are going through. When strong, this leg supports them in selecting the best activities, doing the right things and managing their physical energy effectively to get the outcome they want. However, when this leg becomes loose, it can impact on how and what they eat, how well they sleep, and cause them to behave in a manner that can get in the way of achieving their ideal result.

To build and maintain the ideal platform to support a successful life, career or business, it is important for individuals, teams and organisations to know how to *work to order* in terms of the three legs of their stool. Each leg is equally important, and their true success can only be achieved when all three legs are strong, tight and solid. However, from time to time they will be aware that they are on a stool that is wobbling or not as stable as they need it to be. So which leg do they tighten first? For successful results and outcomes, they should always go straight to their strongest leg, the leg that they know they can always count on, as this will be the easiest and quickest leg for them to tighten. It should be the first leg to tend to. With one leg now solid and strong, their second leg (likely to be the emotional leg) begins to tighten quicker and, with two stronger legs, the third leg becomes less of a concern and begins to tighten as a consequence. They can tighten all three legs, but success comes from knowing in which order to do so best.

Working on the *strongest leg first* is key to getting the three legs of the stool in the right order. This first leg is likely to be either 'psychological' or 'physical' because, almost always, the second leg tends to be 'emotional'.

- If there is a crisis or a challenging situation where positive outcomes are required, they do best when they get their thinking straight or understand better what is going on, and this then makes them feel better, which in turn leads to their doing things that create a positive outcome; that is, *psychological–emotional–physical.*

- If, however, they are at their best when they are doing something, saying something, exercising or relaxing, this then makes them feel better, which in turn helps them to get their thinking straight; that is, *physical–emotional–psychological.*

Ongoing success depends on *keeping it tight* and once they know the best order for tightening the legs of their stool, they can assess accurately the strength of their first leg by testing the strength of the third leg.

If they are 'psychological', then 'emotional' and then 'physical', they can measure the strength of their thinking (psychological) by how disciplined they are in their sleep, diet, exercise, relaxation, stress levels and appearance (physical). If their thinking is strong, they will be doing all the right things; if their thinking is unravelling, they will not be sleeping well, eating correctly, managing stress properly or taking the time to look good. The approach here would be to get to the cause, in this case 'psychological', and work to get their thinking straight. This will then make them feel better and get them back to doing the right things.

Alternatively if they are 'physical', then 'emotional' and then 'psychological', they can measure the strength of their 'physical' state by the level of quality, balance and clarity of their thinking (psychological). If they are physically strong, they will be thinking all the right thoughts; if their physical state is not as strong as it could be, they will be having negative thoughts, feel confused or mentally drained, and unable to be imaginative, creative or considered. The approach here would be to get to the cause, in this case 'physical', and work to improve the areas of sleep, eating, exercise, etc., to boost their appearance and image so that they feel better within themselves. From there their thinking will become clear, confident and bright.

The greatest levels of success are achieved when *the spiral effect* of the three legs is understood. Most are satisfied with knowing how to improve their psychological, emotional or physical state to the first level; however, a spiral of enhanced levels is also available. If they are 'psychological–emotional–physical' they can build a positive spiral that sees their higher physical state leading to an even higher level of thought, which makes them feel better and drives them to an even higher physical condition, and so on. Alternatively, if they are 'physical–emotional–psychological' their positive spiral can lead to greater levels of thought, inspiring them to improve their physical state even further, which in turn makes them feel amazing and takes their thinking to an incredible level, and so on. Note that spirals will go upwards or downwards depending on the choice of direction.

Coaching tips

- Always start with your own assessment as a coach so that you can understand and empathise with those that you work with on this model.
- Although there are some rare exceptions, it is likely that someone's strongest and weakest legs of their stool will be either

'physical' or 'psychological' because, in almost all cases, the 'emotional' leg sits in between, affected by one and affecting the other.

- Some people find it easier to identify their strongest leg first, while others are clearer on what their weakest leg is; either way, you can then work out the rest of the order.

Factors with big impact

- *Physical:* Exercising, fitness, standing up and moving around, writing, drawing, building, fixing, self-image, weight control, clothes, healthy diet, sleeping well, healthy routines.
- *Emotional:* Confidence, control, process, security, value, trust, ambition and light.
- *Psychological:* Taking time, understanding, asking questions, exploring options, clear context, reading.

The seven levels of awareness

1 **Denial/blame.**
2 **Actions.**
3 **Thoughts/beliefs.**
4 **Values/principles.**
5 **Personal identity.**
6 **Higher sense of self.**
7 **Atonement.**

Focus on your blessings, not your misfortunes. Focus on your strengths, not your weaknesses. Relax and let life come to you . . . Try not to force anything.

Anon

Model 6. The wheel of life model

The big picture

A key success factor of individual management is *balance,* the ability to push in one direction, but with an appreciation that this action must be matched in other areas to maintain stability and a healthy equilibrium. There is, however, an optimal balance for each individual, in that what may appear to be an extreme level for one person may be exactly the right level for another. The role of the coach is to help to find, develop and maintain the optimal balance for each individual, team and organisation.

This model is designed to illustrate the range of components that contribute to finding the optimal balance, where the 'spokes' of the wheel measure where the individual, team or organisation believe they are on a scale of 1–10. When these scores are joined up to draw a wheel, it provides a strong visual representation of why life, teams and business can be bumpy, stop and start, slow to get traction, or travelling great distances at great speed!

Although the components of the wheel have changed and adapted to reflect the most relevant areas of the time, this model has been around for decades. Understandably, coaches quickly adopted it because of its ability to give immediately a 'whole picture' view, providing perspective and structure. An initial assessment of the wheel of life as a coaching tool is only the starting point, because it indicates the *current* status; coaching is about taking this as a baseline from which an optimal *future* state can be reached. The model was developed for coaching in response to the many scenarios that were seen as a symptom of imbalance, low sense of perspective or over-emphasis on only one or a few components of success.

Whether coaching individuals or teams, or across organisations, you will often find that there is too much focus on only one or a few aspects of the wheel, which causes imbalance, lack of direction, the feeling of going round in circles, or grinding to a halt. These symptoms would suggest that there are spokes on the wheel that need some attention or energy injected into them. There will also be some instances where the wheel is in perfect balance, as when all spokes are scoring 2 or 3, but it will be difficult to create momentum and drive to get anywhere special anytime soon when the wheel is so small.

For a coach, the wheel provides a clear example and illustration of how all aspects are related and can play a part directly or indirectly with others. The support, learning, drive and perspective that can be gained by individuals, teams and organisations by

Figure 2.3 The wheel of life model

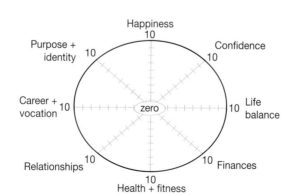

observing their life, teams and business as a wheel that has the potential to drive great distances smoothly, at great speed, can empower people to achieve and perform at an optimal level.

When to use it

- To provide context for why things can feel out of balance, lack momentum or are difficult to get going.
- To manage better the areas that are either neglected or over-emphasised.
- To build a strong and focused future state of an optimal wheel where all aspects are highly developed in balance.

How to use it

The first measure is where individuals would assess their current *health and fitness* on a scale of 1 to 10 (0 at the centre, 10 at the outer edge). This should cover their diet in terms of what and when they eat; their sleep patterns; their daily and weekly exercise routines; all aspects of their physical health and fitness. This measure is how they would score it in their own eyes, not what they think others might say or compare them to.

Next, their current state is assessed in terms of *relationships* on the above scale of 1 to 10 (0 at the centre, 10 at the outer edge). This should cover all relationship areas, namely personal and professional, formal and informal, long and short term, emotional and transactional. Again, this is how they would score this measure, not what they would guess others would.

Finances is the next measure and this is *not* just about how much money they have, but about what they have financially in relation to how much they need or want; it is about what they want to do with what they have. Score on the scale of 1 to 10 on how they feel about their current financial status.

Another important area to be measured is their *career and vocation*: what they commit a large portion of their time, energy and thought to. This is not just about what they do, but about how they feel about it, the value that it has, the difference that it makes and what it allows them to contribute. Again, score on the scale of 1 to 10 and this should be their own personal assessment.

One of the key factors in this model is how they would score their current *life balance* on the scale of 1 to 10. This is about getting the right balance between keeping what is important at the top of their list and still making the time, space and energy for the other key components in their life. This area is about what is important to them, not what they think others would judge as being important.

It is possible to assess accurately the level of direction they have in their life by how they score their sense of *purpose and identity* on the scale of 1–10. This is about how well they are living their life to achieve the goals that really mean something to them, and in a way that is aligned to them personally. It is a good indicator for assessing their current psychological health and fitness. (See also **Model 14: The identity decisions model.**)

Confidence can be key to many opportunities, so a current score from 1 to 10 will indicate where they are in terms of knowing what they can achieve, what they can contribute, what they can be counted on for, and the value they can bring. This is a measure of how good they feel inside rather than what others may see from outside. (See also **Model 7: The confidence v self-confidence model.**)

Finally, *happiness* is the point where the level of challenge meets their level of confidence. Score on the scale of 1 to 10 based upon how they *do* feel rather than how they think they *should* feel. This should include how happy they feel in all their personal or professional pursuits. It is a good measure of their emotional health and fitness. (See also **Model 4: The happiness model.**)

Coaching tips

There are three main symptoms that you will face when coaching with this model, and each has some common causes:

- Symptom 1: Over-emphasis on one or a few aspects of the wheel, causing 'spikes'. Likely causes:
  - The belief that scoring high on these aspects will compensate for neglecting or ignoring others; that is, 'If I have enough money, then I can buy the rest'.
  - The belief (often reinforced by bosses and peers) that there are only some areas that really matter right now; that is, 'These are the years to focus on your career; the relationships and fitness can be looked at once you've made it.'
- Symptom 2: Under-developed or neglected aspects of the wheel, causing 'dents'. Likely causes:
  - The lack of awareness of how many spokes there are in the wheel.
  - The lack of awareness of how the spokes relate to and impact on how the wheel performs.
  - The lack of connection to, or value in, key spokes of the wheel, such as 'purpose', 'happiness' or 'health'.
- Symptom 3: Consistent low scoring on all aspects of the wheel, resulting in low momentum. Likely causes:
  - Low awareness of what higher scores look like.
  - Low confidence that higher scores can be achieved and maintained.
  - Comfort on having a balanced wheel, albeit small and slow.
  - Fear of creating some spikes that initially may cause imbalance.
  - Fear of failure.
  - Fear of success.

Scoring: Always ensure that the scoring is based upon the opinion of the person taking the assessment and what they themselves believe to be an accurate score, rather than what they believe to be the opinions of others.

Based on average life expectancy, if you were to work each week and leave education until the day you retire, the percentage of your life that you work will be under 11 per cent.

Maslow's hierarchy of needs

1 Physiological.
2 Safety.
3 Love/belonging.
4 Esteem.
5 Self-actualisation.

Never get so busy making a living that you forget to make a life.

Anon

Confidence management (confidence)

3

[**Confidence: Being clear and secure in worth, value, capability and potential.**]

Confidence management is a critical platform on which to build greater performance through coaching. Developing individuals, teams and organisations to have greater confidence is to make them more aware of the worth, value, capability and potential they have, and then to achieve greater outcomes with conviction, determination and resilience.

Individuals with a greater sense of confidence and deeper level of self-confidence consistently perform at the higher levels of their potential: they know who they are, what they are worth, what they bring to the table and what they can make happen; they do not panic; and they deal with all the results they achieve with maturity and perspective. Low confidence in individuals leads to erratic behaviour and approaches, and, when they are desperate for things to go well, often stops success from happening. In such a difficult place, individuals can hold back themselves and others from achieving things as their fears begin to dictate their level of ambition and drive.

Confident teams see a challenge as positive – an opportunity to shine, a chance to learn. Teams that lack confidence will see a challenge as a criticism – a reason to blame, something to avoid. When a team is confident it is open to the diversity in all the individuals and resources available to it, whereas a team with low confidence will expend its energies in arguing for its preference for fear of being marginalised or left out.

The benefits of confidence can be applied across organisations, because, with a high level of confidence and a deep understanding of self-confidence, these businesses will set out, drive and deliver clear strategies to make things happen, while others are left to react, compete or imitate.

As a coach, you, and the individuals, teams and organisations you work with, should feel that bit more confident about what you are doing each time you engage with them; only then will they then be able to develop and challenge themselves to achieve what they are truly capable of.

Model 7. Confidence v self-confidence model

The big picture

Key to the management and then development of confidence is first of all to appreciate the difference and relationship between *confidence* and *self-confidence.* For most people, their understanding of confidence is one-dimensional, wrapped up as one single thing, and therefore they do not distinguish between *external* confidence and *internal* self-confidence. As a coach, you can apply this model to enable and empower the individuals, teams and organisations you work with to develop specific strategies to manage and develop their confidence, and their self-confidence.

This model was designed to illustrate the difference and the relationship between confidence and self-confidence. It shows the difference in terms of the volatility and activity of the two forms of confidence and highlights the 'feel-good' line by which we tend to measure how we feel about how things are going.

The model was created in response to the many coaching scenarios that involved fluctuations in the levels of confidence and the apparent disconnect or contradiction at times between how things were and how people actually felt. Being able to define what confidence is, and how this differs from self-confidence, offers insight and perspective firstly into why it is how it is, and, secondly, into what can be done to build and discover how it can be.

Coaching individuals through this model helps make clear what they can control and affect – and what they can only react to. Understanding and developing both internal and external strategies will enable them to build strong and sustainable self-confidence on which to maintain highs in confidence more consistently; in short, feeling good more often. Without this appreciation of confidence and self-confidence, individuals, teams and organisations can find themselves on a continual roller-coaster driven by the external ups and downs of life, relationships and their career, desperate for something good externally to happen, or to 'get lucky'.

Teams that appreciate the value in building a higher level of self-confidence also develop greater levels of resilience, determination and creativity so that the external fluctuations may take them from feeling fine to feeling fantastic. Teams with lower self-confidence, however, will either stop believing that they can make great things

Figure 3.1 The confidence v self-confidence model

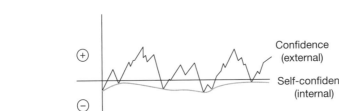

happen and go into a slump, or become so desperate for a boost of any kind that they take wild and unnecessary risks for just a moment of feeling good.

This can also be applied across an organisation. A self-confident business understands its identity, its value, its worth and what it is capable of. It is this level of self-confidence that enables it to launch new products and services, to specialise, to redefine industries, to challenge, to innovate and to break new ground as part of its strategy and not just as a reaction or imitation.

As a coach, you should work to ensure that you engage with individuals, teams and organisations keeping your own self-confidence at a high level so that you then trust your intuition, creativity and resourcefulness for the benefit of the people you work with. If you allow your self-confidence to diminish, you will find that you are desperate for the 'one question' or 'light bulb moment' that will boost your confidence in the moment. But where next? Take time regularly to reflect upon your own worth, value, identity, capability and potential as a coach; there will be plenty there for you to build a strong platform of self-confidence.

When to use it

- To provide context for the difference and relationship between confidence and self-confidence.
- To manage better the level of self-confidence so that fluctuations of confidence remain positive.
- To develop strategies of greater confidence and higher self-confidence so that all projects, initiatives and situations can have an optimal approach.

How to use it

Firstly, it is important to understand what 'confidence' is, what it does, how it works and what can and can't be done with it:

- 'Confidence' is an *external* thing that is driven by, and responds to, events that occur externally, such as results, outcomes, situations, conversations with others, the weather, people's opinions, the economy, a compliment or criticism, clothes worn, car driven, etc.
- 'Confidence' fluctuates wildly due to all the external drivers that it has; it is not possible to *control* it, although steps can be taken to *manage* it. If a compliment is paid, confidence will go up; if a criticism is made, confidence will go down. It is not possible to stop this happening. Achieve a good result and confidence will increase; achieve a disappointing result and confidence will reduce. Again, it is not possible to stop this happening.

Next, it is important to understand what 'self-confidence' is, what it does, what impacts it has, and what can be done to build it and maintain it:

- 'Self-confidence' in an *internal* thing that is built and maintained by inner thoughts, inner words, inner assessment and self-awareness of all that can be offered – all intentions and efforts.

- 'Self-confidence' also fluctuates, but in a far more gradual and far less dramatic fashion than confidence. Self-confidence builds brick by brick, at a pace that will not be noticed each day, but every so often feelings of greater self-confidence will be realised. These gradual fluctuations can also lead to a lack of awareness when self-confidence has declined on a daily basis until it reaches a level that can be far lower than needed. It is possible to increase and maintain levels of self-confidence at any time.

Success comes from the level of *combined confidence,* so it is important to appreciate how confidence and self-confidence work together. The level of confidence is determined by external factors and thus it will naturally go up and down based upon what happens externally. This is natural. The level of self-confidence is determined by internal feelings regardless of external factors. Fluctuating confidence sits on top of the foundations of self-confidence, using it as a base or platform: the higher and stronger the base of self-confidence, the higher the level of confidence that can be reached.

In appreciating how both confidences work together it is important to be aware of *the feel-good line,* a level above which the feelings go from good to great, and below which they drop from being not-so-good to terrible. As self-confidence is the base and platform, then if it can be built and maintained close to the level of the feel-good line it will not matter how low the fluctuations of confidence may fall – they will not drop beyond the base level of self-confidence. And with a high and healthy level of self-confidence, those moments of high confidence fluctuation will feel amazing! However, if the base of self-confidence is allowed to drop far below the feel-good line then it is natural to become desperate for something to happen, anything that will give a momentary glimpse of feeling good, and the slightest external disappointment or upset will bring those feelings down further than they should.

Although it is not something that can be controlled, it is possible to *manage* confidence by retaining a healthy perspective on all the external stimulations that are encountered. Firstly, by keeping in mind that all fluctuations in the level of confidence are momentary; that no matter whether they are positive or negative, whether they increase or reduce the level of confidence, they do not need to last long. Secondly, by being able to keep all the feedback, results, comments, material things and situations that are external (positive or negative) in the context of a bigger picture, this will help balance out some of those emotional fluctuations that affect the level of confidence. If playing a bigger game, it is less likely to get out of hand or lose perspective.

To get a needed break, or when desperate for some external success – something or anything to make the feelings of confidence better from a short-term stimulation of winning – it can be helpful to go shopping, do something distracting, run away or towards something else or someone. This will produce some level of 'high' confidence but it will naturally fluctuate back down before long, and that is when individuals may wish that they had instead put in the work to develop a higher level of self-confidence.

As the base and platform of self-confidence is for the individual, team or organisation alone to build and maintain, it is vital that they learn how to *increase* self-confidence. This is most effectively achieved by conducting regular inventories, compiling mental lists and internally acknowledging all that they know that will boost and retain their level of self-confidence as one of the main keys to achieving all that they are truly capable of; it will determine how they look at their world, how high they can fly and how resilient they can be when they need to see things through.

External events going really well do not alone improve the levels of self-confidence, but they will boost feelings of confidence for a time. Great things can be achieved externally yet still not lead to feeling great inside because the level of self-confidence is so low. Individuals, teams and organisations can also go through a difficult time with external results yet still feel fine due to a high and healthy level of self-confidence.

- Know who you are, what you are really about, all of the great things that you bring and are capable of.
- Know your positive intentions, your skills and attributes, the values that are important to you, the energies and passions that you have to offer.
- Know what you are really aiming for, what is most important to you, the bigger picture of what success will look like for you, your aspirations and affirmations.

Coaching tips

- An individual's *sense of service* can play a part in this model because someone with a stronger sense of service to themselves is likely to find doing the internal work on their self-confidence easier as it involves what they think are their strengths, worth and capabilities. For someone who has more of a sense of service to others, they will be best advised to consider what others would say about them in terms of their strengths, worth and capabilities. (See **Model 43: The sense of service model.**)
- Some individuals, teams and organisations have been reacting solely to their levels of confidence for such a long time that their level of self-confidence has gradually diminished to quite a distance below their feel-good line, so be patient, consistent and positive, and remain determined for them; it will take time as it is a gradual build.

Signs of low self-confidence

- The peaks of confidence no longer reach so high, nor do they last as long or are enjoyed as much.
- The 'buzz' of possessions, promotions, purchases and compliments are lower, shorter and lose meaning.
- The lows of confidence go deeper, are devastating and feel like they last for ever.
- The disappointments become personal and long-lasting failures.
- The drive, resilience, ambition and strategies get lost quickly.

Top 10 steps to build self-confidence

1 **Focus on positive self-talk.**
2 **Do not compare yourself to others.**
3 **Exercise.**
4 **Do not strive for perfection.**
5 **Do not beat yourself up when you make a mistake.**
6 **Focus on the things that you *can* change and control.**
7 **Do things you enjoy, in a way you enjoy.**
8 **Celebrate the small stuff.**
9 **Be helpful and considerate.**
10 **Surround yourself with supportive people.**

The more you work at just being yourself, the more likely you'll feel purposeful and significant in your life.

Wayne W. Dyer

Model 8. The five key differentiators model

The big picture

Being able to define the value of what can be offered is a key attribute to building, maintaining and developing confidence. While there is benefit in being able to list all that someone can bring to a situation or opportunity, their value can be subjective or determined by personal preference. There are, however, five key and objective points of value that specify and differentiate most effectively. As these are defined objectively, they will *protect* and *develop* the levels of confidence rather than be directed or restricted *by* the level of confidence.

This model was built to clarify the most important and objective measures that differentiate people, teams and organisations and communicate their value beyond personal or emotional preference. The model was created in response to the various coaching scenarios involving the periods of doubt and lack of confidence experienced by individuals, teams and organisations. With a clear understanding of what someone can bring in terms of these five topics, they will know where they are currently, and what they need to do to get to where they really want to be.

Coaching through this model empowers individuals to know all that they can bring to each situation and opportunity; for teams, to approach their targets and outcomes with all the resources and capabilities at their collective disposal; for organisations, to have the confidence to create and achieve great results and outcomes.

As a coach, as much as in any profession or endeavour, it is important to know all that you can possibly bring to each session or event so that you are ready, willing

Figure 3.2 The five key differentiators model

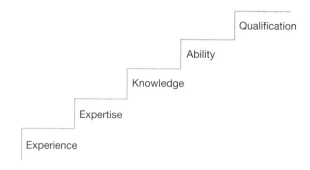

and prepared to offer everything that could be of value. To be the coach you can be, you will know clearly what your five key differentiators are.

When to use it

- To define what the objective differentiators of value are, above personal and subjective measures, to increase awareness.
- To establish the current level of the value proposition to increase confidence and performance.
- To develop each of the key differentiators to increase opportunity and outcomes.

How to use it

For individuals, teams and organisations, the first component is their *experience*: the number of years that they have been involved in something relevant, the variety of situations that they have been through and the lessons they have learned.

The second component is what they consider to be their areas of *expertise*: the specific and relevant skills they have developed to a higher standard, the specific and relevant situations that they excel in, the attributes that they are renowned for and counted on.

The next component is their *knowledge*: all the relevant things that they now know for sure, that they now know work, that they are now certain about and can deliver, all the relevant things that they know how to apply to any situation.

The key component to add now is their *ability*: all the things they can do that are of relevance and value, the relevant impact that they know they can have, the real difference that they can make – all the valuable things that can be expected of them.

The final key component is their *qualification*: all that they believe makes them qualified to do what they do. This may in fact be a formal and recognised qualification, but is equally likely to be a combination of their relevant experience, expertise, knowledge and ability that clearly demonstrates why they are qualified to do something, and do it well. Of course, if they have the advantage of also having a formal qualification to add to this mix, then all the better!

What makes every proposition that bit more distinctive and memorable is when they add *passion and commitment*: the things that they love, the things that matter most to them, the emotions they have about what they do, and how what they do makes them feel when it all works!

Great leaders and managers rely upon fantastic presentation, and to ensure they create the impact that leads to success they should continue to work on their *elevator pitch*: the succinct statements that differentiate them above all others. 'I have this much experience doing this . . . My areas of expertise are these . . . I know how to do these things and make these things happen . . . What I am able to do for you is . . . These are the things that qualify me to do this for you . . . And I truly love what I do!'

Coaching tips

- The key question for this model is 'What do I have?' or 'What do we have?' so that it opens up the thinking to all aspects that can be allocated under that topic. Be aware, however, that most individuals, teams and organisations will have been restricted for some time by asking the question, 'Do I?' or 'Do we?', a question that can often result in a resounding and closing answer of 'No'. You may have to repeat the key question more than once!

- *Experience* and *expertise* are two different things: someone may have been doing the same thing for years, but it does not automatically follow that they are experts.

- *Qualification* can be a formally recognised endorsement, accreditation or award; it can also be the combination of the experience, expertise, knowledge and ability that qualifies the individual, team or organisation to do what they do. Having both is often ideal, but either can be valid.

- All five differentiators can overlap at times, but the power is in defining and combining all five rather than diluting them by bundling them together and losing the amplification and distinction. In effect, five strong reasons why.

The three points of being a credible expert

1 You produce *results.*
2 You continue to *research.*
3 You are a *role model.*

Self-confidence is the first requisite to great undertakings.

Samuel Johnson

Model 9. The optimal appraisal model

The big picture

Too often, the future aims of individuals, teams and organisations are largely dictated and limited by their past results, hopeful that good outcomes continue, mixed outcomes get a bit better and all bad outcomes cease. Being able to assess and appraise with an optimal approach ensures that all future aims and results reach far beyond anything that has been achieved in the past.

The model of optimal appraisal was built to illustrate how the learning from the past can be used to create a springboard for future aims, enabling individuals, teams and organisations to reach all that they are truly capable of. The concept of this model was created in response to the many coaching situations that were a symptom of individuals with low confidence, teams that lacked belief and organisations that had lost or become disconnected with their desire and ambition to achieve truly great things – all because of past performance.

Coaching individuals through this model, where they are introduced to the value of the present as a catalyst for greater achievement, helps them understand that they are in the strongest position that they have ever been in, and thus what they could now be confidently aiming for. Teams will realise that all that they have learned, experienced and gained collectively can provide a platform that will catapult their performance and results to a whole new level in the future. And any organisation that is able to grasp the full value of optimal appraisal will be able to make game-changing decisions and launch competitive blue ocean strategies to render the competition irrelevant by realising the value that their combined knowledge, ability, experience and expertise presents.

As a coach, this model presents you with a fantastic opportunity to reach your full potential by realising and taking on board all the learning and development you can from each and every session.

When to use it

- To ensure that the *past* is being objectively appraised to gain a healthy perspective and to protect confidence.

Figure 3.3 The optimal appraisal model

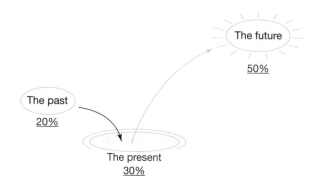

- To ensure that the *present* is being fully and optimally appraised to build greater confidence in the strongest position to date.
- To ensure that the *future* aims are appropriate and relevant from being in the strongest position ever.

How to use it

Individuals should review all the things that have happened in the *past*: what has gone well, what has not gone so well, the good, the bad and the indifferent. It will all be of use as they move forward and learn from it. This allows them to discard the weight of the past, or to try to leave it behind; they will succeed *because* of their past, not *in spite* of it. This should take up about 20 per cent of the appraisal of a situation. (See also **Model 63: The three-boxes model.**)

Next, consider where they are at *present* in terms of what experience they now have as a result of the past, what expertise they have now developed because of the past, what they now know for sure because of the past and what they are now able to do because of what they have learned from the past. Finally, assess why their present qualifies them as being in the strongest position that they have ever been in to date in terms of the experience they have now gained, the areas of expertise they have now developed, what they now know for sure, and what they are now able to do as a result of all that they have learned. Pulling all of this together to confirm that they are now in the strongest position that they have ever been should take up about 30 per cent of the appraisal of a situation.

Finally, using the present (the strongest position they have ever been in) as a springboard, they can project what the *future* should look like. This positioning and use of their springboard enables them to avoid their past and determine their future. Creating what their future can be should take up around 50 per cent of the appraisal.

Coaching tips

- The past is still 20 per cent of the optimal appraisal process; it should not be ignored, disregarded or omitted. This is *not* a 'get over it' or 'let it go' approach.
- The present should take up more time (30 per cent) than the past so that an appreciation of the present is thorough enough and powerful enough to act as a springboard from which to project the future.
- Then 50 per cent of the appraisal should concentrate on what the future should look like based upon being in the strongest position ever. The expectations for the future should reflect a 'bounce' from such a strong position.
- Having presence of mind is something that most individuals, teams and organisations need to develop more. Developing the present that does not drift back either into the past or into the future will in time provide the 'bounce' of optimal appraisal.

The six steps for presenting high self-confidence

1 Acknowledge what you have achieved.
2 Acknowledge the fears and obstacles you have overcome.
3 Acknowledge what you now know and understand.
4 Acknowledge that you are now better prepared than before.
5 Acknowledge that no future failure will finish you.
6 Acknowledge who you are, what you are capable of and what you really want out of life.

Accept your past without regret. Handle your present with confidence. Face your future without fear.

Anon

[PART TWO]

Developing the
leadership core

[
Control: The ability to manage or redirect
disruptive impulses and moods, to be able to
suspend judgement and to think before acting.
]

Control is the second of the six key areas of development for individuals, teams and organisations. Individuals with a high degree of control are able to lead with authenticity, consistency and flexibility, always focused on their desired outcome. Teams that develop a strong sense of control are able to create an environment where optimal outcomes can be achieved through fostering higher levels of trust, conscientiousness and adaptability. Organisations that have a strong leadership core will retain a clear sense of identity, establish conditions and measures for success and remain focused on reaching their destination.

Whereas the previous part of this book focused on the management of emotion, thought and confidence, this part looks at how to build further and develop the capability to control so as to determine the emotions, thoughts and energy that will drive individuals, teams and organisations towards their optimal outcomes.

In this part we present control as the combination of four elements:

This selection of *Key Coaching Models* has been specifically designed to develop a higher degree of control.

Emotional leadership (control of emotions)

4

[
Control of emotions: Selecting the right emotion, to the right degree, for a situation, to get to the outcome you desire while keeping your disruptive emotions in check.
]

The ability to control and channel emotions is a key component of successful leadership for individuals, teams and organisations. Coaching this ability enables the direction and focus of all emotions to be targeted, applied and executed for the achievement of key objectives and goals.

Individuals with greater control of their emotions are able to make intelligent decisions that are then supported and driven by the power of their emotions, whereas those with less control allow their emotions to determine their thoughts and reactions. Teams with stronger emotional control remain objective and keep a balanced perspective, whereas those who lack such control allow the highs and lows of situations to determine what happens next. Resilience, focus and calmness that come from being in control of emotions shine through at an organisational level in the consistency and level of consideration involved in the decisions and strategies implemented. An organisation without such control makes emotionally based decisions on issues of risk or opportunity.

Emotional leadership is part of being a successful coach so that you continually select and introduce the right emotions, at the right level, at the right time for the individual, team or organisation to achieve their desired outcomes. Every coach has emotions, fears and sensitivities; these need to be controlled and channelled in order to coach at an optimal level.

Model 10. The five steps to manage emotions model

The big picture

To be able to enhance emotional leadership, there has to be, first of all, the ability to manage emotions. By doing so, individuals, teams and organisations are then able to allow their intelligence to decide and the power of their emotions to help drive and support their thinking. (See also **Model 1: The EI model.**)

The five steps to manage emotions were adapted for coaching from the many and varied psychological approaches to the management of emotion and stress available today. The practical process was designed in response to that most common of all coaching scenarios: the inability to think straight and logically beyond the level of emotion. By mapping out this quick five-step programme, individuals, teams and organisations can observe what they are experiencing as part of a process to be understood logically rather than felt emotionally. This approach then provides the opportunity to make intelligent, considered and objective decisions and choices.

For individuals, this process ensures that each emotion is managed for what it is and what it is worth, rather than leading to additional layers of emotions that then lead to emotional behaviours and choices. For teams, the five steps provide a guide from which they can take control of their emotions and allow their intelligence to drive their decisions rather than their choices being driven or restricted by how they are feeling. Also with teams and groups, there may be some confusion from having to deal with a variety and range of feelings. For an organisation, the ability to ensure that decisions and strategies are not just emotionally driven increases significantly their chances of success because it will reduce unnecessary risk and cost. With strong management of emotion, organisations will encourage the resilience, determination and consistency that makes the organisation easier to follow and commit to.

Coaches should invest emotion in every coaching session that they facilitate so that they do what it takes to help individuals, teams and organisations move towards their desired outcomes. This is best achieved when the choice of question, content, example or risk is one that is intelligently considered rather than emotionally driven.

Figure 4.1 The five steps to manage emotions model

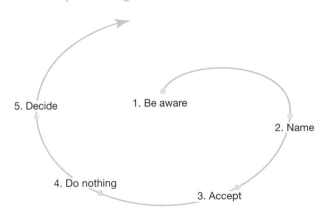

- As a practical model for putting emotions into context.
- To ensure that the unhelpful layering and compilation of emotions is avoided.
- As a clear process for making intelligent and considered decisions.

How to use it

The first step in managing emotions is to *be aware* that there are emotions involved. This level of self-awareness permits the management of the emotion. Signs of temper, anxiety or nerves, or a lack of concentration, patience or focus, are good indicators that there is a feeling of being 'emotional'.

To be in control of an emotion, it is necessary to *name* it, as this enables the emotion to be viewed and considered objectively rather than just felt. This separation of thought and feeling is very powerful.

The third step in the process can sometimes be difficult, but it is necessary to be successful. No matter what the emotion is, one must learn to *accept* it; that is, to understand that whatever the emotion is, it is OK and understandable to feel it. Whether it is an emotion that should or should not be present, know that it is, and accept that, given the circumstances, it is fine for now.

The fourth step is the one that is most likely to seem unnatural from the start: to *do nothing*. This is an important part of being able to manage emotions, since this 'pausing' enables intelligence to get in front of emotion. 'Pausing' may only be momentary, but that is all it takes for intelligence to take the lead in a situation.

With the first four steps complete, the fifth step is to *decide* what is now needed to get to the desired outcome. With intelligence leading the process, all of the emotions can fall in behind to drive and support the intelligent, strategic and considered choice of action.

Coaching tips

- Allow time to be sure that they are dealing with their 'base' emotion rather than one of the 'layers'. Asking 'Why do you feel this emotion?' will help them identify if this is the base one. If they have not been dealing with it they will not have done any harm, but it will remain unmanaged, although possibly clearer. Someone may feel *anger* because they have been asked to do something that they are *insecure* about and they *fear* failing at it. Asking questions or progressing by a process of elimination are both effective.

- Naming the emotion is an important action, but the value is in doing so to objectify the emotion rather than debating or challenging the name chosen for it. Whatever the individual, team and organisation choose to name it, the value is that it has now been named, even if done so subjectively.

- Ensure that the 'do nothing' step in the process is sufficient enough for intelligence to take the lead, but do not to allow this to be perceived as doing nothing at all!

The top 10 emotional signals

1 Discomfort.
2 Fear.
3 Hurt.
4 Anger.
5 Frustration.
6 Disappointment.
7 Guilt.
8 Inadequacy.
9 Overwhelmed.
10 Loneliness.

Feelings are much like waves; we can't stop them coming, but we can choose which ones to surf!

Anon

Model 11. The SARA model

The big picture

The ability to control emotions when delivering a message or communication can be prepared for and managed in advance; however, being able to remain in control of the emotions when receiving feedback or communication requires another level of control. In a world of ever-increasing comment, posts, feedback, analysis and opinions, the ability to control emotions when on the receiving end of what others think has become a necessary attribute for success today.

The practical four-step process of SARA (Shock, Anger, Rationalise, Accept) was adapted for coaching in response to the significant increase in sources and volume of feedback, data and comment that individuals, teams and organisations now have to deal with. Whether perceived as negative feedback or positive comment, it is crucial to be able to deal with, understand and respond in a way that protects and progresses the individual, team or organisation towards their desired outcome. Setting out these steps helps to explain the natural and emotional process involved and allow the process to be observed and understood with greater objectivity and less emotion.

For individuals, the steps set out each part of a natural process so that they do not need to add further layers of emotion unnecessarily. Understanding that this is a logical order, and that there is a destination to reach in the process, increases their ability to deal with feedback and comment with greater objectivity and to respond constructively. In the absence of understanding this process, individuals will often respond emotionally and irrationally, losing perspective, taking things more personally than intended, or lashing out to make others feel how they have been made to feel.

For teams, the process enables a more open environment for communication because each member of the team can identify where they or another team member are in these four steps and know what support to offer for the next step. Without appreciating these necessary steps when dealing with feedback, others' feelings can often be disregarded, under-estimated, ignored, criticised or even disrespected with consequently negative effects on morale, relationships and performance.

Organisations that appreciate the natural order and process of dealing with feedback will communicate with greater context and consideration of the message they want to get across. They will anticipate the reactions of their employees and be ready to support them in a constructive, objective and more positive position of acceptance. (See also **Model 60: The context–consideration–conclusion model.**) They will also understand how to deal positively with the feedback, comments and criticisms that their employees may offer in their formal appraisals, assessments or surveys. An organisation without an appreciation of the SARA model will tend to suffer from low engagement and higher conflict when its employees are stuck in shock, feel anger or engage in arguments.

Coaching is not a scripted environment, so coaches need to be well prepared for dealing with the wide range of scenarios, issues, opportunities and situations that can brought to a session. To coach at the highest level, it is important to go quickly through the steps of the SARA model in order to provide the most helpful and constructive response.

When to use it

- As a practical illustration of the emotional process regarding feedback.
- To provide a quick, easy-to-understand technique to manage feedback.
- As a method for dealing with, and responding to, feedback in a way that is objective and constructive.
- As a strategy for getting the most out of feedback, both giving and receiving.

How to use it

The first and automatic reaction to receiving feedback, no matter whether it is praise or criticism, is *shock.* This may range from being 'totally out of the blue' or 'not really expected'. It may also be because of what feedback has been offered, how it has been offered, why it has been offered, when it has been offered, or by whom it has been given, but overall, to a greater or lesser extent, the cognitive reaction to

Figure 4.2 The SARA model

1. <u>S</u>hock
2. <u>A</u>nger
3. <u>R</u>ationalise
4. <u>Accept</u>

feedback is a variable degree of shock. This is natural and should be expected before moving on to how the feedback is felt.

The next reaction that follows is *anger* as emotions kick in before intelligence. When individuals, teams and organisations receive positive or negative feedback, they can feel uncomfortable or embarrassed, making them the centre of attention or holding them up as an example of something good or bad. They may disagree with the feedback, or just disagree with how it was said or shared. They may actually agree with it, but wish it had not been said in the way it was. Again, the extent of anger can range from major to minor and it can grow or recede over time if dwelled upon. The emotions here are natural and to be accepted before intelligence is allowed to enter the process so that they can move on to what they think about the feedback.

Everyone is wired for their emotions to kick in before their intelligence, so once beyond the emotional stage of anger they can get to the *rationalise* part of the process where their intelligence gets to grips with things. Again, this reaction happens no matter whether the feedback is good or bad, positive or negative, as praise or criticism – either way their mind will now start to process all the reasons, known and imagined, for the feedback given. A lot of time and energy can be spent in this part of the process. This can lead them to dismiss feedback that could be valuable; it can also lead them to build up the feedback in their mind into something that it should never have been and way out of proportion, good or bad. This is also a natural part of the process to learn, accept and appreciate, but, at the same time, staying in this place too long can become a barrier to the next and highest value stage of this process.

For individuals, teams and organisations to achieve and enjoy success it is important for them to learn to *accept* feedback as constructively as possible. This is not about their accepting all feedback as 100 per cent true (this is not a healthy approach to feedback), it is more about learning that there is value in at least considering that there *may* be an element of truth or value in the feedback. This balanced and considered approach allows their mind to remain open to possibilities without inflating or deflating their self-confidence or self-esteem; it is just feedback based upon an opinion, and therefore it may be interesting, but it does not need to be assumed to be totally true.

The secret to success for individuals, teams and organisations with this process is to *avoid getting stuck,* as this is one of the main stumbling blocks they will encounter when dealing with feedback. Too many times they will get so hung up on the shock and surprise that they freeze and later still do not know how they felt about what has been said. More often, however, they will stall in the anger and not get beyond how they have been made to feel, or their emotions will fester and they will fail to take away any healthy context or perspective. The biggest hurdle they will face, though, is becoming consumed by their eagerness to rationalise feedback: to make sense of what has been said to them, by whom it was said, why it was said and the way or the time that was chosen to say it. Whether known, but more often guessed, assumed or imagined, this ability to create a rationale, story or theory for the feedback will falsely inflate or diminish the value and importance of the feedback offered. Only beyond rationalising will they get to acceptance.

- Feedback is feedback, and there is never a shortage of opinions and comment. It happens, and it is to be expected; it should not come as too much of a surprise or shock.

- Some feedback will feel good, some will feel bad and some will create mixed emotions. People are entitled to feel what they feel when receiving feedback; whatever they feel is natural, OK and more often may not be how the feedback was intended. There is no need or value in adding emotions to emotions, feeling annoyed about feeling angry, etc.

- It is natural to want to think things through, but it is unlikely that anyone will ever know the complete truth behind the feedback they receive; understanding that it is useful is the key – awareness is more valuable than analysis. It is what it is; it says more about the person providing the feedback than the recipient. Being able to move on to acceptance as quickly as possible saves more than just time.

- Accept feedback for what it is: the opinion of others. Accept that people are entitled to their opinion, but that this is not something that has to be adopted or rejected wholesale. Healthy acceptance is the ability to say, 'Well, maybe . . . ' It is also healthy to see feedback as interesting rather than judgemental. With healthy acceptance it is easier to manage emotions confidently with regard to feedback and grow from the process.

The three drivers of an emotional state

1 **Your physiology: stand tall, breathe fully.**
2 **Your focus: be positive, look for the opportunity.**
3 **Your language: be kind, optimistic, compassionate.**

You will not be punished for your anger; you will be punished by your anger.

Buddha

Model 12. The spectrum of fear model

The big picture

Psychologists have for many years suggested that there is only a small set of basic or innate emotions, and fear is considered to be one of the most common and powerful. Fear is an emotion that is induced by a perceived threat, in the present or in the future, which causes a change in brain and physical function, and ultimately in behaviour. Understanding and being able to control fear is a key attribute that will determine the level of emotional leadership that can be achieved.

This model was created and developed for coaching in response to the many scenarios where decisions, actions, ambitions and well-being were affected, restricted or driven by fear. The practical illustration of the range and scale of fear presents this powerful emotion as an intelligent force that can be managed and channelled to deliver the thoughts, strategies and behaviours aligned to achieving successful outcomes. As with all successful approaches to the management and leadership of emotions, this is about having the right amount of fear applied in a way that is appropriate to the situation and in turn drives towards a clear and desired result. (See also **Model 1: The EI model.**)

By understanding the range of fear, from fearless to fearful, and the options in between, individuals, teams and organisations are empowered to avoid the paralysis and complacency of fear and make intelligent choices in how they manage and channel this powerful energy to do the right things. With such an appreciation of this powerful emotion, the fear of fear itself is controlled and diminished. (See also **Model 10: The five steps to manage emotions model.**)

When to use it

- As a practical model for putting fear into context.
- For avoiding the paralysis of fearfulness.
- For avoiding the complacency of fearlessness.
- To appreciate the value and power of being specifically frightened.
- As a method for being frightened enough to channel thoughts and actions towards desired outcomes.

How to use it

At one end of the spectrum of fear, individuals, teams and organisations can be *fearful*. This is when they are so full of fear that they can actually freeze or become paralysed by their fear. At this end of the spectrum they emotionally expand specific into non-specific and imagined fears to create such a powerful mass of fear that their intelligence looks for ways to avoid the issue or for evidence that it is just something they will have to learn to live with, or without, depending on the fear.

Figure 4.3 The spectrum of fear model

100%
Fearful
(emotional)

Frightened
(intelligent)

0%
Fearless
(emotional)

At the other end of the spectrum of fear, individuals, teams and organisations are *fearless.* This is when they are so unaware of any specific things to fear that they become oblivious to risk or danger. At this end of the spectrum they can become a liability and run the risk of being unaware of, unprepared for, or naive to, the dangers and pitfalls that are around them. This is often the case when they are so emotional that they just do not want to consider that there may be any risk or danger involved in what they want to do, which leaves them exposed to many unnecessary and easily avoidable pitfalls.

The healthiest position to populate on this spectrum is the range of being *frightened,* which sits between 'fearful' and 'fearless' as the area where individuals, teams and organisations are specific about their fears so that they can prepare and plan for how to deal with them. Being frightened is what keeps us alive and free from unnecessary harm and danger; it enables us to deal intelligently with our emotion of fear so that we can decide the appropriate level of emotion to apply for the outcome we want. Successful people understand the value of being frightened as it gives them the courage to do things that others fear, and the confidence to avoid unnecessary harm in the process. (See also **Model 1: The EI model.**)

The difference between being at the extremes of fearful and fearless, to becoming just frightened, is determined by the level of specification involved. If individuals, teams or organisations talk themselves out of doing the things that they are fearful of, then being specific about what it actually is that they fear allows them to start working out ways to deal with, mitigate or divert around those bite-sized chunks that they fear. If they are running headlong into situations but hitting walls or getting their fingers burned then they are fearless, and being specific about the potential risks, pitfalls, dangers or disappointments will allow them to plan for, anticipate and mitigate the risks of the hurdles that may otherwise cause them to stumble or fall.

Fears are not always there to be conquered; they can be managed so that there is *no holding back.* Fear is good and healthy as long as it is managed within the range of being frightened, and all it takes is to become specific about the risks, dangers and potential pitfalls. If something has become such a fear that it has caused a block, then individuals, teams and organisations should be specific so that it becomes just something to be frightened of; they should not live trapped by fear. However, if they keep getting caught out by the complacency and unpreparedness of being fearless, then they should consider the specific risks and potential dangers so that they can put in the work to prepare well and work out a plan. If something is worth doing, it should be worth doing successfully.

Coaching tips

- To move from being fearful to frightened, the coaching questions should focus on making specific what it is exactly that is feared.
- To move from being fearless to frightened, the coaching questions should focus on identifying specific things to be concerned about.
- Overcome resistance to this model by communicating the value and power of being frightened.

- Be specific to avoid the reaction of going from one end of the spectrum to the other.
- Deciding not to do something can be a strong choice when it has been thought through. This model is not intended to get people to do everything, it is to help them make more considered decisions and choices rather than be a hostage to their fears.

Acronym for fear

- **F**alse
- **E**vidence
- **A**ppearing
- **R**eal.

The seven levels of fear

1 Doing the wrong thing (paralysis).
2 Wasting time (inefficiency).
3 Things getting worse (catastrophe).
4 Letting go (holding on).
5 Not being able (self-doubt).
6 Being different (normality).
7 The unknown (disbelief).

Courage is not the absence of fear but the triumph over it. The brave are not those who do not feel fear, but those who conquer that fear.

Nelson Mandela

Authentic leadership (trustworthiness)

[**Trustworthiness: Staying true to convictions with integrity and congruency.**]

Authentic leadership is described as an approach that emphasises building legitimacy through honest relationships that value an ethical foundation, truthfulness, openness and consistency. By building trust and enthusiastic support, authentic leaders are then best placed to improve individual and team performance.

Trusted individuals benefit from the support, drive and confidence that comes from having a strong following and so are more likely to remain consistently true to their own values and principles, whereas those who are not trusted enough will often compromise to obtain consensus or will become isolated. Teams that have built trusting relationships benefit from a bonding culture of openness and honesty that encourages ideas, challenge and innovation rather than a divided environment and blame culture that will develop within a team that does not remain true. Organisations are also affected by their level of authenticity because their relationships internally and externally will be far stronger when the organisation drives and behaves in a manner that is congruent with what it believes in and stands for.

Authentic leadership allows individuals, teams and organisations to be clear about their identity and trusted to remain true and aligned to that identity. This strength of connection and clarity of purpose provides a focus and channel for emotion, thought and behaviour to drive towards specific outcomes and results, and in a way that others can engage with, support and follow.

Trustworthiness and authenticity are of key importance in any coaching relationship, so being clear on identity, values and philosophy is a major contributor to the success of coaching and of the coach.

Model 13. The intelligent trust model

The big picture

Trust is described as having a number of connotations: reliance on the actions of another party; the relationship between two people; relationships between social

Figure 5.1 The intelligent trust model

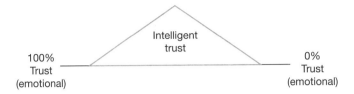

groups; the expectation of a product, service or technology. More than any other component between people, 'trust' is considered the most important, the most essential, the most non-negotiable. An assessment of trust, however, is typically emotionally driven, where the result is either 'complete' trust or 'not at all' and often swings from one end of this spectrum to the other.

This model was created and developed for coaching in response to the various scenarios where relationships, people, products, services or technologies were presented as either totally trustworthy, or never to be trusted again. The practical illustration of the range and scale of trust presents the opportunities and choices to be considered on this most important topic of trust so that the approach can be more intelligent than just emotional, and as with all intelligent strategies, defining the right level of trust to put into specific people and situations can enable great outcomes to occur. With trust, thoughts, ideas, emotions and actions become powerful drivers of positive reactions; without trust, very different thoughts, ideas and emotions become powerful drivers of lesser reactions and behaviour. (See also **Model 2: The feel–think–react model.**)

Trust is such a critical component in relationships between individuals, teams and organisations that this model presents a valuable opportunity for coaching greater performance, support and potential. It is also imperative that the coaching relationship is built upon a level of trust that is intelligent and specific so that it can be sustained and relied upon throughout each situation and scenario.

When to use it

- As a practical model for putting trust into context.
- To avoid the emotional condemnation and barriers of 'cannot be trusted'.
- To avoid the emotional pressure, disappointment and exposure of total trust.
- To appreciate the value and power of intelligent trust.
- To build sustainable relationships and strategies based upon what can be trusted.

How to use it

There is a *spectrum of trust* on which people, relationships, products, services or technology can be placed and categorised as 'can be totally trusted' at one end and 'never to be trusted' at the other. Often, when any of these are somewhere in between these two extremes, the decision will then be to play safe, put them at the 'low-trust' end of the line and wait to see if they earn trust over time. Alternatively it may be decided to give them the benefit of the doubt and put total trust in them from the start to see if they can handle it or whether they will ultimately disappoint over time. Individuals will also do this when wondering whether they can trust themselves in certain situations or scenarios.

As emotion kicks in before intelligence, it is natural to place *emotional trust* in people or products, services or technologies; this will place them wholesale at either end of the spectrum (100 per cent or 0 per cent trust). This is an emotional assessment driven by what is either wanted most (positive), or what is feared most (negative).

The emotional trust question: 'Can I trust this?'

The use of *intelligent trust* is one of the key success factors to master, as it will enable the accurate assessment, management and strategic planning required to successfully get the best results from every situation and relationship. This intelligent approach to trust opens up the full range of the spectrum so that there can be an accurate assessment of not how much it *feels* that someone or something can be trusted, but what they can be trusted *to do* in a specific situation based upon what is *known for sure.*

The intelligent trust question: 'What can I trust?'

Building trust is a key attribute to success, and when established effectively, it will consistently get the best out of people, relationships, products, services and technologies. Intelligent trust is not something that is *earned,* it is something that is *established* based upon what is known for certain. To build trust effectively is to create a balance of what can be intelligently trusted to be done, and what can be intelligently trusted *not* to do.

The value in knowing what can be intelligently trusted is that a strategy can then be built around it so that no one or nothing is left exposed. What can be intelligently trusted should be current rather than based purely upon previous experience or reputation. Assessing what can be intelligently trusted should be considered objectively and calmly rather than at the moment of either delight or disappointment, as this will emotionally skew the thinking involved.

Relationship trust is one of the most fulfilling and rewarding aspects of trust. Emotional trust is a high-risk strategy in relationships as there will be very few people who deserve, can match or can cope with 100 per cent trust being placed in them in every situation. Those few people who can are truly special individuals who should remain precious and highly valued. There are also a few people who truly deserve 0 per cent trust in every situation. Those who do are the people who will be incapable of adding, or refuse to add, any positive value until it is found what they can be trusted to do. Relationship trust is best achieved by taking an intelligent, considered approach as this enables a sustained relationship to be built with appropriate and accurate levels of intelligent trust so that it can adapt and remain relevant as the relationship evolves. The intelligent trust question is: 'What can I trust this person to do?'

- Be specific in all coaching relationships as to what you can be trusted to do so that a sustainable, clarified and consistent level of intelligent trust can be established.
- Clarify what you intelligently trust others to do so that they know they are trusted, but not weighed down with the burden of never letting you down.
- Trust can be a very emotive subject, often being described as something 'lost' or 'betrayed', and therefore these emotions will often have to be managed before you can look at trust intelligently. (See also **Model 10: The five steps to manage emotions model.**)

Acronym for intelligent trust

- **T**rust based upon
- **R**ational
- **U**nderstanding of
- **S**omeone's
- **T**endencies.

The four degrees of being trusted

1 **Distrust (knowing you will not support).**
2 **No trust (doubting that you will support).**
3 **Blind trust (hoping that you will support).**
4 **Proactive trust (knowing that you will support).**

A relationship with no trust is like a car with no gas; you can stay in it as long as you want, but it won't go anywhere.

Anon

Model 14. The identity decisions model

The big picture

To develop authentic leadership, and to build trusting relationships, it is essential to behave, think and react congruently and consistently with the ethics, values, principles and qualities believed in; that is, to behave in a manner that is clearly aligned with the stated *identity* of the individual, team or organisation. When behaviour is out of line with that sense of identity, or there is no clear sense of identity to begin with, then the ability to trust or be trusted becomes an issue.

The model of *identity decisions* was developed for coaching in response to the scenarios and dilemmas caused by a lack of clarity and direction within individuals, teams and organisations. This simple illustration of a strong and clear sense of identity offers a way of making decisions that can channel energies, emotions and behaviours towards powerful and optimal outcomes.

When individuals have a strong sense of identity they have a focus and clarity on what the best choices and decisions are, and they will know that success will be achieved by being themselves throughout the process. Without that sense of identity, or a strong enough connection, they will continually face dilemmas and feel confused as to the best path to take, and success will feel fraudulent for them. For teams, this can also be the case: a strong sense of identity and the determination to behave in a way that is congruent and aligned makes it easier to make decisions and to behave consistently to get the best out of the team. Without this sense of identity and direction, the team can often feel compromised or troubled with the range of options and choices that they face, many of which will be conflicting and divert them from the potential they have as a team. A sense of identity is one of the components that has a significant impact on the success of an organisation, one that knows and understands what it is focused on, and stays true to its values so that it can be trusted and considered genuine in its ambitions. An organisation that does not have this will likely follow any path, and often many different paths in many different directions, without ever reaching a desirable destination. When an organisation is inconsistent in its behaviour or strategies, the path becomes hard to follow and it is even harder to trust.

When coaches are clear and connected to their identity, they then have only to be true to that identity to become the best coach they can be. When that clarity or connection is missing, the coaches' questions become inconsistent in quality and intent, and the sessions delivered will be sub-optimal.

When to use it

- As a practical model to establish or re-establish a sense of identity.
- To develop an identity-based approach to decisions and dilemmas.

Figure 5.2 The identity decisions model

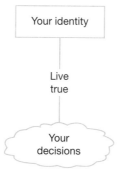

- To increase energy, confidence and self-worth.
- To build a strategy for sustained success and aligned growth.

How to use it

Successful decisions are made when a strong *sense of identity* has been developed; this is about an individual, team or organisation knowing who they are, what they are about, how they see themselves, what is most important to them. The first requirement in this process is for them to consider how they see themselves, how they would want to describe themselves, etc.

Success comes when an individual, team or organisation consciously *lives true* to that sense of identity; if individuals see themselves as 'nice' people then all they have to do is what any nice person would do, say what any nice person would say, behave as any nice person would, etc. This will allow them to align with and channel all their energies by being true to themselves. This is just as true for teams and organisations.

Being wonderfully imperfect, when an individual, team or organisation says or does something that does not align with their sense of identity, all they have to do is *reconcile and reconnect* to get that drive and alignment back. If, as a nice person, they say something mean about someone, they will not feel good about themselves as they are now out of alignment with their sense of identity. But, as a 'nice' person, they can then do what a nice person would do, and say sorry to the person they have been mean to and commit to doing better next time. They will then be immediately reconciled and reconnected with their sense of identity.

With so much going on and so much pressure to deal with, individuals, teams and organisations can forget or lose the connection to their sense of identity, and in doing so then lose their barometer or point of reference for what direction is right for them. They will know this when they try on another identity for size, trying to be something that they are not. They should *avoid getting lost* and remind themselves regularly of who they really are, what they are really about, what is important to them, what they are counted on for, etc.

What individuals, teams and organisations have, what they achieve and what they do can often provide a distraction or cause confusion as to who they really are. This will result in their feeling trapped by expectation or newfound reputation and make them feel they no longer have the same choices. This state of depression reduces their alignment and energy as they experience a sense of suffocation by what they now have or do. (You are a comedian, so make me laugh; you are a parent, so you can talk only about kids and schools; you are a successful company, so it must all be about money.) Individuals, teams and organisations can *escape the traps* by remembering that they are not what they do; that they are not what they have; that they have a specific identity and do things and have things, but are not defined by them. They are successful but sometimes deliver a disappointing result; this does not define them as a disappointment. Separating who they are from all the temporary distractions of what they currently do, or have, helps them retain a connection to their clear and powerful sense of identity.

Coaching tips

- A consistent strategy of 'affirmation' is key to the power behind ongoing success for teams, individuals and organisations. Whether in writing or in the mind, there is power in listing regularly up to seven positive statements of identity so that the connection is reinforced for each situation. (See also **Model 34: The affirmations model.**)
- Creating a sense of identity can often be a case of trying something on for size as a start to see how it feels before developing it further over time.

Suggested starting points

- *For individuals:* A good person; a strong leader; an experienced professional; an entrepreneur; someone who wants to make a difference; someone who does the right thing, etc.
- *For teams:* A team that delivers; a strong unified team; a creative team; a team that leads; a team that makes things happen; a team that makes a positive difference, etc.
- *For organisations:* A good business; an honest business; a strong business; an ambitious business; a disruptive player in the industry; an innovative business; a business that cares; a business that has a positive impact; a quality brand; an exclusive business; an aspirational brand; a value brand; a service company, etc.

The power of affirmations is unleashed when written as . . .

- Personal (I . . .).
- Present (as if now . . .).
- Positive (fantastic, great . . .).
- Passionate (with emotional meaning . . .).

Table of personal identities (estimated)

1 **Absolutist: strong sense of right versus wrong.**
2 **Materialist: aspirational; keen to succeed.**
3 **Egocentric: individualistic, looking for power and respect.**
4 **Personalistic: wants fairness, equality and freedom from exploitation.**
5 **Tribal: follower of strong leaders; seeks safety and security.**
6 **Systematic: in pursuit of knowledge; sees the bigger picture.**
7 **Holistic: seeks spirituality; strives to eliminate oppression.**
8 **Reactive: inward worldview; dependent on others for support.**

Who you are will always trump who you think people want you to be.
Bruce Brown

Model 15. The future self-identity model

The big picture

Authentic leadership and trustworthiness in the context of transformation is the ability to create fundamental change by being consistent, now, to the values, behaviours and principles desired in the future. Whether as an individual, as a team or across a whole organisation, *being* the change that is desired enables the trust, engagement and support to remain throughout the most trying and uncertain times.

Authentic leaders will live and demonstrate the transformation they require so that it is clearly understood, trusted and affirmed. Leaders who fail in this area will appear incongruent to the transformation and will not be wholly trusted in terms of their belief and commitment to the cause.

This model was designed as the next level on from identity decisions (see **Model 14: The identity decisions model**) where the focus on identity is based in the future, but where living true alignment in terms of behaviours, values and decisions starts now. Developed as a coaching model in response to the variety of scenarios that would benefit from having a higher sense of vision and purpose beyond the present, this clear illustration sets out the value of having, and being connected to, a higher sense of identity that will drive successful behaviour, greater momentum and more strategic decisions.

Individuals with a sense of future self-identity have a greater sense of direction which can then inform their choices, behaviours and decisions rather than be influenced, restricted or dictated by where they are now or what they have gathered to date. Teams with a future self-identity can work towards being the team they aspire to be, by committing to those choices, behaviours and decisions right now, whereas teams that are only in the 'now' will often lose the belief, desire and commitment to

Figure 5.3 The future self-identity model

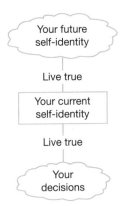

becoming more than they already are. The big opportunity for organisations here is truly to transform their business or their industry by *being* the change they want to achieve, and in doing so they will build the trust, commitment and following of those who can see that there is action beyond the words.

At some point, individuals, teams and organisations will achieve the success and results that they were aiming for. With that success, and all that comes with it in terms of possessions, titles, awards, rewards, status and reputation, it is common for them to accept this as their identity and look to be true to what they should do, positive or negative. Over time they will become trapped by this sense of identity, and their choices, behaviours and decisions will be driven by this persona. The result of not achieving goals can also have a powerful impact on the identity that an individual, team or organisation aligns with and lives true to. A future self-identity empowers the individual, team or organisation to decide what they want to become and make their choices from there.

For coaches to develop a genuine connection to their own future, self-identity is a key strategy in realising their full potential. With this sense of focus and direction, their choices, decisions and behaviours will be clear and instant, their performance consistent and of great impact. This level of commitment demonstrates their credibility to encourage and challenge the individuals, teams and organisations they work with to create and connect to their own future self-identity.

When to use it

- As a practical model to create and connect to an aspirational sense of identity.
- When an individual, team or organisation is being judged only by their current results.
- To develop a future-based approach to choices, behaviours and decisions.
- To increase energy, confidence, self-worth and sense of purpose.
- To focus on a strategy for long-term success and alignment.

How to use it

Define the identity that would be considered as *aspirational*. This should encompass as many aspects as possible in physical, psychological and emotional terms, purpose, etc. It should also outline aspirations in terms of character, approach and demeanour, level of confidence, ambition, drive, personality and happiness.

Consider then the individuals, teams and organisations that truly inspire and be clear on the characteristics they have that would be considered *inspirational*. This is not about what they have or what they have done, it is about the characteristics they have that inspire. (See also **Model 18: The admiration model.**)

Paint, list or imagine this aspirational *self-portrait* of what will be in this future self-identity. The picture should show what the future identity will look like at that point in terms of what is done or had, the relationships, the diet, the lifestyle, the sounds and senses that are wrapped up in it, etc. The ability to engage emotionally with this portrait will determine how much of this picture can be brought to life and have genuine meaning.

The next step is to *be true and aspirational* with this portrait as the guide. For the individual, team or organisation in the portrait, how would they deal with the situations and opportunities they face today? The connection and discipline in this area will determine how quickly the future self-identity can be made real.

The confidence to keep going, the resolve and resilience, the determination and drive to succeed, and the motivation to do even more will depend largely on the ability to *recognise progress* throughout this process, identifying and acknowledging the things that have been done as a direct result of having an aspirational future self-identity.

A further step to protect confidence and motivation is to *avoid perfection,* as aiming for perfection will lead to focusing more on areas that are judged as 'lacking' rather than progressing. Individuals, teams and organisations will always remain as wonderful pieces of work in continual progress. Seeking perfection is only the ego talking; continual improvement is how successful people achieve more and travel further!

Coaching tips

- The most important distinction within this model is that future self-identity is about what an individual, team or organisation aspires to *become*, not what they aspire to *have.*
- Be patient – building, defining and enhancing an 'ideal' will take more time than determining all the things that are to be avoided.
- It is important to reinforce the context that this future-based approach is to enable individuals, teams and organisations to *learn* how to be all that they can be. Consequently, the thoughts, behaviours and choices may not all fit into place right away.

The personal alignment model levels

1 **Environment.**
2 **Skills.**
3 **Behaviours.**
4 **Beliefs.**
5 **Identity.**
6 **Sense of purpose.**

Be the best possible version of you.

Anon

Consistent leadership (conscientiousness)

6

[**Conscientiousness: Being thorough, careful and vigilant, with a desire to do things well.**]

Consistency in a leader is considered to be one of the most important characteristics of success: it allows for measurement; it creates accountability; it establishes a reputation; it ensures relevance; and it maintains the message. Consistent leaders are conscientious: they exhibit self-confidence, act dutifully and aim for achievement through planned behaviour; they are generally organised and dependable. Conscientiousness is demonstrated in behaviours such as being neat and systematic, careful, thorough and thoughtful.

Individuals who become consistent and conscientious leaders develop and maintain habits for success that will enable them to achieve good results time and again. Individuals who are seen as inconsistent and less conscientious are viewed as 'laid back' and less goal orientated or results driven. Teams that are consistent and conscientious in their approach take what they do seriously and systematically measure their performance and monitor progress towards their desired outcomes, whereas inconsistent teams are seen as being less reliable and likely to be disorderly. Consistent and conscientious organisations aspire to be the best that they can be and continually look to what is considered to be 'best in class' as their benchmark. Organisations that lack consistent leadership will lack the focus, discipline and achievement orientation required to deliver on goals and promises.

Coaching individuals, teams and organisations through consistent leadership is about developing great habits for success and approaches that deliver good results, namely the strategies for care, discipline, efficiency, achievement, planning, organisation, thoughtful consideration and measurement.

Model 16. The habits model

The big picture

Consistent leadership is built upon the ability consciously to apply discipline to the behaviours that drive desired outcomes and become habits for success. Whether as an individual, as a team or across a whole organisation, when their character is perceived positively, they will be able to reach positive outcomes and opportunities. However, if the perception of character is negative, the outcomes and opportunities made available will be restricted or removed. This perception is vital therefore in opening up or closing down the opportunity to achieve desired outcomes, and is based upon the habits demonstrated by the individual, team or organisation.

This model was developed and applied to coaching as a practical illustration of the impact that the habits of individuals, teams and organisations have on future opportunities. In addition, the model sets out the process that creates, drives and develops the habit. In setting out what leads to a habit, and then what the habit leads to, this model empowers individuals, teams and organisations to appreciate and protect those habits that take them to where they want to be, and to challenge the validity of and cost involved with those habits that no longer work for them.

Individuals who understand the value and impact of their habits are able consistently to maintain and demonstrate their character and preparedness for being successful; they can continually assess and modify their habits to ensure that their true character and value can be appreciated and understood. Individuals who are less aware of how their habits lead to a perception of their character, and that this will either work *for,* or *against,* what it is that they want to achieve, are not aware of how they are holding themselves back, or that their strongest habits are so vital.

Applying this model for teams and organisations allows a greater sense of awareness of when they need to 'step up' or 'raise their game' to realise the opportunities they desire. Knowing that what used to be good enough is no longer good enough provides the opportunity to redefine and create a 'step change' for success. Without this level of awareness, teams and organisations can aspire to many things but will not be able to convince others to trust and believe in them when their habits are not clearly aligned with success.

Many coaching scenarios involve issues and opportunities around behaviour: what an individual, team or organisation does, or can do, to make happen what they want to happen, or not. It is often the case that those being coached are themselves the

Figure 6.1 The habits model

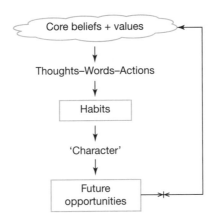

main block to their own success, as their habits do not take them to the outcome they desire. Coaches learn that attacking or criticising or trying to change the habit is not the solution, as they understand what has created and driven the habit. They understand how to challenge in a manner that encourages individuals, teams and organisations to question the validity of the beliefs and values behind the habit. Coaches also know how to help to identify those powerful and productive habits that have become a cornerstone of success and deserve to be maintained or developed even further.

When to use it

- As a practical model to illustrate what creates a habit, and the consequences that follow.
- To develop the awareness and assessment of habits in terms of value and impact.
- To define the habits of success that need to be protected, developed further or communicated better.
- To identify the habits that have become barriers to success.
- To create a strategy for the development and demonstration of habits for success.

How to use it

Habits are driven at source by the *core beliefs and values* of the individual, team or organisation. What they really believe in and what they hold as fundamental values provide the foundation from which all their behaviours that develop into habits derive.

The next step in forming a habit is their *thoughts, words and actions* that follow. When a particular behaviour sits well with their core beliefs and values it is because they *think* the behaviour is right, they will *say* it is right and therefore they will keep *doing* it.

Habits are then formed when the individual, team and organisation think, say and do something enough times that it becomes consistent and almost feels automatic.

The impact a habit has is that it encourages others to create a perception of *character*; good habits lead to positive perceptions, while bad habits project more negatively on character, and therefore reputation.

The perceived character of an individual, team or organisation then has a direct influence on the *future opportunities* they are given. If they have a habit that encourages a positive perception of their character in relation to an opportunity, then that habit is working for them. However, if they have a habit that leads to a reputation that is not appropriate for a particular opportunity then they will not be considered for it.

To *change habits* that work against getting the future opportunities desired, the individual, team and organisation must firstly define what opportunities they want to have, and the benefits that would arise. If the opportunity means enough, this can then be the driver to decide that what used to be acceptable or have value now needs to be challenged. 'Stepping up' occurs when it is realised and accepted that what once used to be good enough is no longer good enough. Even the most comfortable and long-standing habits can be changed when it is realised that they are now blocking a successful outcome.

To *protect habits* that work towards a successful outcome, it is necessary to define further the future opportunities that the individual, team or organisation wants to create and the benefits that would come as a result. If these opportunities mean enough, they can be the drivers to believe in and the habits can be valued even more, so they are not forgotten, neglected or taken for granted. Remember that some habits that were once protected, or are now being protected, may have to be changed at some point in the future. Even good habits can have a shelf life.

To *create new habits* that would open up future opportunities, define what those opportunities are and clearly what they would look like. The benefits and further opportunities that this would in turn lead to can then be explored. If these opportunities mean enough, consider what perception of character and what reputation would need to be established for the individual, team or organisation to consider. Decide then what habits would best create the perception of character to support this desired perception and reputation, and, again, if the outcome means enough, upgrading the core beliefs and values will be less difficult to do.

To develop a *habits strategy* means conscientiously and considerately deciding on the habits that lead to positive results and successful outcomes. To ensure that others can trust that this is a strategy they can believe in and depend upon, it should be communicated and reinforced regularly. Without communication of the thought process and the decision taken, even the best habits of an individual, team or organisation can be perceived as easy, lucky or lacking real thought. (See also **Model 60: The context–consideration–conclusion model.**)

Coaching tips

- Changing a habit requires a change in the core beliefs and values of the individual, team or organisation. As a coach, you cannot challenge or intrude upon their core beliefs and values; this is their space. What you can do is ask the question of whether a particular habit is taking them towards what they want, or somewhere else. It is then up to them to decide either to change that habit, or to continue with it.

- Many individuals, teams and organisations do not have a clearly defined picture of the future opportunities they want to be ahead of them; even those who do are unlikely to appreciate the relationship between the future they want and their current habits, so be patient and work it through step by step.

- It is often the case that some will see their identity as being defined by *what* they do, rather than *who* they are. This can lead to the emotional protection and justification of a habit. (See also **Model 14: The identity decisions model.**) They are, in truth, an individual, team or organisation that can choose to change what they think, do or say without losing or having to change their identity. Separating *behaviour* from *identity* is key.

The perception of your character may not actually be true or accurate, but it is what people will go on, so take care with this:

- Perception is not truth.
- Perception is someone else's reality.
- Someone else's reality becomes their truth.

The top five habits of highly conscientious people

1 **Decisiveness.**
2 **Punctuality.**
3 **Appreciation of formality.**
4 **Holding clear values.**
5 **Demonstrating virtue.**

We are what we repeatedly do. Excellence therefore is not an act but a habit.
Aristotle

Model 17. The strategic measures model

The big picture

One of the clearest methods of demonstrating consistency and conscientiousness is through measurement: if an individual, team or organisation is serious about something, they will have a measurement for it. If someone is serious about becoming faster or stronger, they will measure their current performance, and then their progress. If a team is serious about making a great contribution, it will measure its contribution today and aim for a specific increase tomorrow. And conscientious organisations will consistently measure and monitor the aspects of their people and their business performance that they are really serious about and committed to.

Today, there are more forms and methods of measurement than ever before. To avoid measurement becoming a distraction from performance improvement, or just analytics to record demise, individuals, teams and organisations who succeed in reaching their full potential understand how to apply strategic measures: that is, measurement as a genuine means, method and process to achieve a clearly defined result.

This model was developed and applied to coaching in response to the many projects and aspirations that either lacked a robust level of measurement, or where the amount and complexity of measurement were so heavy that they got in the way of improving the performance or the result. In setting out the four levels of strategic measurement, and their relative importance and interdependence, this model makes clear how to distinguish strategic measurement from the extensive array of things that can now be measured. When individuals, teams and organisations understand what to start, and then where to build next, they can develop a strategy of measurement that is aligned to achieving their desired outcomes and results.

Measurement in coaching has accelerated in recent years, and successful coaches ensure that their selected measures focus on these four key levels, and are related. Such coaches develop a healthy quantity of questions, from which they determine higher quality questions that they can ask. From there, they can begin to assess and understand the real value of the questions they ask, and ultimately appreciate the genuine impact that the questions had. The full effect of their strategic measurement of questions is realised in the combination of asking the right number of questions of the right quality that add real value and ultimately have high impact; all four levels are required to ensure there is a strategic measurement of their questions.

Although individuals, teams, organisations and coaches can achieve success and deliver positive results at any one time, to be consistently successful there has to be a strategy for success; and for a succession of success, there has to be strategic measures in place.

When to use it

- As a practical model to illustrate the four levels of strategic measurement.
- To make clear the relationship between the four levels and hierarchy of measurement to ensure they become strategic.
- To apply strategic measures to a project, initiative or area of performance.
- To develop a strategic approach to measurement for performance improvement.

How to use it

To ensure that success is not just something that is tasted every now and again, individuals, teams and organisations have to be serious about becoming successful. Having decided this, they then have to prove to themselves and others that it is *more*

Figure 6.2 The strategic measures model

than just words this time; to do so they will have to measure, otherwise how would they know? Strategic measurement starts with setting out the desired goal and then establishing the current reality. From there it is about monitoring and measuring progress and performance against the goals.

The first strategic measure is *quantity,* as a level of activity has firstly to be consistently reached to become successful. If someone wants to reach a level of fitness successfully, they will need to exercise more; if they want to be more successful in any aspect of their life or career, they need to do it to a level that will help them become successful and then to maintain it.

When they are happy that they are consistently hitting the level of activity required, the next level of measure, *quality,* is added. This is about improving the standard of what they are doing to become successful while still retaining the necessary quantity. If someone wants to reach a specific level of fitness then it is about measuring the quality of their workouts as well as how often they exercise.

When the right things are being done to the standard required for success, it is important to realise and recognise the *value*: the defined returns gained for getting the quantity and quality right. Someone who is exercising often enough and putting the work into each session will benefit in a range of ways, from feeling more confident, more in control, greater self-esteem, clearer thinking, increased energy, less stress, greater focus, etc.

When someone reaches a level where they are doing the right things as often as they need to be done, and feels that they are gaining the full value from all their efforts, they should move on to the measure of *impact*: the desired result of doing all the right things as often and regularly as needed. Someone who now feels more confident, energised and focused may be able to create conversations, relationships and opportunities, and engage in activities that were previously beyond them.

Continued and ever-increasing success only comes from the *winning combination* of achieving the right quantity of activity at the right level of quality and value designed to have the highest impact. The discipline to keep all four levels of measure as important defines a strategy for a succession of successes.

Consistent success relies upon the individual, team or organisation *redefining success* to retain and refresh their momentum. If at any point they feel that they have reached as high as they want to go in a particular area, they will need to decide on another area to become successful in before 'successful' becomes what they used to be!

Coaching tips

- The key to continued success comes from being able to focus on and develop all four levels of measure. Most will want to progress to the impact level of measurement but often forget about keeping the quantity at the level where it needs to be.

- There will also be some who believe that if they keeping hitting a high quantity then the quality, value and impact will automatically follow; this is neither a strategy of measurement, nor a strategy for success!

The top five facets of highly conscientious people

1 They follow the plan.
2 They stick to the plan.
3 They work to the plan.
4 They take responsibility for the plan.
5 They respect the reason for the plan.

Success has always been easy to measure. It is the distance between one's origins and one's final achievement.

Michael Korda

Model 18. The admiration model

The big picture

Admiration is described as a social emotion elicited by people of competency, talent or skill exceeding normal standards. Admiration is credited with being able to facilitate social learning and motivate self-improvement through people observing and appreciating the abilities and characteristics of role models. The use of admiration can therefore be a powerful driver of consistent and conscientious leadership, acting as a guide and barometer for performance, behaviour and choice.

Being able to admire specific characteristics enables individuals, teams and organisations to connect intuitively with the attributes that can enable them to become what they want to be, to contribute to what they want to be a part of, and be proud of what they represent.

This model was developed as a coaching tool to help individuals, teams and organisations to apply all their capabilities to specific situations and scenarios in order to perform at their best when it matters most. A practical and intuitive process, this model illustrates how to find and get the best from within themselves by connecting to the characteristics that the individual, team or organisation admires most.

As a method for development, the model encourages the admiration of specific characteristics rather than the wholesale admiration of any one individual, team or organisation. This avoids searching for the complete 'ideal' and then pretending to be something that they are not, or missing out on the great characteristics that others have, just because they also have characteristics that are not admired. This more specific and individual approach encourages the search to find admirable characteristics in all people, teams and organisations so that a connection to all the resources within can be utilised. This can create the consistency of results that comes from having developed 'success habits' (See also **Model 16: The habits model.**)

As each coaching session is a 'live' event, there is great value for coaches to be connected to all the characteristics they admire so that they can deal with and excel in all the scenarios and situations that they are presented with. They can then develop their clients by encouraging them to connect with the characteristics they admire in others, open their minds to what they can do, and intuitively connect to all the strong characteristics they themselves possess.

When to use it

- To connect intuitively to inner characteristics of strength.
- To get beyond the flaws and connect with the strength characteristics and attributes of others.
- To establish best practices, approaches and barometers for success.
- To increase confidence and overcome indecision.
- To build a portfolio of success characteristics for optimal performance.
- To perform consistently and conscientiously.

How to use it

The first step in this process is to help create a list of the people, teams or organisations that are *admired*. Write out a list of those that are held in the highest esteem: the people who have inspired; the teams that have done something special; or the organisations that have demonstrated special attributes. The list can include those who are known directly and those admired from afar.

Figure 6.3 The admiration model

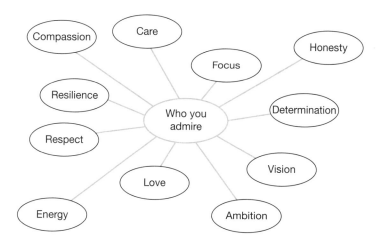

From the list, decide on the *characteristics* that are admired in each one, the attributes that they have. Do not be concerned that there may be some guesswork or imagination involved in deciding what those characteristics are; this is partly an intuitive process.

By listing the people and their admirable characteristics, *intuition* is being engaged to connect these attributes within. For someone to be able to admire a characteristic, they have to be able to recognise it; to recognise it they have to be able to connect with it; and to connect with it, they have to have it. This is why they may select the same person as someone else would, but they will see and admire different characteristics. What they can see and relate to tells you what they have within them, and with confidence and belief in the characteristics they admire, they can create their own authentic version.

The *application* of this model involves deciding on the person they would want to connect with intuitively in a particular situation, issue or opportunity because they admire them for how well they dealt with similar or relevant scenarios. Considering what characteristics the person, team or organisation would bring connects them to those same characteristics they have within themselves. That is, thinking of a friend they admire, a great speaker, a top performer, a great leader, or a celebrity who has always inspired, and considering then what advice they would offer.

To connect to and develop further their own attributes and characteristics for success they can build their *success team* by collating all of the people they admire for their success in specific situations, and then keep them in their mind as their team of advisors. Great success is rarely achieved in isolation, so encourage them to gather together their 'board of advisors' to provide them with an intuitive connection to all the advice, guidance and wisdom they will need to achieve amazing things. They will not have to do it on their own ever again!

Coaching tips

- When someone struggles to admire a person, team or organisation, it may be that they are looking 'wholesale' rather than at specific areas or circumstances and because they are seeing flaws that cannot therefore lead to admiration. Encourage them by suggesting certain well-known people or colleagues and asking, 'What could you admire about them?'

- This model is for connecting to inner characteristics, strengths and attributes by observing and appreciating them in others so that an authentic version can be applied. This is not to encourage imitation or impersonation, or the pretence of being something or someone else. (See also **Model 14: The identity decisions model.**)

The top 10 admired characteristics

1 **The ability to learn.**
2 **Humility.**
3 **Integrity and honesty.**
4 **Resilience.**
5 **Compassion for others.**
6 **Big vision.**
7 **Respect and concern for others.**
8 **Responsibility.**
9 **Inspiring others.**
10 **Reinventing oneself.**

Admiration is the powerful and polite recognition of another's resemblance to ourselves.

Ambrose Bierce

7

Flexible leadership (adaptability)

[**Adaptability: The willingness to show flexibility when dealing with change.**]

Flexible leadership has been described as an ability to lead and manage in a non-rigid manner; however, this can often be wrongly perceived as having a negotiable, consensus-driven or popularity-focused approach. Leadership flexibility is being able to access, implement and execute a full range of strategies and approaches to get optimal responses, returns and results from any given situation or scenario. Flexible leadership is about trusting and being trusted to adopt and adapt whatever style and approach is required to deliver optimal outcomes – to protect the results as 'non-negotiable' by keeping the process as 'negotiable'.

Individuals who demonstrate flexibility and adaptability understand that to be results focused they may need to allow their preferred process to remain open to negotiation. They understand that as soon as they become fixed in their process, the result can be exposed to risk. Teams with the ability to adapt understand the value of defining their desired result first, in order to define a range of strategies, actions and methods that could get them there. Teams that fall short on delivering successful outcomes tend to stick with the process too long and blame the desired result for being too big or unrealistic for their process. Successful organisations learn how to anticipate future likely scenarios so that they can define alternative strategies in advance to ensure that hurdles to overcome do not become barriers. This anticipation of flexibility and willingness to adapt ensures that their approach to success will see them get beyond the many pitfalls and minefields that less successful organisations stumble into.

Coaches who can demonstrate the confidence to be flexible and the ability to adapt give their clients and colleagues great assurance that they will adopt the approach, and be willing to do what it takes, to help deliver optimal results. Understanding the coaching process is a fundamental requirement of good coaches, but any unwillingness to apply that process in a way that works best for the client will be limiting for some, and cause others to disengage or de-select.

Model 19. The negotiable and non-negotiable model

The big picture

A key component of being able to lead with flexibility and to adapt where necessary to achieve a desired outcome is being able to determine and hold true to what is negotiable and what is non-negotiable. The most commonly recognised definitions of 'negotiable' all indicate that when something is considered to be negotiable, it is still open to discussion, debate or modification; it has yet to be confirmed or set in stone. This infers that something considered as being non-negotiable is now confirmed and set in stone, and no longer open for discussion, debate or modification.

This model was developed for coaching to clarify the definitions of each component and the direct relationship between them. Designed as a response to the many coaching scenarios where what was up for debate, and what was not, was either confused or not communicated clearly, this model illustrates the importance of choosing what you want to hold true to, and what happens by default from there.

For individuals, teams and organisations, the model presents the opportunity to make an informed choice of what will be made non-negotiable, and, as a result, what then must be made to remain negotiable. This also provides the facility to avoid the risk of allowing both the process and the result to be perceived as either negotiable or non-negotiable.

For coaches, the model allows you to position options in a way that is fair for men and that offers a choice for women. (See also **Model 3: The men v women model.**)

When to use it

- To prioritise what needs to be non-negotiable and accept that need for flexibility in other areas.
- To get beyond the desire to control all things.
- To provide focus and clear prioritisation.
- To be results driven and to allow the process to breathe.

Figure 7.1 The negotiable and non-negotiable model

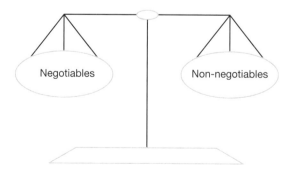

- To provide clear direction and room for others to contribute.
- To manage, communicate and lead effectively.

How to use it

Success becomes far clearer when what is deemed to be *non-negotiable* is distinct from all other aspects and components. List the things that are truly not up for negotiation, discussion or compromise. This should not be an extensive list of non-negotiable things so the approach remains reasonable; however, it should be made clear what these things are. If everything is presented as non-negotiable it will lack the clarity and power of knowing what is most important, and ironically everything becomes negotiable, variable and optional.

To emphasise what is important, now list all the aspects and components that are *negotiable.* This is not to label these things as being unimportant or of no value, just of less importance than what has been deemed non-negotiable. Remember that negotiable means to discuss and agree to find a mutual and satisfactory conclusion, it does not mean that these things do not matter or hold little value. The list of what is flexible and adaptable is recommended to be a more extensive list in order to appear fair and reasonable, and that there is clarity and focus on what is most important.

It will be of great value to remain aware of *the default decision,* when by making something non-negotiable, something else then becomes negotiable by default. If you have in your non-negotiable list that everything must be carried out in a certain way, the level of engagement from others will become negotiable by default. If, however, the non-negotiable list is that everyone is fully engaged to deliver the result, then by default there will have to be room for some negotiation in how things are done and decisions made. Be clear on what exactly is genuinely non-negotiable.

To be sure that this is clear and understood, avoid *the double positive* of making *everything* non-negotiable. When this happens there is no real clarity, direction or focus on what really should be non-negotiable as everything is relegated by default to becoming negotiable, flexible or optional.

The art of *communication* is key in emphasising the balance and consideration of what is non-negotiable and what therefore remains negotiable. For men, this will then be seen as *fair,* while women will have a sufficient element of *control* that can be attained from what is understood to be negotiable.

Coaching tips

- Having things as negotiable, flexible or adaptable can be liberating and allow for a stronger focus on what really is non-negotiable. However, allowing things to be negotiable can be difficult when there is a strong emotional desire to control. By directing this desire onto the result, it becomes easier to find comfort with a more flexible process.

- Letting go of a process so that it becomes negotiable is easier to do when the result being made non-negotiable is significant, important and meaningful enough. If being flexible on the process is still too difficult, then the desired result, and the connection to it, need to be made bigger and stronger. (See also **Model 20: The result v process model.**)

- Having everything as non-negotiable increases pressure, stifles innovation and creativity, hinders growth, undermines self-confidence and restricts the level of success that is available.
- Having everything as negotiable increases anxiety, lacks focus and direction, reduces the perception of value and meaning, undermines self-worth and restricts the sense of achievement or growth available.

The four levels of adaptability

1. **Openness to new ideas.**
2. **Adaptation to situations.**
3. **Handling of unexpected demands.**
4. **Adapting or changing strategy.**

Creating success is like using a camera; focus only on what is most impor-tant and you will capture it perfectly.

Anon

Model 20. The result v process model

The big picture

Consistent and successful leadership in terms of being flexible and adaptable is not achieved by just following a process that will hopefully reach a result; neither is it just about achieving a result at all costs and in any way possible without a method or process. Successful leadership is about having the dual appreciation of the value of focusing on the result and having a robust system or process, but knowing which one to make set and definite and which one to allow some leeway or flexibility. The most successful leadership strategy is results driven and outcome focused, while having the confidence to allow the process to breathe with some flexibility. This approach means doing what it takes to make outcomes happen, rather than having blind loyalty to a process no matter what result it produces.

This model was created in response to the many coaching scenarios where the 'result' and the 'process' were confused, ill-defined or emotionally driven rather than intelligently selected or understood. A practical illustration makes clear the relationship between the result and the process: the importance of the order; the conscious and subconscious choices made; and the defaults and consequences that then occur.

Whether for individuals, teams or organisations, the model enables and informs the choices available to be truly successful and to deliver excellent outcomes. When results driven, there is a healthy appreciation that the process may have to be flexible or adapted along the journey in order to ensure that the desired destination is reached. When choosing to prioritise the process over the result, it may still be possible to achieve the desired outcome, but while the process is made steadfast and non-negotiable, the result becomes negotiable and therefore open to change.

For coaches, the model is best illustrated by the coaching process and the desired results from each session or situation. When the process is kept rigid, there is a risk that what could have been more beneficial in terms of questions or approaches is not considered, and although all the boxes were ticked in terms of process, the outcome is potentially sub-optimal. The coaching process is very important, but the main value of coaching is found in the results and impact that it can have.

When to use it

- To be aware of the choices involved, and the consequences of being either results or process driven.
- To identify whether something is a process or a result.
- To make more informed choices and decisions as to what should be non-negotiable and negotiable.
- To drive a results-driven approach with an appreciation for process.
- To create a flexible process for achieving desired results.

How to use it

Appreciating whether to make something negotiable or non-negotiable is best illustrated using a *piece of string.* At one end of the string there is *a clear result,* and at the opposite end, *a specific process.*

A *nail of focus* is used to pin the string at the point deemed to be non-negotiable.

From all the components involved, *identify* what the desired result is, and then place the other components as being 'process'. If in doing so it becomes clear that there is a better result to be achieved, then change the current result and reposition it now as part of the process. Be sure not to create multiple results by selecting the biggest, most important outcome.

Figure 7.2 The result v process model

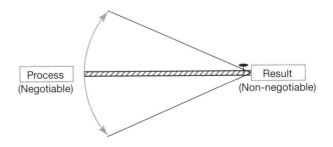

Focus on result is illustrated by pinning the 'result' end of the string; this will make the result non-negotiable and, as a consequence, the process negotiable. With the nail in the result the available range and scope of process are now clear.

Focus on process is illustrated by pinning the process end of the string; this will make the process non-negotiable but, as a consequence, the result negotiable. With the nail in the process the available range and scope of possible results are made clear.

Any components that do not fit properly at either end of the string should be put to one side as they may be *unnecessary distractions,* but, if not sure, it is best to treat them as a potential process.

Coaching tips

- Defining 'result' from 'process' can be difficult and take some time, but it is worth doing well to establish the genuine result required.

- What used to be a 'result' can later become part of a 'process' to achieve even greater results, and vice versa. Ensure that it is the current definition that is being worked on.

- If there appear to be multiple results, explore what the outcome would be if these results were achieved. Focusing on this greater outcome would then allow for these multiple results to be seen as part of a process and become negotiable and flexible. (See also **Model 29: The responsible v accountable model.**)

- Many people have an emotional drive to make the process non-negotiable: men, because it is fair to expect or hope that by sticking to a designed process, good results should follow; women, because it feels easier to control a process than it is to control a result. (See also **Model 3: The men v women model.**) So be persistent and be patient to get there.

The top 10 questions of adaptability

1. What do you want to change?
2. Is this something that you really want to change?
3. What is it that you really want to do?
4. What skills and capabilities do you have for this?
5. Do you want to use your existing skills and capabilities?
6. What are you interested in?
7. What values do you hold dear?
8. Are you prepared to start from scratch?
9. What will it take to make this happen?
10. Will you regret it if you don't?

When obstacles arise, you change your direction to reach your goal; you do not change your decision to get there.

Zig Ziglar

Model 21. The avoiding de-selection model

The big picture

Flexible leaders who demonstrate the ability to adapt their approach, and have a willingness to negotiate the process in order to secure their desired result, will consistently progress further than those who set out a plan that is rigid and inflexible. Flexible leaders appreciate that leading and managing are strategies; choices to make; approaches to consider; part of the process. Those who do not allow themselves the option to choose to lead, or to choose to manage at any point in the process, are making their process non-negotiable and risk de-selection from success.

Flexible leaders understand that there are times to lead and times to manage, and their decision is driven by what they believe is the best approach and process for achieving their desired results. Leaders who lack flexibility and who are less willing to adapt often find themselves forcing a process because of their determination always to lead, or alternatively they do not take the opportunity to step up or forward because they would prefer to manage the process rather than lead.

The concept of *avoiding de-selection* was created initially in response to the coaching scenarios around the topic of recruitment. When this was applied naturally to a recruitment process it became clear that the principles were just as relevant to the many situations that involved any form of process: where there is a non-negotiable, inflexible process, the desired result immediately becomes negotiable.

For an individual, a team or an organisation to implement a rigid, inflexible process they risk having this process being de-selected; they risk those involved de-selecting themselves; they risk being de-selected as the individual to follow, the team to be part of, or the organisation to be with. With an understanding of how to avoid de-selection, individuals, teams and organisations benefit from having an approach that is flexible and adaptable to drive towards the desired results with greater levels of engagement, commitment and contribution; by avoiding de-selection they can then be selected.

Figure 7.3 The avoiding de-selection model

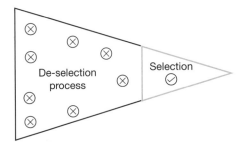

The coaching relationship, particularly in the early stages, will encounter and have to manoeuvre around many pitfalls that could lead to sudden de-selection. These minefields could be in the from of your manner, your choice of words, your use of humour, your intensity or directness, etc. This model provides a guide for traversing the first 90 per cent of the selection process so that you can be selected and committed to as the coach.

When to use it

- To illustrate and then manage the stages of every selection process.
- To develop a strategy for selection.
- To explain how and when to adapt a process.
- To be able to communicate a process and set clear expectations along the way.
- To improve negotiations.

How to use it

No matter what the process of selection is for – a job, a relationship, a supplier, a buyer or seller – *the first 90 per cent* of the process is to look for a reason to 'de-select'. For example, when looking to hire someone and 40 people have decided to apply, the process has to begin by looking for reasons to reduce that number quickly down to a shortlist before the process of selection can begin. The reasons for de-selection will be variable, subjective and emotional, as their purpose is purely to find reasons not to hire at this stage. Only with a small number of applications can the actual selection process begin.

The first stage in avoiding the risk of de-selection is to *understand the stages of the process* so that you know when the time to de-select moves to the time to select.

Next, make sure to *clarify each stage* of the process so that you neither go too far too soon, nor get left behind and therefore get de-selected.

Each stage of the process will have a purpose, thus it is critical to *understand the expectations* involved so that these can be met effectively first time.

The ability to *listen and match* during the process plays a big part in avoiding de-selection so as to work *with* the process rather than *against* it.

As the process moves forward, be aware of the signs that the time for de-selection is nearing its end, which typically is when options and scenarios to consider are introduced. These 'Would you?' questions are a strong indicator that you are now moving towards the start of the selection process. It is vital to remain *open to con-sideration* to avoiding closing things down or becoming too difficult or conditional. These are not yet decisions to make; they are opportunities to intimate willingness and positivity, ensuring that de-selection is avoided.

The reward for avoiding de-selection lies in *the last 10 per cent* where getting selected takes place, as there are now no reasons not to do so; or, even better, hav-ing avoided the de-selection process, there is now the choice of whether to accept the offer, relationship, sale, or whatever.

Successful people focus on the strategy of *win it, then decide* as opposed to talk-ing themselves into, or out of, opportunities in advance of the de-selection part of the process. This approach develops a winning mentality and great self-confidence from knowing how to get to the stage that offers them the options and choices of the last 10 per cent of the selection process.

Coaching tips

- There is an emotional drive to want to get to the selection part of the process, or to see the whole process as being one of complete selection, so it helps repeatedly to frame avoiding de-selection as part of the overall strategy to get selected.

- There is also an emotional push to want to make decisions; to think through things in advance; to run through scenarios as though they were already real. But while there are a number of assumptions or unknowns involved, there are as yet no decisions that can be made. Only once a specific situation is presented, an offer made, a proposition tabled, something to sign up to, or pay for, is there then a real decision to be made.

- Avoiding de-selection is *not* about playing hard to get, it is about working in sync with the whole process. It is always beneficial to intimate interest early in the process, interest in progressing to the *next stage* of the process.

Adaptability is the fusion of two key attributes: flexibility and versatility:

The two attributes of adaptability

Flexibility

1 **Open-minded.**
2 **Collaborative.**
3 **Content.**
4 **Approachable.**
5 **Comfortable with ambiguity.**

Versatility

1 **Objective.**
2 **Considerate.**
3 **Helpful and constructive.**
4 **Compassionate.**
5 **Calculated risk taking.**

Make sure you are consciously rowing your boat, and not subconsciously drilling holes in it.

Anon

[PART THREE]

Results-driven coaching

[
Motivation: The passion to work for internal
reasons that go beyond money and status; an
inner vision of what is important in life, the joy
in doing something, the curiosity in learning,
being immersed in an activity, and the pursuit
of goals with energy and persistence.
]

Motivation is the third of the six key areas of coaching development. Individuals with higher levels of motivation achieve greater results and are fascinated with and driven towards taking the initiative and finding solutions. Teams that have strong motivation use their high levels of commitment as a catalyst to inspire innovative ideas and concepts to achieve successful outcomes. And the most consistently successful organisations have in abundance the optimism and resilience that come from being hugely motivated to keep delivering results.

This part focuses on outcomes and results: the mindset for winning and the behaviours for achievement. Where some may consider the previous two parts as good preparation, this part on motivation is where most people expect to see the impact of coaching really kicking in.

In this part we present motivation as the combination of five elements:

This selection of coaching models has been specifically designed to develop higher levels of motivation.

Goal setting (achievement)

8

[**Achievement: The drive to improve or reach excellent standards.**]

The ability to set goals has long been regarded as an essential attribute for any individual, team or organisation that wants to achieve great things, because, without goals, there is very little motivation to do what needs to be done to be successful. The focus, drive and clear direction that come from having a specific goal is often the visible difference between those who may hope, wish and want, and those who desire, believe and expect. As the late, great author, salesman and motivational speaker Zig Ziglar was known to ask, 'Are you a wandering generality? Or are you a meaningful specific?'

Achievement is found in any hard-won success that faced difficulty or opposition before reaching its goal. Without the goal, there is no real sense of achievement. Coaching is very much goal oriented and results driven, so coaching presents a fantastic vehicle for individuals, teams and organisations to discover the motivation to achieve ambitious and meaningful goals.

Individuals who set goals are easily distinguished from others by their level of motivation and sense of purpose in what they do. Teams that are focused on their goals rise to every challenge and create opportunities to achieve their desired outcomes, while goal-oriented organisations channel their efforts and align their decisions and choices with what can make them successful. Those who do not set goals can only drift in the hope that they will end up somewhere better.

It is difficult to see how a coach could operate without being able to set goals; it would be like being a driving instructor who does not know how to drive. A coach needs to set goals to understand what it is like, and what it takes, to set out and achieve hard-won success.

Model 22. The GROW model

The big picture

A key component in the creation of motivation for any individual, team or organisation is to be able to set and achieve meaningful and impactful goals. With a clear destination in mind that has an emotional connection to a number of gains and benefits, there will be the motivation to work out what it takes to get there, and then to get started. Without a goal, there is nothing to aim for.

GROW (Grow, Reality, Options, What next?) is considered by many to be the fundamental model for coaching as a simple goal-setting and problem-solving process that is easy to share and communicate. There have been several claims since the 1980s as to the originator of the GROW model, and although it is not possible to identify any one author, the likes of Graham Alexander, Alan Fine and Sir John Whitmore are all regarded as having made significant contributions to it.

When applied to coaching, this model provides a simple structure for each session, conversation and line of questioning, producing a clear psychological framework and a process for getting things in the right order. This is a model for any coaching situation, and can also be applied as a clear framework for all forms of communication.

There has been a range of coaching models developed over the years that clearly derive from the GROW model (see also **Model 40: The coach16 model**) and where they have remained true to this process, they have proven to be effective.

When to use it

- As the basic framework for any coaching session.
- As an effective problem-solving process.
- As a model for clear communication or presentation.

How to use it

Be clear and specific on what the *goal* is in terms of what it looks like, what it will mean, what impact it will have, and how it is going to be measured. A written goal is 42 per cent more likely to happen according to the 2015 research of Dr Gail Matthews, at Dominican University in California.

Consider what the current *reality* is in relation to the goal: the progress made so far, the relevant knowledge, experience, expertise and abilities that have been gathered to date. Focus on what has been gathered rather than any perceived gaps. Put more thought into defining why this is a better position, with better preparation, and is better equipped now than ever before in order to achieve the goal.

Figure 8.1 The GROW model

G — Goal

R — Reality

O — Options

W — What next

Explore, design and decide upon the *options* that that will work best to reach the goal. These options may not be what everyone would agree with, but they are about doing what it takes to achieve the goal.

To make sure that things are moving, be clear on the first *what next?* to move towards the goal. These first steps, and the steps that will then follow, provide momentum and a sense of travel that will demonstrate the direction of travel towards success!

Coaching tips

- Stick to the model, and the order: you must always start with the goal.
- Not everyone has a goal to begin with, so be patient and ask questions that will help inspire what the goal could be.
- Make sure the options are not yours.
- Check that 'what next?' is actually the first thing that needs to be done.
- Once complete, recap what the goal, reality, options and 'what next?' are for greater clarity.

The value of a GROW conversation

- **G**oal: Purpose.
- **R**eality: Context.
- **O**ptions: Consideration.
- **W**hat next?: Conclusion.

The seven levels of achievement motivation

1. Staying alive (survival).
2. Staying safe and loyal (relationships).
3. Beginning to separate self from others (self-esteem).
4. Exploring who you are (transformation).
5. Aligning fully with who you are (personal cohesion).
6. Aligning with similar others (making a difference).
7. Fulfilling your potential and giving back (service).

Setting goals is the first step in turning the invisible into the visible.

Tony Robbins

Model 23. The goal-setting questions model

The big picture

The process of setting goals is the development of an action plan designed to motivate and guide individuals, teams or organisations towards a specific, desired and meaningful outcome. The quality of goal setting is largely determined by the quality and order of the questions asked in the process. For goal setting to have the maximum impact on motivation, to have the influence to make things happen, and to be considered as a genuine objective rather than just another dream, there has to be a greater depth of questions beyond just 'What do you want to achieve?'.

This process of *goal-setting questions* was designed for coaching in response to the many scenarios where individuals, teams or organisations had set, or often been given, a goal to aim for yet this had not then generated any increase in motivation or commitment. This practical model illustrates why it is important to go beyond the question of 'What?' because having direction alone does not lead to the achievement of a goal.

By coaching through this model the power of direction can be combined with the motivation, influence and commitment to succeed. (See also **Model 41: The power of 'why?' model.**)

When to use it

- As the basic framework for setting goals.
- As an effective way of increasing direction, motivation, influence and commitment.
- As a model for inspiring greater motivation.
- To re-energise existing goals.

How to use it

Successful goal setting begins by asking the 'what?' question: what is it exactly that you want to achieve? This question provides the important ingredient of *direction* to goal setting.

Figure 8.2 The goal-setting questions model

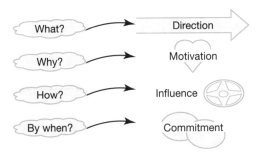

The next step in the goal-setting process is to ask the 'why?' question: what is the reason for this goal, its value, the benefits and opportunities it brings, the impact it will have on you and others, the future successes that then become possible, the knock-on effect, the ripple effect, the biggest picture value for your goal? This question provides the necessary ingredient of *motivation* to goal setting. There cannot be too much of this, but there can be too little, so it is always best to create as many reasons as possible for 'why?' a goal has importance, value and impact.

The third stage in goal setting is to explore the 'how?' question: what are *all* the ways, the options, the strategies, the plans, the ideas and considerations for achieving the goal? With a full list of the many ways in which the goal will be successfully achieved, the options that are believed best suited to achieve it can be selected. This part of the process introduces the ingredient of *influence*; without influence there is then a heavy reliance on the ingredient of 'luck'.

To complete the goal-setting process there must be a specific answer to the question 'by when?' to clarify the date and time by which the goal will be achieved. Only with a clearly stated deadline can the speed, direction and method of travel be assessed as sufficient for a successful outcome. This date demonstrates the level of *commitment* to achieving the goal; this is what separates goals from wishes.

Coaching tips

- Spend time on the 'what?' question until you feel that it is specific and big enough to be remembered and connected to.
- Spend even more time on the 'why?' question; the more reasons for achieving the goal, the more likely the goal will be achieved.
- Spend time on the 'how?' question to explore a range of options; try to avoid going immediately with the first or most obvious option until alternatives have also been given consideration.
- Be determined to get a specific date and time for the goal to be achieved; this is often the most difficult part of the process to nail down, but it is vital.
- Many individuals, teams and organisations drop goals when they are not motivated or monitored. Re-energise previous or existing goals by asking the goal-setting questions.

The five stages of achievement

1 Set your goal.
2 Analyse the ultimate benefits and impact.
3 Put together your strategy for reaching your goal.
4 Implement your strategy with energy.
5 Continue to evaluate and control your strategy.

The four targets in goal setting

1 **The immediate target.**
2 **The definitely achievable target.**
3 **The intermediate target.**
4 **The ultimate target.**

A dream is just a dream. A goal is a dream with a plan and a deadline.

Harvey Mackay

Model 24. The ART in SMART model

The big picture

The greatest sense of achievement comes from having accomplished something that required superior ability, special effort, great courage or extraordinary determination to overcome all obstacles and challenges. The level of ability, effort, courage and determination required, however, is dictated by the size, scale and impact of the goal itself: if it is a big or ambitious goal then it can generate a lot of motivation towards an ambitious achievement; if it is a small and logical goal then it can only generate a relatively small amount of motivation towards something that could have been considered a likely outcome anyway.

Since the November 1981 issue of *Management Review* there has been almost a universal acceptance that all goals should be set to the criteria of SMART (Specific, Measurable, Amazing, Ridiculous, Time-preferred). Going back even further to Peter Drucker's 1954 book *The Practice of Management,* where the concept of 'management by objectives' was first made popular and to whom the concept of the SMART criteria is commonly attributed, there is a strong belief that all goals should be set as specific, measurable, attainable, realistic and time-bound.

When we look at the definitions of goals and then objectives it becomes clearer as to why SMART objectives work so well, yet to restrict goals to being attainable or achievable, realistic or reachable, and then be bound to a specific and non-negotiable time, makes clear why so many individuals, teams and organisations fail to reach the level of motivation and momentum through the goals they set. (See also **Model 53: The momentum model.**)

The ART in SMART model was designed for coaching in response to the most common scenarios and situations where goals were lost or where the goals being set were failing to generate the motivation and momentum required to achieve great things. The most frequent causes included a lack of clarity in the goal; a lack of measurement in terms of starting point, progress or desired result; a lack of aspiration in the goal; a lack of excitement or sense of achievement in the goal; or the disconnection or loss of faith in the goal as time and progress do not appear in sync.

Figure 8.3 The ART in SMART model

S — Specific

M — Measurable

A — Amazing!

R — Ridiculous!

T — Time-preferred

This simple, practical and effective model instantly re-energises, re-emphasises and reinvigorates the goal-setting process, stimulating the emotions, energy and momentum that drive superior results.

When to use it

- As an energising framework for setting goals.
- As an effective way of increasing the emotion, energy and momentum in a goal.
- As a model for building ambitious, stimulating and inspiring goals.
- To re-energise, re-emphasise, reinvigorate or replace existing goals.

How to use it

The first stage of SMART goal setting is the same as with objectives: they should be *specific*. Only when a goal is clearly specified will it provide a strong sense of direction and consistent focus.

Also of equal importance to SMART goals and objectives is that they are *measurable*. Only when a goal can be quantified is it something that can be considered genuine and taken seriously.

While a SMART *objective* may have to be considered attainable, a *goal* should really be thought of as *amazing* so that it goes beyond logic and stimulates emotional engagement and excitement.

Consistent with defining goals as being more energising than objectives, the next ingredient for SMART goals is for them to appear almost *ridiculous,* whereas an objective should be more realistic.

Although SMART objectives are logically time-bound by one specific and manageable deadline, SMART goals should be considered *time-preferred* so that the goal can 'breathe'. This more flexible approach allows the goal to arrive earlier than expected as well as to happen at the right time rather than be pre-ordained. If the goal is big enough and amazing enough it would still be taken even if it were to arrive a few days earlier or later. When goals are time-bound they are often compromised by the pressure of time, whereas time-preferred goals can remain non-negotiable.

- Most individuals, teams and organisations are comfortable, and often defensive, with the concept of SMART goal and objectives setting as long as this means attainable, realistic and time-bound. The quickest way to progress is to differentiate between SMART objectives and SMART goals. SMART goals should be amazing, ridiculous and time-preferred.
- The risk of setting attainable goals is that, once they appear unattainable, they stop being goals.
- The risk of setting realistic goals is that, once they appear unrealistic, they stop being goals.
- The risk of setting time-bound goals is that, when time starts running out, the goals appear to be unattainable or unrealistic (see above) and are then compromised or lost.
- Not everyone can immediately shift their thinking to what would be amazing or ridiculous, so be patient and consistent; it is great practice and great development.

You have a genuine goal when:

- You know what it looks like . . .
- . . . but you don't yet know how to get there.

The three levels of goal setting

1 What you *know* you can do.
2 What you *think* you can do.
3 What you *really want* to do.

It's not enough to want to make the effort, it is in the doing, not just the thinking, that we accomplish our goals. If we constantly put our goals off, we will never be fulfilled.

Thomas S. Monson

Creative leadership (initiative)

[**Initiative: Action taken when presented with, or when creating, opportunity.**]

The ability to come up with a new plan or process to achieve a specific outcome or to solve an issue is an attribute that continues to increase in both value and demand. With the desire to achieve pioneering results in a world where the volume and complexity of issues accelerate faster than ever before, being able to develop and demonstrate initiative has become one of the most powerful attributes of successful leaders.

Creative leadership and being able to take the initiative are seen as clear indicators of motivation and the desire to deliver results. Individuals who develop initiative think creatively and consider alternative ways in which a result can be achieved or a solution found. Teams that are motivated and results driven create an environment that encourages higher performance and higher attainment. Organisations that are considered to be creative leaders avoid the distractions of busy-ness by being clear and focused on making the most important things happen and creating strategies of priority and impact.

Many scenarios brought to a coaching session have reached the point where all existing, traditional or known strategies have fallen short. Being able to develop individuals, teams and organisations to get on the front foot and take the initiative is an important and valuable facet of coaching as it opens up the opportunity to create a clear competitive advantage. To do so with greater credibility, coaches should work continually to develop their own ability to take action when presented with, or when creating, opportunity.

Model 25. The egg-timer model

The big picture

Creative leaders have two attributes which set them apart: the ability to imagine what could be possible and the desire not to accept how things are as how they will always be. Their drive for continual improvement and their ability to have this as a method and an approach rather than just an emotional preference form their clear competitive advantage.

This model was designed and developed for coaching to provide a framework for greater creativity and imagination for those who wished to be known as creative leaders. Where the concepts of 'brainstorming' and 'blue sky thinking' are defined as 'Thinking that is not grounded, or in touch with, the realities of the present', this model takes a starting position from real and present scenarios and from there follows a three-question process to arrive at the optimal solution.

With practice and discipline, the model enables individuals to start from an open-minded, bigger picture perspective in regard to any scenario so that they have a broad range of options to consider and select from. Teams that apply this model are more inclusive and engaging as a team when they start with a large quantity of ideas and input from which they can select the highest quality options. Organisations that adopt this approach have greater conviction and confidence in what they decide as their best option, because it has been selected from a broad range of considerations. Without this model, the pressure of gravity forces the thinking to become very narrow, very quickly, and therefore to restrict options, ideas and creativity.

It is imperative for the coaching process that consideration is given to imaginative, creative and all possible options so that better and best solutions can be created or discovered. This model is a highly effective, popular and easy-to-share process.

When to use it

- As a model to illustrate three levels of initiative.
- To raise the level of approach from all as a 'must do'.
- To open up the mind to what could be possible.
- To connect and combine imagination, thought and action.

How to use it

To open the mind to the possibilities that can be created, *the power of 'could'* needs to be considered. This is the ability to resist the immediate temptation and pressure to know what should or must be done. In as many situations as possible and practical, make sure that the first ask is about what 'could' be done. This is a quantity, high-volume part of the process, so encourage an open flow of ideas and possible solutions without judgement or justification, including the obvious, the creative, the

Figure 9.1 The egg-timer model

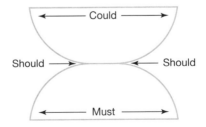

sensible and the outrageous, and everywhere in between. The 'could' question stimulates the imagination to create solutions.

With a sufficient volume of all the things that could be done, move on to *the importance of 'should'* as this question acts as a filter to let only the highest quality options make it through. This crucial filter may be based upon the amount of time available, the scope of the situation, the resources available, or the scale and size of the desired outcome. Some ideas may just not be quick enough, wide enough, viable enough or big enough to make it through this time, but maybe next time, so they should be stored for easy access when the filter changes or is different. The 'should' question stimulates thoughts to consider and evaluate options.

Finally, at the bottom of the egg-timer there should be the purest and highest value ideas for the situation that have been selected and filtered from all the possible options rather than just from what has been done before. *The value of 'must'* ensures that the possible options have been filtered to capture the strongest solutions available, resulting in 'must-do' actions. The 'must' question stimulates action and commitment.

When asking 'must' questions, it is possible to reach what can be considered a right answer. When asking first of all a 'should' question, it becomes possible to find what can be considered a better answer. Only by first of all asking a 'could' question will it be possible to come up with what can be considered *the best answer.*

Coaching tips

- Always start, and stay longest, in 'could' whenever practical, because the process will flow easier when in 'should' and then 'must'

- For many people who have been under the constant pressure of 'must' questions, being asked 'could' questions might take some getting used to; be determined and patient.

- Be strict and consistent with the filter of the 'should' question as this will determine the quality of what 'must' be done. No matter how attractive, engaging or exciting a 'could' is, if it does not make it through the filter it is not a 'must' this time.

- Whatever is collected in 'could' should be kept safe and available for future consideration, especially what does not make it through the filter of 'should' on this occasion. If it is feared lost or forgotten, ideas or suggestions can be forced through the process just in case.

The three Fs of the egg-timer model

- **Free (open and accessible for all).**
- **Filter (sorting value).**
- **Fortune (making value happen).**

The six levels of initiative

1. **You wait until you are asked, or told.**
2. **You ask.**
3. **You suggest or recommend.**
4. **You act, then instantly feed back.**
5. **You act, then feed back when necessary.**
6. **You act on your own.**

Imagination is more important than knowledge. Knowledge is limited: Imagination encircles the world.

Albert Einstein

Model 26. The conditions for success model

The big picture

Leaders who show initiative are able to create and influence the conditions that can allow successful outcomes to occur. These leaders do not accept conditions that they believe hinder the chances of success, neither do they give up on what could be successful because of existing or historical conditions or rules. Leaders with initiative do not take on all challenges under any or all circumstances, terms or conditions, they know what it will take to succeed and make such things their clear conditions for success. With these conditions, successful decisions can be made more consistently.

This model was designed and developed for coaching to encourage positive decision making through the creation of terms, environments, relationships and any other impacting conditions that support successful outcomes. Individuals who are clear on their conditions for success can remove all the unnecessary hurdles and drawbacks so that their focus and energies are geared for success. Teams that understand their best conditions for success set the ground rules and the environment that gets the best out of all the components within the team, and organisations with a focus on creating conditions for success are able to get the maximum return from all their resources and investment to achieve their goals.

Too often, individuals decide to walk away from good opportunities for fear that the conditions may not suit them. Too often, teams take emotional decisions that do not allow them to fulfil their potential as they fight against restrictive conditions that have been put in place by others. Too often, organisations make reactive decisions and are left puzzled and disappointed that what used to be an environment for success has become a haven for mediocrity. With a clear, current and powerful set of conditions that are geared for success, individuals, teams and organisations can channel their focus and energy, and make intelligent decisions, on delivering the outcomes desired.

From the outset in a coaching relationship, conditions for success need to be set out. The fundamental points around confidentiality are a clear example of setting the conditions for success, because, without this, the relationship will only be dealing with varying degrees of failure. For any client, it is of great value to get beyond decisions based purely upon their emotions or perceptions, and to get to a more intelligent decision-making process.

When to use it

- As a model for making intelligence-based decisions.
- To maintain leverage and influence.
- To avoid emotional decisions that are never going to work as they could.
- To create the conditions and environment where success can occur.

How to use it

Take two pieces of paper and at the top of each piece write the current *variables*. This will be the variables of 'yes' and 'no' or 'stay' and 'leave' or 'take it' and 'leave it'. So on one page write at the top the variable 'yes' and on the other page, the variable 'no'.

At the bottom of each piece of paper write out the *constant* as the description of what success is to be; this will be identical on both pages whether or not the ultimate decision is a 'yes' or 'no'.

With one page with a 'yes' at the top and the clear definition of success at the bottom, and the other page with a 'no' at the top and an identical definition of success at the bottom, decide which one will be the *first choice* to work on to create the conditions for success. Both will be worked on, but trust that the one chosen to work on first is likely to be the emotional preference. (This process will ensure that a more intelligent decision is made.)

Working on the first-choice page, start to list *what a person would need to do* to make this choice achieve the definition of success. It should include the things that

Figure 9.2 The conditions for success model

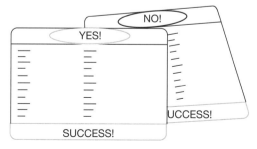

would need to change or be kept the same, the things that would need to be protected or let go, the things that the person would need to be prepared to take on and make happen.

Continuing to work on this page, list *what others would need to do* to make this choice achieve the definition of success. It should include the things that they would need to change or keep the same, the things that they would need to protect or let go, the things that they would need to be prepared to take on and make happen.

Finally on this page, list *what else would need to happen* to make this choice achieve the definition of success. It should include the things that would need to change or stay the same, the things that would need to occur or be avoided, and the things that would need to be assumed in order for things to happen.

With a clear, intelligent, considered and comprehensive strategy which includes all that the person, and others, would need to do in addition to the other things that would need to happen or be assumed, there is now a way of making this decision result in the success that has been defined. But for now, it is *time for a break*; step away from the process and allow some time and space to cool off and refresh.

On returning, refreshed and open-minded, turn to the page with the *secondary choice*.

Focusing on this choice, *repeat the process* of what the person would need to do, what others would need to do, and what else would need to happen, to create an intelligent, impartial, considered strategy for making this choice a success.

Lay both sheets of paper together to compare the differences and similarities of each one. With two intelligent and considered lists of conditions that could make either decision (yes or no) successful, consider what set of conditions the person feels better about, is more confident in, is inspired by and is most excited about. This permits *an emotionally intelligent decision* to be made.

Coaching tips

- Most people make decisions based upon whether they feel they can do something, or they cannot. No matter how they feel, it will be whether they have the right conditions for success that will determine the outcome.

- Everyone is entitled, and best advised, to review their own individual conditions for success rather than accept or work with, or against, the conditions that have been seen as sufficient for others.

- Many people have never consciously set out their conditions for success, so be determined and patient as their coach; what is important to them will come out.

- Many people do not like saying 'no', either because they do not want to offend, or because they are left feeling vulnerable or under pressure. This model allows people always to be able to say 'yes' in future, but always with conditions.

- Having the opportunity to shine.
- There is a clear problem to be solved.
- Having a level of relevant expertise.
- Having good people to call upon.
- Being able and willing to learn quickly.

The real winners are the people who look at every situation with an expectation that they can make it work or make it better.

Barbara Pletcher

Model 27. The task v test model

The big picture

Taking the initiative is something that enables one person to stand out from others; it is a demonstration that one person is asking a different kind of question to everyone else; it is a level of energy, drive and focus that has delivered a type of performance that sets someone apart from the rest.

This model was developed as a model for coaching in response to the many situations where the performance, output and result were crucial for success. The model was then also applied to the many situations where activities, roles and responsibilities were not being viewed as anything other than a chore, or an event to get through, yet these could prove to be vital opportunities to show great initiative.

When individuals understand that they are facing a test, they will prepare accordingly; however. for many of the tasks they are given, they will only do what they feel is expected of them to get through it or get it done. When a team sees itself as being tested, it gathers together all the energy and resources it has to refocus and recommit to doing whatever it takes to deliver the desired result; however, for the many other tasks the team has, these are likely to be delegated and ticked off when complete. Organisations that know that the product they are about to launch is a test of their credibility and ambition will be all over the communication and positioning of that product, they will have everyone at the top of their game and they will be committed to grasping every opportunity. Organisations that see this as just another product launch to get through will be more likely to do only what they have done before.

This practical and easy-to-share model enables individuals, teams and organisations to tap into the additional 16 per cent performance available to them when they decide to treat something as a test rather than just another task.

Figure 9.3 The task v test model

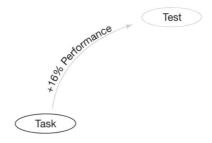

When to use it

- To create opportunities that stand out.
- To increase performance in terms of focus, energy and application.
- To ensure that tests are not failed by not turning up.
- To make clear what the tasks and tests are.

How to use it

A *task* is something that has to be completed or made to happen. The task element for a student is the studying, attending lectures, the reading, etc. The task element in learning to drive is the lessons and studying the Highway Code. The task element of a sports star is the training, the diet, the preparation, the warm-up, etc. The task element for a stage performer is the training, the rehearsing, the warming up, the diet, channelling the nerves, etc.

A *test* is something that has to be delivered to a certain standard and assessed as a pass or a fail. The test for a student is not the study, but the exam. The test for a learner driver is not the lessons, but the driving test. The test for a sports star is not the training, but the performance when the whistle blows, the bell rings or the starter gun sounds. The test for the stage performer is not the rehearsal, but the performance when the curtain rises and the spotlight is switched on.

From an *operational view,* all this is about appreciating that tests and tasks are two different things and understanding whether something we are about to do is a test or task or what components are a test and what components are a task. People may not ever knowingly want to fail a test, but they will fail in all of the tests that they do not turn up for!

From a *management view* it is about appreciating that there are no amount of tasks that can be completed to ever compensate for failing the tests. If a student passes the exams there is less importance attached to how much studying had been done; however, if a student fails the exams it is assumed that whatever amount of study was put in was not enough – grades, certificates, qualifications and degrees are awarded on results. Tasks are important, but not as important as passing the tests.

From a *strategic view* it is about the ability to determine whether a person sees what they do as a 'task' or a 'test' in whole or in part. This is not about assessing a task as testing or challenging, but about deciding that something will be seen as more than just a task and deciding to see it as a specific test. A salesperson may see a presentation to a prospect or client as a task to complete well, in that they should make sure they can make clear to the client everything about the product and services they are selling. A more successful salesperson will see this as more than just a task, but more an opportunity to shine, a chance to pass the test of how much they believe in their product or service, how influential and compelling they can be, how seriously they take what they do, how much commitment they can generate and how big an order they can enthuse the client to place. This salesperson will have a different approach to and energy in their pitch, and their client will know it.

Setting out what is the test and what is the task is a process in *self-selection*: it is about what a person chooses to see as a test, more than just a task required by others. Some people may clearly set specific tests of what they want a person to prove and demonstrate, and give them a definite chance to shine; however, this should not restrict the person in setting out what they want a test to be. Everything cannot be made into a test as this would only downgrade everything to a task, so select the tests that the person would want to take and excel in!

Self-selecting and prioritising tests above tasks opens up the capacity to deliver 16 per cent extra to everything. When something is self-selected as a test, it encourages a person to up their game, to prepare more sharply, to focus more intensely, to aim that bit higher, challenge that bit further and set more specific outcomes to be achieved. A person will see situations as being more important, of higher value and a fantastic opportunity to shine! When a person performs 16 per cent better or higher, they pass those tests!

Coaching tips

- A difficult or challenging task, or something that a person does not like doing, may make it testing, but that is not the same as setting it as a test; a test has a pass or fail.

- Many people miss the opportunity to pass a test because they were so busy with all the tasks they had to do; always prioritise tests above tasks.

- The clear benefits of setting a specific test will show a 16 per cent increase in performance in areas such as preparation, focus, rehearsal, practice, research, presentation, creativity, energy, attention to detail, scope and impact.

- Be careful not to set all things as tests. The point is about peak performance. There should always be many tasks to complete and get through as preparation for when there is a real test.

The top 10 personal tests

1   Character.
2   Integrity.
3   Ambition.
4   Commitment.
5   Drive.
6   Courage.
7   Belief.
8   Determination.
9   How much you care.
10 How seriously you take yourself.

Initiative is doing the right thing without being told.

Victor Hugo

Driving results (commitment)

10

> **Commitment: Willingness to give time, energy and personal reputation to something that is believed in, or a promise or firm decision to do something.**

Being able to do what it takes to make something happen is a key and valuable asset for success. In a world where there is never a shortage of people who operate on a level where they either agree or disagree about something, but as yet do not bring the value of commitment to do anything about it, those who are willing to step up and step forward, really do stand out.

Being results driven is about committing to the delivery of the desired outcome, doing whatever it takes to achieve what has been promised. This sense of accountability brings with it a focus and clarity that ensures that the decisions taken mean the most important things remain as the most important things.

Those who are committed to driving results are more opportunity focused than risk focused, because they see the outcome as the reason to get moving and the thing run towards more than as something dangerous to run away from. This mindset ensures that they will see things through to the conclusion they are aiming for rather than just staying far enough away from danger to feel safe again.

Model 28. The agreement and commitment model

The big picture

Agreement is a positive and valuable reaction and the definition of 'harmony or accordance in opinion or feeling' confirms that gaining agreement is a good thing to achieve or reach.

Commitment, however, can be a far more positive and powerful reaction as the definition of 'the quality of being dedicated to a cause or activity' suggests.

This model was designed for coaching in response to the many unfulfilled situations and missed opportunities where agreement was secured but a sufficient level of commitment was not. A clear and practical model that illustrates the difference between agreement and commitment, it provides insight into making an informed choice between what is required and what is being asked for.

Individuals who appreciate the difference between agreement and commitment know what to ask for rather than project their own judgement onto others. Those individuals who automatically assume that if they have committed, then others will have also, are often left disappointed or exposed. Teams that get beyond their emotional desire for agreement will test quickly to know for sure if there is genuine appetite and commitment to take their ideas forward rather than just be listened to. Organisations that value commitment above agreement go further and engage and assess the level of commitment across their employees because they know that just getting agreement can be cheap and far easier, but of far less value than having a fully committed workforce.

This is a vital topic for coaches to understand fully, because the value, impact and results of each session will be significantly different if the clients are fully committed to growth and success from when they may have just agreed in principle with a concept.

When to use it

- To differentiate clearly between agreement and commitment.
- To define what is required and needs to be asked for; agreement or commitment.
- To avoid projecting or assuming agreement or commitment.
- To avoid over-committing.

How to use it

Agreement is a logical, intellectual and widely available decision used to endorse a thought, idea, initiative or principle. Agreement is an important component that gives credibility to how something or someone is.

Figure 10.1 The agreement and commitment model

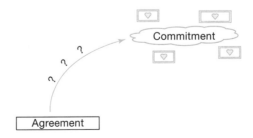

Commitment is an emotional and powerful decision used to create, drive and deliver results and outcomes that were at one stage a thought, idea, initiative or principle. Commitment is a highly valuable component that powers someone or something to what it can be.

For some people, agreement and commitment are *one and the same*; when they agree to something, they also commit. These people are quick to sign up to do things, but they can often become over-committed.

For other people, however, agreement and commitment remain *two different things*; they may be quick to agree in principle with something or someone, but they have yet to make any commitment to getting involved. These people are quick to agree with things but their agreement should not be assumed as a level of commitment to take action.

To *know for sure* whether someone is in agreement and is committed, or whether they just agree with you, requires you to add some questions to the assessment. The difference between agreement and commitment is most clearly indicated by *pictures in the mind*: if someone is committed, they will have begun to paint pictures in their mind about what they need to do, or what this will look like, and what the outcome will shape up as. If someone has only agreed but not yet committed, they will not have these pictures in their mind, because what is being asked of them still remains just a concept. Having gained agreement to meet someone for lunch, for example, questions such as 'What?', 'When?', 'Where?', 'How?' or 'With whom?', and the quality of their response, will give an accurate indication of whether lunch is going to happen or not.

To *develop commitment* ask these questions to help someone begin to build and expand the pictures in their mind with the answers they give; big pictures lead to big commitment.

Coaching tips

- People who commit quickly and easily will often project their approach onto others and end up disappointed, frustrated or exposed; they need to ask two or three questions to know for sure.

- People who agree quickly and easily but are reluctant to commit will often project their approach onto others and end up being criticised for letting others down or not doing what was expected of them; they need to ask two or three questions to know for sure.

- Asking for agreement is a good and positive thing when agreement is all that is sought or needed.

- People who are capable of strong commitment are often difficult to get to agree because they know that by agreeing they are likely to commit. Being difficult to get to agree can be a good sign of someone who can commit.

- People who are very quick to agree (almost too quick) are unlikely to want to commit. Although in the moment of agreement this feels positive, it is best to remember that this is only an agreement.

The six levels of commitment

1 Interested.
2 Informed.
3 Involved.
4 Immersed.
5 Invested.
6 Innovating.

Opportunity is missed by most people because it is dressed in overalls and looks like work.

Thomas Edison

Model 29. The responsible v accountable model

The big picture

Driving results successfully is very much about being able to hold what is most important above all the other aspects that remain important. This subtle differentiation can be applied to being responsible or accountable where in one there is an obligation to do things (responsible) while in the other there is a requirement and expectation that things will be done (accountable).

This model was designed for coaching in response to the many scenarios where individuals, teams and organisations remained unclear as to what they were accountable for, and what then they were responsible for. The confusion and lack of understanding or differentiation between these two components has proven to be commonplace, so this model has been of widespread value in terms of providing clarity and enabling clearer communication, understanding and acceptance.

When individuals are clear about what they will be held to account for, they are then able to manage all that they are responsible for, but not to the detriment of what is their accountability. When teams understand what they are accountable for, they know what their most important measure is above all others and can focus and prioritise accordingly. When organisations develop a culture of accountability, they have all their resources performing interdependently but focused on delivering their part of the equation successfully. Without this appreciation of accountability, individuals, teams and organisations develop a sense of being overly responsible for too many things, leading to process becoming the most important thing above their results, and creating a feeling of being overwhelmed and under pressure. (See also **Model 20: The result v process model.**)

In the scenario of a coaching session, the coach is accountable for the session going well and responsible for being well prepared and alert to picking up all the signals from the client. The client is accountable for bringing to the session the two or three things that are to be worked on, and from there responsible for the level of engagement, focus and interaction.

When to use it

- To be clear on the most important thing to focus on.
- To know the key measure that will be assessed.
- To provide clarity on what is negotiable, and what is non-negotiable.
- To be liberated from overwhelming responsibilities.

How to use it

To be successful, there must first be an acceptance and appreciation of all the things that an individual, team or organisation is *responsible* for. These will be the many key components that play an important part in the things that they do. These components are important, and when they are dealt with in a responsible manner, by providing an appropriate amount of care and attention, they will give in return a strong base for success.

What enables the next level of success to be achieved is being clear on what an individual, team or organisation holds themselves, or is held by others, to be *accountable* for. This will be the singular result that they alone are depended upon to deliver and is treated as their highest priority among their responsibilities. This does not reduce the importance of what they remain responsible for, but elevates the one thing that must be delivered above all else.

The key word to confirm accountability is *consequence*: when there is accountability, there will be consequence. So, when an individual, team or organisation delivers what they were accountable for, there will no doubt be a conversation to be had. When they do not deliver what they were accountable for, there will also no doubt be a conversation. What responsibility lacks is any sense of clear consequence.

Figure 10.2 The responsible v accountable model

Getting the combination right between responsibility and accountability is what develops a genuine winning mentality. To be successful in sport, there is the need to compete to win. There is the responsibility for doing all the things in order to compete and perform to the best of ability, but winners will hold themselves accountable for the result. They will always want to perform well, and are willing to accept variables in what they are responsible for, as long as they are winning.

Being clear on accountability unleashes *the power of singularity,* where the one thing above all others that must be delivered is known and made clear. This power increases focus, drive and resilience while providing enhanced perspective.

Overall, when individuals, teams and organisations are clear on what they are accountable for above all the things that they are responsible for, they experience a sense of *liberation* from the stresses, pressures and anxieties of the many responsibilities that are attributed to them.

Coaching tips

- Many people fear their perception of what being held accountable means, so be prepared for an initial reaction of resistance. If you are determined and patient, there will be a big door to walk through with a great sense of liberation on the other side.

- Many people have the idea in their head that they are either responsible *or* accountable, and so would rather be responsible and avoid the consequences. They are already held responsible *and* accountable but often without clarity on which is which. With clarity they can focus and apply their efforts to the most important aspects with confidence. (See also **Model 19: The negotiable and non-negotiable model.**)

- Holding yourself to account for the one thing you want to deliver is the best way to understand and experience the liberation of being accountable.

Five levels of accountability

1 **For a result.**
2 **For yourself.**
3 **For a team.**
4 **For an organisation.**
5 **For a community.**

Everything in life is a reflection of a choice made. If you want a different result, make a different choice.

Anon

Model 30. The motivation to move model

The big picture

Those who deliver results are known for having their eye on the prize at all times, focusing on what they want and being determined to do what it takes to get to where they want to be. Those who deliver results have great levels of motivation to succeed, great levels of drive and ambition, great resilience and optimism to overcome any challenges, and they will hold themselves accountable rather than look for excuses.

This model was designed for coaching to illustrate why some people are motivated to be successful, while others seek comfort. This practical model makes clear the role of the comfort zone and the impact of focus on either the dangers or opportunities faced. The model was developed in response to the many risks and opportunities faced by individuals, teams and organisations that weighed up the perceived pros and cons before settling down in their comfort zone so that they could motivate themselves and others to commit to their opportunities and become motivated to move.

When individuals develop enough reasons for achieving something they will then overcome their fears and work out how to make it happen; when they do not create enough reasons they will not be motivated enough to do so. When teams are clear on all the benefits and gains of winning, they will summon the strength and find the application to compete and come out on top; however, when they are focused more on the danger of losing, then they will be quickly just holding on and often caught out or come up short. Organisations that lead, communicate and promote opportunity above danger are able to encourage the innovation, creativity and emotional power that make extraordinary things happen. The alternative focus across an organisation only fosters a culture of fear, blame and cynicism.

A coach is best placed as someone who is definitely opportunity focused, but who also has an appreciation of dealing with comfort and perceived danger.

When to use it

- To become opportunity focused.
- To be able to make things happen.
- To overcome fears and manage the perception of risk.
- To understand why you do, and why you do not.

Figure 10.3 The motivation to move model

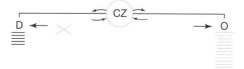

How to use it

Every individual, team or organisation sits on a *line* where at one end there are what is seen as *dangers* and at the other, what is seen as *opportunities.*

Everyone tends to stay in their current *comfort zone,* far enough away from their dangers and also far enough away from their opportunities.

From this place of comfort they will then *weigh up the pros and cons* of the situation, and when such drop-down menus balance out, they will want to stay where they are, in their comfort zone. Only when the opportunity is far greater than the danger will they want to move towards that opportunity.

There will be some situations where they find themselves *stepping out* of their comfort zone, moving towards the potential opportunity, but then their inner voices will talk them back into their comfort zone to avoid the risks that may be involved.

There will also be some situations where they find themselves *falling out* of their comfort zone, drifting towards the dangers they fear, but will then take some sort of action to move away from those dangers, towards their opportunities, only to stop again when they return to their comfort zone.

The drop-down menus of both danger and opportunity are a result of how well an individual, team or organisation can *focus to expand*, and whichever is the greater will become their motivator.

When they are more *danger focused* they will create an extensive list of all the fears, risks and negative outcomes that could come from the situation they are facing. This creates a drop-down menu of reasons 'not to' and of things that they want to avoid, so then they will begin to eliminate the possible benefits of the opportunity from their thinking.

When they are more *opportunity focused* they will create an extensive list of all the benefits, rewards and positive results that could become possible from the situation they are facing. This creates a drop-down menu of reasons 'to do' and of things they want to achieve, so they will begin to eliminate the possible risks of the danger from their thinking.

To make the most of an opportunity it is important to keep an *eye on the prize.* Individuals, teams and organisations can be motivated and *driven by fear* when they want to get away from a perceived danger; however, once they reach their comfort zone they will stop running.

These same individuals, teams and organisations can also be driven and *motivated by success,* and when they are focused on the opportunity and all the benefits and possibilities that become available to them, this approach drives them to achieve sustained success and positive results.

Respect in this regard is earned by being fully aware that there are always both risks and dangers in a situation, but being willing and able to build a compelling drop-down menu of reasons to still go for the opportunity. Pretending or believing that there are no risks involved, or that there are no gains to be had, does not earn that respect.

- Most people believe that circumstances and situations are what determine their choices and decisions. While some people find this model immediately empowering, for others it may take a little time.

- The model is not about letting go of fears or ignoring risks, it is about putting the work into compiling a drop-down menu of reasons to go for an opportunity that is compelling in respect of the dangers involved.

- If an individual, team or organisation has been weighing up a situation for quite a while, or has done so several times but has not been motivated to move any further, it may be because the drop-down menus are currently balancing each other out. If so, they should focus on the opportunity.

- If the drop-down list of danger is greater than the list under opportunity then it would be wise to consider not doing it at all.

- Whatever is focused on will expand: opportunity, danger or comfort.

The seven key personal motivators

1 **Competency.**
2 **Autonomy.**
3 **Relatedness.**
4 **Purpose.**
5 **Meaning.**
6 **Rewards.**
7 **Power.**

Don't ask what the world needs. Ask what makes you come alive and go do it. Because what the world needs is people who have come alive.

H. Thurman

11 Inspirational leadership (innovation)

[
Innovation: Creating new ideas and applying better solutions to meet new requirements or existing needs.
]

Inspirational leaders have the ability to move situations forward towards more positive outcomes, opportunities and results. Their ability to have a clear view and connection to where they want to be enables them to create new paths to reach their desired destination quicker or more smoothly.

From a bigger picture viewpoint, these leaders ask questions of themselves and others that inspire the thoughts, ideas and plans that would otherwise not have existed or been given consideration. This ability changes the dynamics to make success more available and then to extend the possibilities even further.

Comfortable and confident in the chaos that inspirational leadership can create, these leaders have a healthy appreciation of the value of new habits and approaches, understanding that existing habits and approaches will use the same amount of time and energy to maintain as could be invested in new and improved ones.

Great coaches always begin with the end in mind (See also **Model 22: The GROW model**), always look for questions that will open up further possibilities, and always look for the opportunity to develop better habits for greater results. (See also **Model 16: The habits model.**)

Model 31. The end in mind thinking model

The big picture

Inspirational leaders develop strategies, options, solutions and approaches to deliver results that would otherwise not have been given the opportunity to be tested or, in time, trusted. This ability to focus on the desired outcome and take a view from there so that they can reverse-engineer solutions and pathways is what sets leaders apart from others who would prefer to manage.

The concept of this model is the application for coaching of Habit number 2 from Stephen R. Covey's bestselling book *7 Habits of Highly Effective People,* where the reader is directed to 'Begin with the end in mind.' Stephen Covey was a renowned educator, businessman, keynote speaker and author. This model is an ideal model for coaching that fits perfectly with the ethos of the GROW model and all results-driven approaches. (See also **Model 22: The GROW model, Model 40: The coach16 model** and **Model 30: The motivation to move model.**) When applied as a coaching model, what is a logical management tool transforms into a motivating, inspiring and compelling process for achieving extraordinary outcomes.

A simple and practical process, the concept of this model illustrates the power and capability that comes from taking a 'top-down' view on any given situation or scenario. When successfully connected to that desired outcome, individuals, teams and organisations gain a healthy and innovative perspective of where they are now and all the potential steps that they can take to succeed.

When a coach approaches each session with this model they will be open to all the possible questions, pathways and learning that can lead to successful coaching outcomes rather than just taking it one question at a time, where the next question is restricted by the one that came before.

When to use it

- In each and every coaching session.
- At all formal and informal meetings and presentations.
- To provide context for all forms of communication.
- To connect with all the energy, motivation and sense of purpose throughout all projects and initiatives.

How to use it

The full power and benefit of this model becomes available when *ridiculously fantastic outcomes* are set. Make clear what a ridiculously fantastic outcome would be; what would be amazing, phenomenal, crazy, special, tremendous and magical. This should be full of everything that could be imagined and desired to happen. The further the outcome is pushed in terms of scale and impact, the more power, perspective and motivation will come from it.

Figure 11.1 The end in mind thinking model

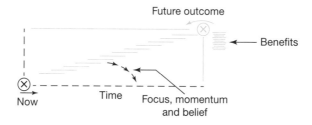

The recommended *timescales* for the desired end in mind should be no less than three years to avoid being too small and short term, and no more than five years to avoid being too distant and vague:

- If aiming for something that has to be sooner than three years, project beyond the current goal to what you would then want three years to be.
- If aiming beyond five years, work out what the goal would be for year 5 within that longer term outcome.

With the desired outcome clearly defined, imagine that it has a *drop-down menu of success* that, when clicked on, lists in detail what it looks like, feels like, tastes like and sounds like when achieved. Continue down that list to explore and expand all the benefits and gains that will then become possible for those that will be involved, touched or affected directly or indirectly by this success. This 'ripple effect' of benefits and gains will determine the level of engagement and motivation generated.

From the ridiculously fantastic outcome with a lengthy drop-down menu of benefits, begin to *work your way back,* detailing step by step in chunks of time. From a desired three-year outcome, determine where progress would need to be at 30 months, then at 24 months, then at 18, and so on until it can be seen where things need to be 6 months from now. This makes clear what needs to be started now to make those first steps. It may then become apparent that there are too many steps and layers currently in place; in fact the outcome may be closer than first imagined.

With all the steps now in place there can be a *mountaintop view* from the summit of the desired end in mind in three–five years, looking back down the mountain to where things are today. This provides the level of resilience required to achieve such great outcomes. This reconnection to what is being aimed for, and all the benefits and gains that will come with it, becomes a powerful source of energy and drive to see things through and keep the result in front of mind.

From the mountaintop view, looking back down to where things are currently helps to gain the healthy perspective that there are indeed 'many winding paths' and options that could all lead to the summit. This provides a valuable reminder to keep the process and journey flexible so that the outcome can remain non-negotiable and set. (See also **Model 19: The negotiable and non-negotiable model.**)

When beginning with the end in mind, all that needs to happen, and the timing of what needs to happen, can be seen in *variable chunks* rather than in set blocks of three–six months at a time. All steps leading up to the summit can then be used as building blocks of preparation for success: sometimes they will happen sooner than expected, sometimes they will take a little longer, and sometimes they turn out not to be needed at all, but the process will remain negotiable to ensure the outcome remains constant. (See also **Model 20: The result v process model.**)

Coaching tips

- When any next steps are presented as being 'critical' or 'make or break' then they are being viewed from the bottom up and lack the perspective from an 'end in mind' view looking top down.

- Many people emotionally want to make their plan linear, in equal and sequential chunks, and always heading in a straight line, yet this is rarely, if ever, a successful strategy. However, it should be anticipated that these emotions will be present to begin with.

- When you begin with the end in mind and work your way back, there are no gaps between where you want to get to and where you are now. When beginning from the bottom, there is always a gap.

- More motivational than the desired outcome is the list of wide-ranging gains and benefits that come as a consequence of success. (See also **Model 41: The power of 'why?' model.**)

The four steps of successful innovation

1 Think *big*!
2 Start small.
3 Test quick!
4 Scale to size.

We may be very busy, we may be very efficient, but we will also be truly effective only when we begin with the end in mind.

Stephen R. Covey

Model 32. The paradigm questions model

The big picture

Inspirational leaders understand that individuals, teams and organisations are the sum and substance of the questions they ask; when big questions are asked, big outcomes can occur, while smaller questions will lead to lesser results. Inspirational leaders appreciate the value of asking questions to create paradigm shifts that challenge the existing concepts, thought patterns, theories, research methods, expectations and standards.

The concept of *paradigm questions* is a method designed for coaching to help overcome or get around the existing blocks in any given situation, relationship or scenario. This practical illustration of how a change of question can inspire a change in perspective or mindset provides an effective and impactful coaching tool for individuals, teams and organisations.

As an ideal approach for when an individual is currently over-thinking an issue, a team that cannot see any light at the end of their tunnel, or an organisation that has begun to doubt its capability and capacity, this model opens the mind to all that could be possible and allows the free flow of ideas to start again.

Figure 11.2 The paradigm questions model

When to use it

- To unblock the thought and idea process.
- To inspire more creative solutions.
- To create a paradigm shift and open up new opportunities.
- To generate a whole new focus and outlook.

How to use it

Open up minds to the creative and innovative inspiration that comes from *paradigm shifts* by allowing the current thinking to be challenged and stimulated by disruptive questions and scenarios. These questions are designed to imagine a scenario that is not currently the case.

Paradigm-shifting questions at their core are *what if?* questions: they stimulate alternative scenarios that challenge and open up existing thought patterns.

In any current situation, begin by considering the questions of *more or less*: 'What if I had more time?' or 'What if I had less time?' Beyond time, apply the *more or less* questions in the most relevant and applicable terms: 'resources', 'money', 'people', 'talent', 'options', 'qualifications', etc. These questions open up choices beyond any perceived restrictions or blocks. List what would be done in each scenario as if it were non-negotiable and had to achieve the desired outcome.

The next level of paradigm questions is, 'What if it had to be you?' and 'What if it could not be you?' These *you or not you* questions open up choices regarding ownership and responsibility. List what would be done as if each scenario were non-negotiable and had to achieve the desired outcome.

The long-term value of paradigm-shifting questions is that they empower people to make *considered decisions.* Having worked out what they would do in any situation if they had either 'more' or 'less', and having worked out what they would do whether it had to be 'them' or 'not them', they can assess the range of options that are now available and make a considered decision on what they believe to be best. The scenarios created go beyond current reality and so extend the thinking to be bigger than the current situation faced.

Coaching tips

- People will engage quicker with these questions if they are first given the context of what paradigm questions are for and why they are an effective approach.

- Some people can feel quite foolish about having had a block that was then removed by a single question, so make clear how common these blocks can be.

- Resistance to paradigm questions comes in the shape of responses such as 'But I can't' or 'That can't be done' or 'But that would never happen.' This is a test for the coach to be confident enough to reinforce the scenario with questions such as, 'What if you had to?' or 'What if it had to be done?' or 'What if that could be made to happen?'

- Always ensure that you do return to the current reality having extended the thinking with good paradigm questions. The current situation may not have changed, but the perspective and thinking will have.

The five stages of a paradigm shift

1   **Informed thinking.**
2   **Destabilisation.**
3   **Disorientation.**
4   **Facilitating environment.**
5   **Reorientation.**

When you change the way you look at things, the things you look at change.
Wayne Dyer

Model 33. The new habits impact model

The big picture

Innovation is a key attribute of successful and inspirational leaders, in particular their ability to create new habits and behaviours that are aligned to achieving ever-greater outcomes. While many leaders may be able to make the decision to launch new initiatives or approaches, only the most successful leaders will drive these new habits through and beyond the 'crunch times' that will always occur to reach greater heights. These leaders understand and appreciate that these new habits will require the same 100 per cent effort, energy and focus that old habits do.

This model was created and developed for coaching in response to the many scenarios where individuals, teams and organisations were aiming for far greater results, yet were holding on to older habits that were no longer fit for this new purpose. The model offers a clear illustration of the process and choices involved in creating, driving and maintaining new habits. Too often, new habits are invested in only until they hit a tough patch and at that point they are hit by doubts or the judgement that the decision to do something new must have been wrong. This model explains the choice to be proactive and continue to forge ahead, or to be reactive and return to old habits at those key moments.

This is a key model for coaches, because often the coach is there to encourage, motivate and challenge new ideas, approaches and habits, so that the process and 'crunch times' can be expected, anticipated and prepared for.

When to use it

- To unleash new potential.
- To manage the process of creating and fulfilling new habits.
- To anticipate the hurdles and difficulties that are always likely to occur.
- To understand the trajectory of being proactive and reactive in those crunch moments.

How to use it

Old habits require a high level of focus, energy, effort and discipline to retain and protect. This investment is often under-estimated or lost because old habits make that withdrawal automatically without requiring any decision or authority over time.

Figure 11.3 The new habits impact model

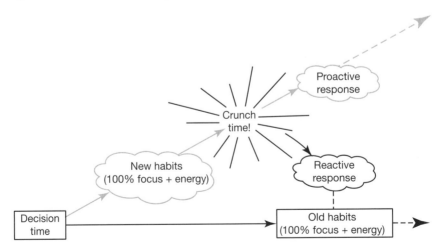

New habits require *exactly the same* level of focus, energy, effort and discipline to create as old habits do to maintain. This investment in new habits is often over-estimated or feels greater because they initially require a decision and recommitment on a daily basis until they become established.

Whether maintaining an old habit or creating a new habit, there will come a *crunch time.* This is when situations, events or circumstances that were not wanted or expected force another decision to be made regarding the habit – whether to continue with it, or to make a change.

There are two responses available at this point. The first option is the *reactive response,* which drives fear, frustration and disappointment, and leads directly back to the 'old habits'. This limiting response erodes confidence, ambition and optimism, and reduces the chances of changes that would lead to success. There is also the choice of taking a more *proactive response,* which drives creativity and innovation, and encourages the creation of new habits. This uplifting response empowers, energises and inspires confidence and belief in success.

Although old habits and new habits require the same amount of focus, energy, effort and discipline, each choice immediately follows a *very different trajectory.* The quality of the choice depends on the destination desired.

It is important to consider that even the most trusted and successful habits will at some point hit a crunch time and a decision will have to be made. Regardless of the emotional or psychological attachment to a particular habit, *all habits get old eventually.*

Coaching tips

- Hitting a crunch time is not a signal of a poor or wrong decision in the first place; if the new habit is going to have any significant impact it is likely to have to go through this tough patch.

- Trying to avoid a crunch time will only lead to trying new habits that are unlikely to be of any significance.

- Anticipating that a crunch time is likely, unavoidable, inevitable or even a very positive sign that the new habit is going to be of significant impact is likely to reduce or eliminate any fear that the crunch time is perceived as a failure or cause for alarm.

The nine personal habits that indicate success

1 You find happiness in the success of others.
2 You continually seek new experiences and learning.
3 You do not think 'work/life balance', you just think 'life'.
4 You are incredibly empathetic.
5 You have something to prove to yourself.

6   You ignore the limiting hype of the 40-hour week.

7   You see money as a responsibility, not just a reward.

8   You do not think you are particularly special.

9   You appreciate that success is fleeting, but dignity and respect last for ever.

You will never change your life until you change something you do daily. The secret of your success is found in your daily routine.

John C. Maxwell

Solution focus (optimism and resilience)

[
Optimism and resilience: Persistence to achieve goals through times of adversity, challenge and setbacks.
]

Being solution focused is the most effective approach to getting results quickly because it is a simple process that emphasises what is already working. As a formal approach, solution focus originated as a therapy model before being applied to coaching and organisational development. Here we will look at the specific coaching models that build upon the following principles:

- Focus on the solution, not the problem.
- Be confident to act upon surface-level information.
- Value the small, sequential steps towards a solution.
- Believe that everything required to work to a solution is already available.

Individuals who have the level of optimism and resilience to remain solution focused are clear on who they are and what it is that they want to achieve. When further developed, they are able to see their desired future as being in the now and living true to this vision. (See also **Model 15: The future self-identity model.**)

Teams with a strong focus on solutions maintain a consistent connection to the results and outcomes they want to achieve to the level of positive expectation. With this, they develop a higher level of awareness of the people, places, situations, conversations and opportunities to help them realise their ambitions. (See also **Model 31: The end in mind thinking model.**)

Organisations that are genuinely solution focused have the strategic and commercial awareness of the value to be gained from investing in ideas and initiatives that offer solutions and potential advancement. These organisations look at the value throughout all phases of these projects and initiatives, not just at the end result. (See also **Model 63: The three-boxes model.**)

Solution-focused coaches look for every opportunity to build on what is already there to help create greater results, growth and sense of achievement. These coaches have an unlimited and unrestricted belief in all that is possible, but with a genuine appreciation that there will be many steps and hurdles along the way.

Model 34. The affirmations model

The big picture

One of the most consistent attributes of those individuals, teams and organisations that drive and deliver good results is that they already believed in advance that they would be able to do so. This is where the power of affirmations comes into its own as its definition suggests: 'statements which affirm something to be true'.

This model of *affirmations* was designed and developed for coaching in response to the many situations and scenarios where the level of belief, optimism and resilience needed to increase before good results could be achieved. This simple and practical illustration sets out the steps to construct powerful affirmations that will become positive self-fulfilling prophecies.

Individuals who build up strong affirmations start to believe and expect that what they desire is here already, or on its way, whereas those without such positive expectation are running a subconscious affirmation of lack and doing without. Teams that regularly affirm and reaffirm who they are and what they are about instil confidence in themselves and so encourage others to support and engage with them to achieve great things. Organisations that clearly state their success and ambition make clear to all that they are committed to success and expect to achieve their goals and outcomes. This generates the positive, solution-focused approaches that ensure that projects, initiatives and products become successful.

A coach can only develop this attribute fully in others if they themselves have powerful affirmations from which to operate. Having affirmations is a major tool for coaches who wish to develop continually and avoid complacency.

When to use it

- To build confidence, ambition, optimism, resilience and positive expectation.
- To support the setting of ambitious and demanding goals.
- To develop a strong solution focus.
- To manifest positive outcomes and results.

Figure 12.1 The affirmations model

How to use it

The first rule of powerful affirmations is that they are *personal*; they begin with *I*. This helps create and establish a positive sense of future identity. Each affirmation must begin in the singular 'first person'.

The second rule is that affirmations are written in the *present*; they are written as 'now'. This is the vital disruptive component that causes the subconscious mind to become active and create connections for realising the affirmation. This ingredient requires imagining what is desired as if it was already in place. The ingredient requires trust and belief in the affirmation process most. This is the part that many people miss out on, or stop adding, but it is the catalyst for making things happen that would not otherwise occur. Adding this component attracts the desired outcome, while omitting this part of the process will only push what is desired further away.

The third rule is that the affirmation must be written in the *positive*: having rather than not having, gaining rather than losing, achieving an opportunity rather than avoiding a danger. While there can be two sides to a coin, positive affirmations are focused on the gains that you want, and your affirmations are wholly positive in their impact.

The fourth rule of affirmations is that they must be written with genuine feelings so that they can be considered *passionate*. This power of emotion will drive and energise the discipline, focus, belief and confidence required to achieve amazing results. If what has been written does not fire passion then it must be expanded until the affirmation becomes something that grabs the emotions and imagination to the point that it is dreamt about at night, and is immediately at the forefront of mind in the morning.

The final rule of affirmations is the need for discipline; if someone is *persistent* enough to write down their affirmations each and every day they will supercharge their journey to amazing outcomes. It only takes a few minutes each day to make the biggest investment possible in the future.

Affirmations will be most *powerful* when there is the right amount of affirmations that offer the right balance and blend. (See also **Model 6: The wheel of life model.**) Writing *seven* affirmations, *seven* days a week, is highly recommended for the most amazing results. If any of these affirmations become less positive or passionate over time, upgrade them to keep them working.

Coaching tips

- Being an expert in what you do not want is very common. Being able to set out what you really do want is, for many people, either difficult or unusual. Be patient and determined; it can sometimes take many attempts to build and upgrade powerful affirmations.

- Writing things down is much more powerful than just thinking them through in your head.

- No matter how good the affirmation, it should be open to review and improvement when something even more inspiring comes to mind.

- What is written down is now on its way, so be alert for all the signs of progress that will remind you that you are on the right track.

Providence is when opportunity meets preparation. Your job is to make sure you are ready and prepared so that the right opportunities can arrive at the right time; affirmations are your preparation.

Desire, Ask, Believe, and Receive – Stella Terrill Mann

Model 35. The gestalt model

The big picture

To develop being solution focused, optimistic and resilient to a more advanced level, those individuals, teams and organisations that are able to make extraordinary things happen combine the principles of affirmation with the applied science of gestalt. (See also **Model 34: The affirmations model.**) With the confidence, ambition and positive expectation that come from writing down a desired future state as 'now', those who stretch far enough, and who are determined enough, will stimulate the power of their subconscious mind through gestalt.

The definition of gestalt is: 'An organised whole that is perceived as more than the sum of its parts.' It is a German word meaning whole, pattern or form and it sits in the subconscious mind. The practical role of gestalt is to help make sense of the world that is seen in the conscious mind, therefore retaining sanity and order. Gestalt acts as a bridge between the subconscious and conscious minds across which they can send messages and communicate.

Where writing affirmations is the mechanism to create a state of reality for the conscious mind to see, gestalt can then be stimulated to create all the connections to what will be needed to bring that reality into being.

The gestalt model was designed and developed for coaching as a powerful tool to create solutions and drive results that would otherwise not occur. As a clear and simple illustration of what can be considered a complex science, this model offers a practical process that can stimulate extraordinary results and achievements for individuals, teams and organisations.

As the science and psychology of gestalt may be no more than a vague concept for many to begin with, it is advisable for coaches to develop some personal experience and awareness of the topic in advance so that the natural questions and queries can be anticipated and responded to properly. Being able to shift dynamics and then manifest outcomes using gestalt presents amazing opportunities and potential.

When to use it

- To expand confidence, ambition and positive expectation.
- To understand the process of manifestation.
- To shift dynamics and create new solutions.
- To channel all available energy to achieving amazing outcomes.

Figure 12.2 The gestalt model

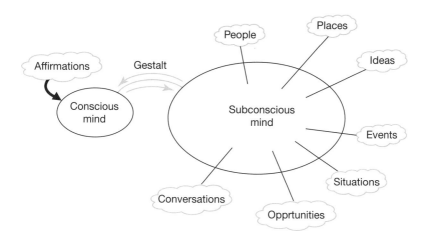

How to use it

As mentioned above, gestalt is 'an organised whole that is perceived as more than the sum of its parts'; it is a German word meaning whole, pattern or form. Gestalt sits in the *subconscious mind,* which is nine times the size and capacity of the *conscious mind.*

The practical *role* of gestalt is to help make sense of the world that is seen in the conscious mind, therefore retaining sanity. Gestalt acts as a *bridge* between the subconscious and conscious minds across which they can send messages and communicate.

Designed to help *make sense* of the world that the conscious mind observes and believes, gestalt responds by sending back concepts, ideas, theories and analogies that build the picture that is being seen and believed. So when someone behaves in a way that was not expected, others will look to create a story or explanation that makes that behaviour make more sense.

To assist further, gestalt creates *connections* to people, places, situations, opportunities and conversations to bring into being what the conscious mind perceives to be true. So when someone comes to mind who has not been seen in years, they then call or email, or appear all of a sudden.

Gestalt provides a very strong power of *attraction* because whatever the conscious mind perceives (positive or negative), gestalt will work to help make that mental picture make sense by connecting the necessary people, places, situations, opportunities and conversations.

- *On the positive* side, this makes gestalt a powerful way of attracting and connecting with all the positive things desired just by imagining and believing in all the best things that could happen.

- *On the negative* side, however, gestalt is equally powerful at attracting and connecting all the negative things feared just by your imagining and believing in all the worst things that could happen. Gestalt does not judge or differentiate between 'positive' or 'negative'; it just works with what someone chooses to input.

To *stimulate and generate* it only requires the creation of pictures in the mind. These pictures are immediately sent from the conscious mind across the bridge to the subconscious mind and gestalt quickly gets to work on it if there is enough desire and belief in the pictures. If the level of desire and belief is not sufficient, however, it is unlikely to have enough energy to stimulate gestalt.

Committing to *affirmations* (see also **Model 34: The affirmations model**) is the most powerful way in which to manifest amazing results through gestalt. The daily writing and conscious connection to affirmations that are *personal, present, positive, passionate, persistent* and *powerful* provides a toolkit for attracting the people, places, situations, opportunities and conversations that create special and extraordinary outcomes.

It is always best to be *in the driving seat* in terms of gestalt so that it is possible to control the direction of travel. That is, to be clear on the fantastic, amazing, illogical and outstanding outcomes and destinations that can be reached; to write out affirmations in the personal, present, positive and passionate; and to do so persistently so that gestalt kicks in and gets to work. Negative thoughts, however, will be at least as powerful as positive thoughts, so make sure that the positive thoughts are in the driving seat pushing the right buttons.

Persistence is key to success with gestalt. When an affirmation station something in the 'now' is consciously written down, the subconscious mind will initially reject this affirmation as being merely a 'wish'. However, by persistently writing this affirmation out, and reaffirming the desire and belief in it, this creates the chaos in the subconscious that stimulates gestalt to help make sense of what the conscious mind sees and believes. This is why writing affirmations down once is less effective; it may actually work out in the long run, but stimulating gestalt is a powerful accelerator that attracts the people, places, situations, opportunities and conversations that bring what has been created in the mind into being.

A clear indicator that gestalt has been generated is when *sensory acuity* has been activated and recognised. This is the heightened awareness that people, places, situations, opportunities and conversations are now beginning to appear. This may be an advertisement on a billboard not noticed before, the friend of a friend who happens to be already doing what is being aimed for, the study class that appears out of the blue, the car in the exact colour desired appearing more and more, or the chance meeting with a stranger or someone not seen in years; all are examples of gestalt activating sensory acuity, designed to encourage to keep up the good work and get ready for successful outcomes.

Coaching tips

- Avoid getting too hung up or obsessed with the science involved (there is a world full of research). Awareness of what gestalt can do and how it can be applied is of greater value as a coach than getting drawn into deep analysis of the topic itself.
- The most effective explanations of gestalt are simple, practical and by example.

- Gestalt is a capability within everyone, but as with all capabilities it may be at varying degrees of development, maturity or strength; it may also vary in terms of being trusted or acknowledged. Keep it simple, and take small steps.

- When coaches practice and develop their own understanding of gestalt they are better placed to help, support and challenge the individuals, teams and organisations they work with.

The five ways to increase your resilience

1 **Pump up your positivity.**
2 **Live to learn.**
3 **Open your heart.**
4 **Develop healthy habits.**
5 **Hang on to humour.**

It is the heart that knows the path. The mind is just there to organise the steps.

Jeff Brown

Model 36. The cupcakes model

The big picture

Those individuals, teams and organisations that drive successful outcomes by being solution focused, always optimistic and reliably resilient all have an astute appreciation of value that goes beyond the singular measure of the end result; they appreciate, value and capitalise on the various stages of gain and benefit throughout the whole process.

This model was designed and developed for coaching in response to the many situations and scenarios where solutions, ideas and initiatives were left unsupported or rejected because a one-dimensional measure of success could not be guaranteed. With a wider understanding of all the positives that come from engaging in each stage of the process when creating a solution, there is greater optimism, resilience and motivation for success.

Individuals who develop a 'cupcake' mentality when building solutions capture all that is to be gained at each and every stage of the process, while others stall and become reluctant to make things happen in the absence of guarantees or certainty of result.

Teams that lack understanding of all the benefits that can be created as a result of setting out to achieve something when there is a lack of certainty will walk away from the opportunity to achieve things of any significance for fear of failing, while those who can see that success is a journey, with a series of levels, stages and checkpoints that could inspire even greater outcomes, make quicker decisions and get started.

Organisations that apply a 'cupcake' approach to the creation of solutions and initiatives understand the richness of the learning experience. Resilient, optimistic and focused on the positive, these organisations encourage and support all endeavours that can lead to a range of successful outcomes, in addition to the ultimate result. Organisations that lack this level of optimism and value in learning will choose only to invest, authorise or sanction what they believe to be a definite and controlled outcome, and although these may be achieved, only the less significant solutions come with such assurances.

A 'cupcake' approach is important for a coach to adopt and develop in order to create and recognise the value throughout each and every coaching session rather than chasing down or trying to force 'light bulb' moments as the singular measure of success.

When to use it

- As an optimal approach for initiatives, launches, solutions and projects.
- To communicate the full and wide-ranging value of an initiative.
- To develop a wider appreciation of value in the learning process.
- To protect the value of creativity and innovation with resilience and optimism.

How to use it

One of the main obstacles to achieving and creating great things is the approach of *one-dimensional success.* This is the sole focus on success being exclusive to the result: the destination; the outcome. With this restricted appreciation of success that sits only in what happens at the end, an initiative is less likely to get started, and even if it does get going, the initiative is unlikely to gain enough support, investment or time to reach completion.

Consistently high achievers go on a *journey of success* where each step has value, learning and progress which are then seen as successes. With this open appreciation of success throughout all that happens along the journey, as well as in reaching the destination, there will always be value to be gained, always valuable possibilities to be explored, always succeeding, always successful.

The *cake* is the largest component and foundation of this model. The cake represents all the benefits, learning and experience that will be gained, even just as a result of setting out on the journey. These successes will range from what is communicated by stating the decision to go on the journey to all the conversations, meetings, ideas, insights and connections that will now occur because of the decision to travel.

The successes that make up the *icing* on top of the cake include the additional skills, understanding and knowledge that will be gained as the journey continues: the

Figure 12.3 The cupcakes model

people that will be met, the situations encountered, even the other paths and journeys that may be discovered, all because of the decision to travel.

The *cherry on top* here is then the ultimate success where the specific outcome that was set is achieved: reaching the desired destination; attaining the final goal.

The *taste of success* can be on several levels: cake can taste good, even on its own, but tastes much better with some icing; cake with icing is a sweet taste, even when there is no cherry on top. The complete taste, however, comes when the cupcake is completed with a cherry on top, when the ultimate goal is achieved as well as enriched with valuable learning and experience throughout the process.

The ultimate aim should always be for 'cake and icing, with a cherry on top', but there should always be the appreciation and value of being able to *eat cake* throughout the journey, always learning, always developing, always growing, always succeeding, always getting better prepared to provide a solid base to future initiatives.

Coaching tips

- This model is not designed to encourage devaluing or forgetting about the ultimate result; it is about developing a healthy appreciation of all that can be gained and learned from the experience in addition to achieving the goal. (See also **Model 30: The motivation to move model.**)

- This model is excellent for developing a stronger awareness, recognition and appreciation of success throughout all stages of a process; this helps deal with the fear of failure that holds many people back.

- Each coaching session should be an example of a cupcake where there is an appreciation of the value in being there, actively listening, and remaining an objective partner throughout; getting to know and understand each other; asking questions that may open up new perspectives or ideas; and yes, there may be some real breakthrough moments that open up a world of new possibility.

The seven habits of optimistic people

1 **Express gratitude.**
2 **Invest time and energy.**
3 **Listen with interest to others.**
4 **Gather with positive people.**
5 **Ignore negative mindsets.**
6 **Forgive.**
7 **Smile – a lot!**

A positive attitude causes a chain reaction of positive thoughts, events and outcomes. It is a catalyst and it sparks extraordinary results.

Wade Boggs

[PART FOUR]

Coaching for greater influence

[
Social skills: The ability to understand the
emotional makeup of others and the skill in
treating others according to their emotional
reactions.
]

Social awareness is one of the five key areas of development for individuals, for teams and for organisations. People with high social awareness connect better, relate better and communicate better. Teams with high social awareness collaborate and create better, and ultimately deliver better results. Organisations that clearly have a high level of social awareness are always in touch with the mood and feelings of their audience and are quick to respond. Coaching for greater social awareness helps develop and empower individuals, teams and organisations to become more connected to, trusted by and of service to their chosen audience. They know how to get the best out people and of a situation; they know how to create environments and relationships for success.

As a coach, many of the scenarios and situations you will work through with your clients will have their root cause, and their gateway to fantastic outcomes, grounded in their level of social awareness. When it is understood how best to connect with people, how situations best work, what the key motivations are, and how to get the best out of all the resources available, then great outcomes become possible. In many ways, social awareness can be considered to be the oil in the machine, without which it will ultimately grind to a halt, while a well-oiled machine runs fast, smooth and effortlessly.

In this part we present social awareness as the combination of these four key elements:

This selection of coaching models has been specifically designed to help develop a higher level of social awareness.

Creating powerful connections (empathy)

[
Empathy: Understanding what another person is experiencing from within the other person's frame of reference.
]

Coaching and developing greater empathy enables and empowers individuals, teams and organisations to connect better with others, and in doing so become more influential. This ability to understand and appreciate the feelings of others helps build trust and extend the options for more effective communication between people. People without empathy, no matter how talented or determined, quickly become isolated and marginalised.

These benefits extend into the coaching and development of teams because, with greater empathy, they can have the optimal conditions required for collaboration, innovation and delivery of collective results. A team that lacks empathy can quickly become a disparate collection of individuals or develop into siloes.

Furthermore, the benefits of empathy are often what drive the success of organisations – internally with their employees, then externally with the customers, partners and suppliers. An organisation that can relate to the emotions and feelings of its audience will always outperform one that lacks that connection and bond.

As a coach, it is imperative to develop and demonstrate a high degree of empathy with your client because, without that bond, rapport, trust and connection, the coaching relationship is not going to be of any significant value regardless of the quality of the content. Being present and actively listening is key. Paying attention not just to what people say, but how they say it, will also give you some indication of how they are feeling, as will all the subtle facial movements and body language. However, the clearest way as a coach to develop and demonstrate your empathy is to do what good coaches do: ask good open questions about how someone is feeling.

Model 37. The creating the common ground model

The big picture

Individuals, teams and organisations that look to establish powerful connections and higher levels of empathy develop strategies and approaches for bringing together the focus and energy of all into a common and shared outcome, above the distractions and divisions of personal preferences, emotional reactions, disagreements and points of conflict.

This model was developed in response to observing so many conversations and meetings where people were actually saying the same thing and aiming for the same outcome, yet became embroiled in argument, debate and emotional conflict around issues that were often incidental to the outcome. This scenario was also noted in many individuals who developed inner conflict and distraction from their desired outcome to their emotional or assumptive preferences.

Whether applied to an individual, a team or an organisation, this model is a highly effective coaching tool to help enhance focus, drive, energy and perspective. The coaching relationship itself is a great beneficiary of the model when applied consistently.

When to use it

- To channel all effort and energy towards a compelling and shared outcome.
- To maintain a healthy perspective of what is essential and therefore non-negotiable, and what is just preferred and therefore negotiable.
- To encourage respect and collaboration towards ambitious outcomes.
- To galvanise others to commit to delivering results.
- To drive the behaviours that will generate success.

How to use it

Define what is currently understood to be *common ground*. This is the outcome that has been committed to, by the individual, the team or the organisation as a whole. This first step may require some development to make common ground clearer or specific. This first step may even indicate that there is a lack of common ground

Figure 13.1 The creating the common ground model

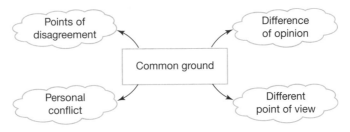

altogether and so this process should be started with the key question, 'What would everyone be able to sign up to as a fantastic outcome?' Common ground is easier to establish the further it is projected forward. Any difficulties in establishing common ground are caused by the emotions around the present and the next steps. It is a future-based destination that can hold gains and benefits for all.

Explore the big picture impact. This is about clearly defining the benefits, gains and opportunities that will be created for everyone involved as a result of reaching common ground. This step generates and strengthens the connection, commitment and ability to communicate the desired outcome.

Extend the big picture impact. This involves looking beyond the immediate benefits and gains involved and connecting to all that will then become possible as a result of achieving the desired outcome. This step stimulates powerful motivation by seeing the desired outcome within an even bigger picture with benefits and gains on a scale that makes the outcome now compelling. This will be most important when hurdles, barriers and detours have to be dealt with on the journey. It is always best to have these compelling reasons captured at the start.

Acknowledge and respect differences. All opinions and points of view need to be acknowledged and respected without judgement so that they do not become an unhelpful distraction, hurdle or barrier. This is easier to do when the scale of the common ground outcome has already been established and accepted as being the most important thing. By comparison, it allows all opinions and points of view to remain important without ever needing to become most important.

Maintain a healthy perspective. From the outset, and then consistently throughout the journey, referring to, connecting to and reminding those involved of the common ground outcome, and all the big picture benefits and gains that have been signed up to and committed to, ensure that a healthy perspective can be maintained, even in the midst of the challenges and detours that may have to be faced.

Coaching tips

- As a coach, it is always powerful to be true to the concepts that you are employing. Establishing a clear and desired common ground outcome with your client will ensure that neither you, nor your client, allow your personal preferences or comfort to become a hindrance to the coaching opportunities ahead. However, throughout you must acknowledge and respect the opinion and view of your client at all times without judgement. Personal mission statements, team projects and company visions are all great opportunities to create common ground.

- Be sure, however, that you have acknowledged and respected your client's opinion and views to the client's satisfaction before you try to move on. Feelings and opinions that appear to have been disregarded or not taken seriously enough by the client will only reduce the relationship over time. This model works quickly so you need not be in a rush to get there.

- Finally, as the coach, your empathy extends to being able to understand and appreciate the opinions and views involved; you are not there to agree or offer your opinion, as this would only serve to emphasise and focus on the opinions and views rather than the outcome.

- As always, be confident with what you are doing; think big, be positive, listen and pay attention.

The four types of empathy

1 **Cognitive: being able to see things from another's point of view.**
2 **Emotional: literally feeling another's emotions.**
3 **Concern: recognising another's emotional state.**
4 **Experiential: gaining direct experience of another's life.**

No-one cares how much you know until they know how much you care.

Theodore Roosevelt

Model 38. The setting emotional contracts model

The big picture

The concept of setting emotional contracts is a vital component in ensuring that value is offered, delivered, received and appreciated. It is a clearly stated agreement between individuals, teams and organisations with their audience that makes clear what is being offered or requested, and what exactly is being asked for, or can be expected in return. Clear emotional contracts protect and develop relationships of value, trust and influence.

This model was developed for coaching in response to the many situations where individuals, teams and organisations were left feeling resentful, under-valued, taken for granted, insulted or made to look like fools, having provided some form of service, product or offering without being clear on what they would want or expect in return. This was also observed within individuals who had done something for themselves without clarity on what they expected to happen next.

Equally, there are as many situations where people feel either overwhelmed or under pressure by how much is being done for them or being given to them; some feel uncomfortable while others have feelings of low self-worth. Some assume what they should give in return and others decide what was probably expected of them, almost always left wondering if they had got it right.

Overall, the lack of setting clear emotional contracts remains one of the major reasons why personal and professional relationships break down or create tension between people.

The setting of emotional contracts is a valuable component for creating successful relationships based upon specific expectations, stated value and the importance of all parties contributing. This model concentrates on the 'giving' situation, but can be easily adapted.

For a coach, the model holds significant resonance between the coach and the client.

When to use it

- To establish a clear understanding of the value, expectation and importance of the contribution between individuals, teams and organisations.
- To avoid 'one-way' relationships which build resentment and destroy trust and value.
- To ensure that relationships are maintained, balanced and fair.
- To create, maintain and develop relationships built upon trust, value, mutual respect and worth.

How to use it

Choosing and communicating what is going to be offered is the first part of setting emotional contracts so as to make clear the extent of the *commitment*: the things that are willing to be done or what is being offered; what the expected contribution is. This is important as it lays out to all parties the specifics of the commitment so that it can be accurately understood, expected and valued.

Knowing then what will complement and work well with this offering is the second part of the process: to make clear *what is expected in return*. This is vital as it communicates the value that the other party can offer: that they play an important and valuable part in the contract, and that they also have a clearly defined role with expectations. This protects people from assuming or guessing what they could or should do to 'pay back fairly'. It also makes clear that there is something to give in return that is of value and would be appreciated.

The secret of success, though, is vital here: the *appreciation of value* must be clearly stated and communicated so that others know specifically what would be valued from them, or the extent to which it is of value. This helps both parties achieve a sense of fairness and parity based upon recipient appreciation rather than level of difficulty or inconvenience to the provider. Appreciation is best measured in terms of value and impact rather than just quantity or complexity.

It is important *always to ask for something* since asking for nothing communicates that there is nothing of value that the other person could offer. Avoid at all costs the perception that there is little or no value in what is being offered or could be offered in return, as this destroys self-worth and ultimately the relationship.

Figure 13.2 The setting emotional contracts model

It is important to understand that *intention does not equate to value.* No matter how positive the intention may be, if what is given or offered in return is not what is needed or expected or relevant, it will not be of any great value. Clear advance communication and agreement of value will enable you to avoid what is one of the most common relationship minefields.

Even as the 'recipient' it remains vital to set a clear emotional contract in advance so that *what is expected* in return can be assured, or made clear otherwise so that feelings of being over-committed or under-valued are avoided. When *making a request* for the contributions of others, make clear what is on offer in return, or alternatively ask for clarity on what they would want.

Coaching tips

- As a coach, setting clear emotional contracts is a key component of a successful coaching relationship. Not every client has a full understanding of what coaching is and is not, but even when they do, it is valuable to make clear what you are able and willing to do as the coach and what you then expect in return. This allows both of you to be assured as to what your contribution and value are to be. It can also be applied to coaching teams and in your relationship with the organisation as a whole. These clearly stated contracts help provide assurance and increase confidence in the people and the process.

- Be careful, however, that both parties are making commitments on their own behalf, as there can be a case of a strained relationship where both parties are focused only on what the other party needs to commit to.

An example coaching contract

I will do all that I can for you as your coach. I will come prepared for each session, focused on you and the topics and goals that you want to work on. What I am looking for in return is that you come to each session with two or three things that you really want to work on that would make a difference for you. This will ensure that you get the most out of the coaching process as each session will be driven by you and I can then bring everything I have to help, support and challenge you to get to where you want to be.

The six habits of high empathy

1 **Cultivate curiosity about strangers.**
2 **Challenge prejudices and discover commonalities.**
3 **Try another person's life.**
4 **Listen hard and open up.**
5 **Inspire mass action and social change.**
6 **Develop an ambitious imagination.**

I've learned that people will forget what you said, people will forget what you did, but people will never forget how you made them feel.

Maya Angelou

Model 39. The connect 2 understand model

The big picture

The concept of first of all making a connection with someone so that you can then begin to truly understand is clearly not a new concept, but it is often forgotten or maligned. Too often people want to judge others based upon what they think they know of them and they never reach the level of relationship that comes from under-standing. Knowing how someone will react may allow you to predict or manage behaviour, but understanding why someone reacts in a certain way allows you to influence that behaviour. To understand someone we first of all have to connect. In the absence of understanding we are left only to project our own reasons why we would have acted in the same way, and often this leads us to make an unfair and inaccurate judgement of others.

This model was developed for coaching in response to the many issues where clients are emotionally wrapped up by what they know has been said, done, or hap-pened, yet they do not yet understand *why.* Without that level of understanding they can only look to predict or manage the situation. Only when they are connected, so that they understand the situation, are they then able to influence.

It takes the same amount of energy and effort to influence a situation or relation-ship as it does to predict or manage it. The awareness and ability to connect so that something or someone can be properly understood opens up fantastic opportunities for individuals, teams and organisations, and of course coaches.

Individuals can become more influential in creating the situations and relationships they want rather than feeling helpless, resentful of or negatively accepting behaviours, reactions or actions that do not work for them. Teams can become more focused and channelled towards high performance with an understanding of how to get the best out of each other rather than having to deal with the disharmony, conflict and strained relationships that can arise with different personalities and skill sets. For an organisation that has a strong connection with its people and its audience, it has the ability to engage and influence behaviour from a strong base of understanding and appreciation.

Figure 13.3 The connect 2 understand model

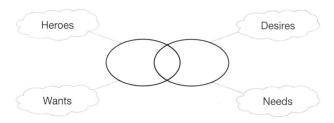

For a coach, the ability to develop the level of connection with clients so that you establish a deep and individual understanding of why they do what they do, say what they say, feel how they feel and react the way they do puts you in a place where you can truly become a strong positive influence.

When to use it

- For individuals, where relationships have become strained due to the behaviour or actions of others that are known, but not yet understood.
- For teams, when behaviour and perceptions of others are causing a distraction or becoming destructive.
- For organisations, where data and feedback have been collated and received on topics such as employee engagement or customer satisfaction, but as yet not understood.
- For coaches, where they need to go beyond just getting to know their client, or when their client would benefit from developing a connection and understanding of what the client is going through in order to be better placed to influence a positive outcome.

How to use it

Ask questions to understand a person's *wants*: the logical things that would sensibly make things better for them.

Ask questions that help go beyond their wants to get to their *needs*: the logical *and* emotional things that would really make things different rather than just better for them.

Connecting further involves asking questions that help tap into the level beyond wants and needs into their genuine *desires*: the emotional and imaginative things that generate compelling energy and passion for them.

The strongest level of connection comes from questions that find out who they regard as their *heroes*: the people or organisations they admire most, wholesale or in specific scenarios. This powerful insight opens up a level of connection that goes far beyond what can be seen on the surface, allowing you to understand and empathise with this person at a deeper level than most others ever will. (See **Model 18: The admiration model.**)

This more detailed and in-depth picture and profile help to go beyond just knowing what someone's actions are, but to understand the cause behind them. The level of connection enables greater influence from a position of understanding.

This level of connection and understanding may not change the 'what' and 'why' something is said, but it will inform 'how' best to do so to achieve the best result.

Coaching tips

- As a coach, connecting with someone so that you can understand them better is a vital component of your coaching relationship. To do so effectively, you must be able to suspend your own judgement and genuinely listen to how they answer your questions. As soon as they feel that you have judged, you will lose that connection. You are there to understand so that you can then be a positive influence.

● Be careful not to be so keen to make a positive difference that you fail to connect with and fully understand your client. It is often the case with coaches that their positive intent drives them in the direction that they want to go in rather than understanding where the client needs to explore. Applying this model with rigour will ensure that you develop a connection and understanding that will endure beyond any one situation to create a long-lasting and positive relationship.

The six steps to empathy

1 **Put aside your own viewpoint.**
2 **Try to see things from the other person's point of view.**
3 **Validate the other person's perspective.**
4 **Examine your attitude.**
5 **Listen.**
6 **Ask what the other person would want to do.**

Empathy is about standing in someone else's shoes, feeling with his or her heart, seeing with his or her eyes. Not only is empathy hard to outsource and automate, but it makes the world a better place.

Daniel H. Pink

14 Establishing success dynamics (situational awareness)

> [**Situational awareness: Reading the mood and feeling of a group, the relationships involved, and the issues present.**]

Coaching and developing greater situational awareness provides the potential to understand the dynamics involved around people, teams, organisations and performance. Being able to make sense of how things really are empowers people to make choices and create strategies that can influence situations to a positive conclusion. When people clearly have low situational awareness they can become unintentionally disruptive or unhelpful, which means they are often left outside or marginalised, or judged as being inappropriate or obsolete. With good situational awareness you will always be involved and included, as you will be trusted to make positive and constructive contributions. If you are ever told that you 'Just don't get it' then you are being judged as having low situational awareness.

The benefits of high situational awareness extend into groups and teams as the ability to read the mood and feeling of the people involved, and, increasingly, for those who are less directly involved will ensure that they develop ways of working that are collaborative and constructive. As a collective unit with high situational awareness, they will produce output and deliver results in a way that is relevant and of high value to their audience.

An organisation with high situational awareness will have the opportunity to lead and challenge its industry, confident in its ability to do so in a way that provides positive direction, motivation, influence and commitment. This strength enables the organisation to make things happen in a manner that its audience want to engage with.

Finally, as a coach, one of the most important attributes you can bring to the coaching relationship is high situational awareness: your ability to ask questions and join dots to help your client paint a bigger, brighter and clearer picture. With high situational awareness you will know exactly how best to coach your client through any scenario based upon your accurate reading of the mood and feelings, the relationships involved, and the issues around them.

Model 40. The coach16 model

The big picture

The aim of this model is to create a matrix structure that illustrates the combined benefits of the two fundamental components of coaching:

1. The base model that all coaching has been built upon, namely the GROW model. (See **Model 22: The GROW model.**)

2. The four base coaching questions of 'what?', 'why?', 'how?' and 'by when?'. (See **Model 23: The goal-setting questions model.**)

The coach16 model is a 16-point process developed in response to the many coaching conversations that were inconsistent and often ineffective. The result, as with many fundamental models that have been around for a long time, was that people were taking bits of coaching models and piecing them together in ways that appeared to be more convenient and comfortable rather than because of the impact they could have. For instance:

- Too many meetings and conversations miss the 'goal' component and start with the 'reality' question of 'Where are we now?' This generally leads to conflict and disagreement because of the lack of shared purpose (GROW becomes ROW!).

- Many meetings and conversations miss out both the 'goal' and the 'reality', starting with the 'options' component of 'What are we going to do about it?' This generally leads to painful experiences because of the lack of purpose and understanding (GROW becomes OW!).

- Then there are those meetings and conversations that skate along on the thin ice of 'what?' questions without ever providing the depth that comes from the 'why?', 'how?' and 'by when?' questions. These meetings and conversations may provide direction on what the goal is, what the current situation is, what the strategy should be, and what the first thing to do is, but they will lack the motivation, influence and commitment required to achieve great things.

When applied either as a coaching model or as a framework for presentation or communication, the coach16 model delivers output that is comprehensive and conclusive. The GROW model was created to ensure that there was always purpose, understanding, a strategy or plan of what to do and then finally some clear actions. The four coaching questions were designed to assess and improve the clarity and sense of direction, enhance motivation, increase the ability to influence and test the level of commitment. The matrix framework of the coach16 model provides a sequential process to combine and amplify the thinking and message of the user.

The coach16 model provides an ideal model and structure for every coaching session or presentation. For an individual, it clearly identifies the components required to be successful and shows in which areas they are strong, which ones they need to work on further, and which ones they are currently missing. For a team, the model provides a common framework to collect and communicate the current thinking of the team so that it can pinpoint the areas that it is strong in, and those to develop further. As with an individual and a team, when an organisation has a strong sense of purpose in where it wants to go, a genuine understanding of where it is, a strategy and plan for the future, and then clear and specific actions to get started on, it is an organisation that *can* achieve things. Combining the organisation's clarity of direction, compelling motivation, confident influence and determined commitment, they then have people who *will* achieve great things.

For a coach, this model provides a comprehensive and conclusive process that ensures each and every session or conversation has optimal value for the client, the group or the organisation.

When to use it

- To provide a structure and process to your coaching sessions and conversations.
- To deliver a comprehensive and conclusive presentation or important communications.
- To build a powerful and compelling strategy for delivering goals.
- To instil a project management approach to issues, opportunities and scenarios.

How to use it

For a strong and clear sense of *purpose,* the first set of questions is goal oriented:

Q1: What is your goal?

Q2: Why is this goal important and of value?

Q3: How will you best achieve this goal?

Q4: By when will you have reached this goal?

Figure 14.1 The coach16 model

	G	R	O	W	
What?	1	5	9	13	– Direction
Why?	2	6	10	14	– Motivation
How?	3	7	11	15	– Influence
By when?	4	8	12	16	– Commitment
	– Purpose	– Understanding	– Strategy	– Action	

To ensure that there is a strong level of *understanding* of the current 'reality' the next set of questions is:

Q5: What is the current situation in relation to your goal?

Q6: Why are you in this current situation?

Q7: How does your current situation impact on achieving your goal?

Q8: By when did you decide to change your current reality?

Begin to establish a *strategy* by asking the 'options' questions:

Q9: What is your preferred option to help you achieve this goal?

Q10: Why is this your preferred option?

Q11: How will this preferred option help move you towards this goal?

Q12: By when will this option begin to make some difference?

With the core components in place, move into *action* with the 'what next?' questions:

Q13: What is the very first thing that you need to do?

Q14: Why is this the first step to take?

Q15: How will this first step move you towards your goal?

Q16: By when will this very first thing be done?

1. Increase and improve the 'what?' answers for a stronger and clearer sense of *direction.* This will involve thinking bigger and being more specific (Q1, Q5, Q9 and Q13).

2. Increase and improve the 'why?' answers for a greater *motivation.* This will involve expanding on the reasons and associated benefits (Q2, Q6, Q10 and Q14). (See also **Model 41: The power of 'why?' model.**)

3. Increase and improve the 'how?' answers for a stronger level of *influence.* This will involve making greater connections and alignment of the things that you do to the desired goal (Q3, Q7, Q11 and Q15).

4. Increase and improve the 'by when?' answers for enhanced *commitment.* This will involve making dates and times clear, specific and non-negotiable (Q4, Q8, Q12 and Q16). (See also **Model 28: The agreement and commitment model.**)

Coaching tips

To get the most out of the coach16 model there are four key questions to focus on:

What is the goal you want to achieve?

This will determine the scale and scope of the following 15 boxes; if it is big, bold and ambitious, there will be great quality throughout the process. If it is small, cautious or unspecific, the rest of the boxes will quickly get into the weeds and get stuck. To be sure, take time to challenge and encourage a big and specific goal before you move to the next boxes. (See **Model 26: The conditions for success model.**)

Why is this goal important to you?

This will indicate whether there is or will be sufficient motivation to achieve the goal. If there are less than seven reasons why it would be a great goal to achieve, then it is highly likely that the goal will not get the effort and support necessary when it needs it most. To be sure, take time to expand on all the reasons and benefits involved. This may be the box that you spend more time on than any other; it is that important! (See **Model 41: The power of 'why?' model.**)

What is the very first thing that needs to be done?

This is an important indicator of how well things will be picked up and moved into action. If you do not know the very first thing you need to do, then there is little chance you will work out the next thing after that. To be sure that what is being offered is the very first thing, keep asking what would have to happen before that until you are convinced that it is indeed the very first thing. Have the courage to make this first thing small and detailed. Then you can move on to the next thing, then the next one, and so on.

When will this first thing be done by?

This is your best indicator of the level of commitment that has been generated. If the answer is vague (asap) or too distant (over the next few weeks or months) then it indicates that there may be a good level of agreement but not yet the necessary level of commitment. Best to be sure by nailing down a specific date and time. (See **Model 28: The agreement and commitment model.**)

The oil of influence

The 'how' line of questions is where the component of 'influence' is assessed and developed. These questions will ensure that the coaching process runs smoothly or otherwise.

All 'how?' questions must be referred back to the goal

Q3: How will you best achieve this goal?

Q7: How does your current reality impact on achievement of your goal?

Q11: How will this option impact on the achievement of your goal?

Q15: How will this first step impact on the achievement of your goal?

The four levels of situational awareness

1 Understand the formal and the informal structure of the situation.
2 Understand the climate and the atmosphere.
3 Understand the formal and the informal relationships involved.
4 Understand the underlying issues and tensions.

The first step toward change is awareness. The second step is awareness.
Nathaniel Branden

Model 41. The power of 'why?' model

The big picture

The importance and value of motivation have been covered in all areas of personal, professional and business performance. The value of having a powerful reason for what you are doing is clearly defined in the book *Man's Search for Meaning,* by Viktor Frankl, an Austrian neurologist and psychiatrist who was also a holocaust survivor. The conclusion is that when someone has a big enough 'why?' they will overcome any 'how?', but when someone has very little 'why?' even the most straightforward 'how?' becomes difficult.

This model was designed and developed for coaching as a way to ensure that coaching sessions and conversations were aimed at motivating people to make a difference in what they were doing rather than just being a comfortable chat or analysis. Many people (but not all) come to a coaching session already knowing what they really should be doing but have not yet found the reason or motivation, so the role of the coach is to help them find this – their big enough reason why.

While the 'what?' to do provides direction, and the 'how?' identifies the opportunity to influence, it is the 'why?' that provides the motivation to do what needs to be done to achieve great things. (See also **Model 50: The what, why and how model.**) For many individuals, teams and organisations it is typical to go straight from the 'what?' to the 'how?' and then wonder why ideas, concepts and initiatives never achieve their full potential. For those with a big enough 'why?' all things become possible. If you have enough reasons to achieve something, you will work out what it takes to get there and be willing to commit to it.

Individuals, teams, organisations and coaches who want to make a really positive impact in life or business learn to appreciate the value of having or generating a big enough 'why?'. Those who had the ideas, the plans, the strategies, the tools at hand, but who didn't have, or lost or became disconnected from, a big enough reason 'why?', would have stopped or walked away from what was possible before success could have been achieved. Overcoming the hurdles in life or business is due more to the level of motivation than any other single component; that is the power of 'why?'.

Figure 14.2 The power of 'why'? model

When to use it

- Throughout every coaching session and conversation. (See **Model 40: The coach16 model.**)
- Throughout every project that would benefit from greater motivation and commitment. (See **Model 37: The creating the common ground model.**)
- When goals, initiatives or projects have run out of steam and would benefit from re-energising.
- When deciding what initiatives, projects or goals to focus on as a priority.
- To increase motivation and resilience for important opportunities, issues and scenarios.

How to use it

Develop *big onion motivation* for any goal by asking on a layer-by-layer basis the 'Why would I, or anyone, be motivated to do this goal?' question.

Start with *individuals*: Why should they be motivated to achieve this goal? What difference will it make? What value does it have? What will then become possible for them? What will achieving this goal communicate? What would they then aim for next? And so on. (This can also start with a specific team or organisation where appropriate.)

Expand the layers with the *others involved* in achieving your goal; Why should others be motivated? What is in it for them? What is the value to them? What difference will it make for them? What then becomes possible for them? What will it communicate? What could they then go on to achieve? And so on.

Extend the layers even further by considering *the wider audience* who will be affected by achieving this goal: those who will gain or receive something from it, those who hear about it, those who get to play some part in it, those who learn from it or those who are inspired by it, etc.

Continue to expand, extend and collate a growing list of reasons and benefits as the reasons why achieving this goal will make a positive difference until the goal becomes truly *compelling* and irresistible – a 'no-brainer'. Only then will someone be ready to do whatever it takes to make this happen. Do not worry if they do not know for sure how they will achieve their goal, because when you have enough reasons why, you will do what it takes to work it out!

- Asking questions to increase the reasons why something should be done helps to generate increased motivation to do it. For all the goals that have been previously set, but not seen through, the dominant reason for these goals not being realised will be an insufficient definition of the goal and its connection to its benefits and associated gains. Help to create these reasons so that they become compelling, then keep referring back to them so that the connection remains strong and current, otherwise they can become weak or forgotten over time.

- It is important to understand that when someone genuinely struggles to come up with enough reasons why to achieve a goal, then they either have to create more reasons, or have to be honest and accept that this is not a real goal for them and something they are unlikely ever to achieve. When this is the case, it is always far more constructive to find a goal that they can be motivated by rather than over-analyse why their current goal just does not work. Over-analysis or judgement only undermines their confidence and you run the risk of having a particular goal because they *should* be motivated by it, rather than because they are. If it does not float their boat, then it is better to help them find what does!

Empowering to remember

If you really had to, you would.

The five steps to build situational awareness

1 Be clear on the desired outcome.
2 Assess the needs and motivations of those involved.
3 Decide upon what is negotiable and non-negotiable.
4 Connect with those involved.
5 Ensure that everyone involved is kept in the loop.

Small moments matter – especially when they remind you of big dreams.

Anon.

Model 42. The dynamic leadership model

The big picture

Dynamic leadership is the ability to connect with and influence others based upon your awareness, understanding and appreciation of what is most important.

This model was developed for coaching in response to the many situations where individuals, teams and organisations are unable to lead positively and influence those around them. The whole focus of this approach is to create a direct link of value from your top priority to that of the person you are looking to influence. This connection is key to being able to influence others on the basis of what is most important to each of you. (See also **Model 39: The connect 2 understand model.**)

The model is the remedy to the three most popular, yet unsuccessful, strategies to influence others:

1. Enforcing your top priority as theirs (bullying and directing).
2. Pretending that their top priority is also yours (insincere and false).
3. Settling for any common denominator (compromised and ineffective).

For individuals, dynamic leadership presents the opportunity to protect what is most important to them while still being able to appreciate and work with what is important to others. Without this ability to connect, individuals are left either to battle with others to get them to agree, or to concede what is important to them. Often the approach that some take is for someone to 'win' and someone else has to 'lose' in these situations, and that is always sub-optimal.

For teams, this model opens up the possibility to get everyone fully motivated and focused on achieving shared and common goals, even though the reasons for each team member to be motivated may be different. This allows teams to have a consistently high level of motivation from everyone involved, with what is most important to each of them being appreciated and acknowledged. Without this appreciation, most teams are left to operate at a varying level of motivation because they only connect to a common thing of importance that is not anyone's top priority.

For organisations, being able to connect their top priority to that of the people, customers and suppliers they want to influence opens up the possibility of high-value 'win–win' solutions and situations. Alternatively, many organisations are left trying to convince their audience that they share the same top priority, which is rarely trusted and often proven not to be wholly true.

As a coach, being able to make these connections is imperative. If clients feel that their coach may be working more to the coach's own agenda then the connection and rapport will quickly disappear. If clients suspect that their coach is pretending to share the same priority then they will take longer to trust and engage fully. If they feel connected with their coach at a lesser level than their top priority, they will not see a great deal of value in that relationship. A coach's priority should be to do great work and be of great value to their clients so that the coach becomes known, recommended and endorsed as a fantastic coach. The clients are there to achieve what is most important to them. Dynamic leadership enables coaches to have confidence in different priorities and the ability to connect their top one with the clients' top one.

Dynamic leadership creates a connection based upon what is most important to each party so that there is the opportunity to influence 'win–win' solutions

Figure 14.3 The dynamic leadership model

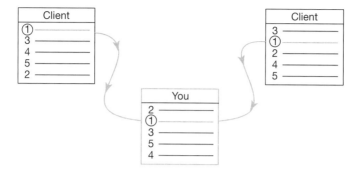

and achievements. (See also **Model 67: The conditions for collaboration model.**)

When to use it

- When establishing new relationships or redefining existing relationships.
- When setting out personal or professional 'conditions for success'. (See also **Model 26: The conditions for success model.**)
- When setting up personal contracts with other individuals or groups. (See also **Model 38: The setting emotional contracts model.**)
- When seeking to increase your connections and influence.

How to use it

List the *top five* things that the client would want at this moment.

Now get *the client's ratings* of this priority list (1–5) in order of importance and value to the client at this moment.

Moving on to whomever the client wants, or needs, to work with to achieve the goal, consider *the top five* things that these people would want on their list of options at this moment. This should be based upon what these people *would* want, not what your client thinks they *should* want.

Now consider or discover what *their ratings* would be on their ideal list (1–5) in order of priority. Again, this should be based upon what they *would* prioritise, not what you think they *should*.

Prioritise clearly by pitching one priority against the other on the basis of 'If you could have only one of these . . . ?', then continue until there is a clear number 1. Then with the remaining priorities do the same until you find the current number 2, then 3, and so on.

Delivering the selections that give optimal solutions is about *reaching the top (the number 1) priority*; this is how well your client makes the vital link between their top priority and the top priority of those with whom they wish to connect or influence.

That is, how they can achieve their most important thing in a way that allows your client also to achieve your most important thing.

Do not be distracted by someone's lower priorities on their list, as these things are of little current value and are unlikely to have any time or energy put into them unless circumstances make them a new top priority.

This vital link must travel in the *one direction* for the best results, starting from the other party's priorities to your client's.

There are several popular choices to avoid:

- Trying to enforce your top priority onto someone else (increases resistance in others and can be seen as bullying).
- Pretending that their top priority is also yours (disingenuous, shallow and can lead to a lack of trust).
- Trying to create a link with your lower common priorities where your number 4 on your ideal list is the same as their number 5 (develops only a low level of connection; too low to have an impact).
- Believing that guessing is better than knowing. It is always best to check what someone's top priorities are if and when there is an opportunity to do so. However, in the absence of knowing, your guesswork should be considered and thoughtful.

Coaching tips

- The successful application of this model relies upon the accuracy of the listed priorities and their current rating. It is advisable therefore to make sure that the top five priorities are continually monitored so that you are not caught out when they change.
- Ideally, you should formalise the process of listing someone's top five priorities so that they know that they have had some input to your understanding of them rather than been judged or assumed. However, if this opportunity does not arise or you cannot arrange it, then you should at least make some considered lists as long as they come from your thinking about what they would want right now, and not what you think they *should* want.
- Be confident in sharing what your top priorities are as this gives your client permission to do the same. This also goes some way in establishing a deeper sense of trust between you.

1 **Learn to predict events.**
2 **Identify the elements around you.**
3 **Trust your feelings.**
4 **Avoid being in too many situations at a time.**
5 **Avoid complacency.**
6 **Be aware of time.**
7 **Begin to evaluate quickly.**
8 **Actively prevent fatigue.**
9 **Continually assess the situation.**
10 **Monitor performance and the response of others.**

To be in hell is to drift, to be in heaven is to steer.

George Bernard Shaw

15 Driving motivation (service orientation)

[
Service orientation: Understanding, anticipating, recognising, accepting and then meeting the needs of others.
]

Being able to coach and develop a greater sense of service orientation opens up individuals, teams and organisations to the solutions and results that can only be achieved by playing to strengths and natural abilities. Greater understanding of service orientation enables people to understand, appreciate and anticipate why they, and others, do what they do. From this strong foundation, they are then better placed to recognise, accept and then respond positively to what drives optimal outcomes.

When individuals understand their own service orientation, they are able to make sense of why they do certain things but not other things, and what questions work best for them and what questions do otherwise. From this level of appreciation, they can then reposition important things in a way that gets the best out of their capabilities. Without a higher sense of service orientation, people are left to try to manage or manufacture the energy and motivation to do things that they do not really want to do. They can then restrict their future to staying with what they do well and just avoid everything else.

The benefits of service orientation have a big impact on relationships with others, because when we can understand, anticipate and appreciate the reasons why they do things, then we can communicate and connect on a level that is of value and impact for them. This level of connection enables us to be more positively influential in getting the best out of others and creating optimal outcomes. When we extend this capability into teams and organisations, the potential to be influential on larger scale situations becomes possible.

Teams with high service orientation will recognise how best to position things and communicate to get the best out of each other. These teams will also engage more positively and effectively with their audience and stakeholders. Organisations that develop strategies, products and services based upon high service orientation will be able to achieve greater success through how they position and communicate their value and impact with their audience.

Low service orientation in teams and organisations leaves them with limited opportunities to influence or succeed on any real scale, as they are only likely to connect with those who share exactly the same service orientation; alternatively, if they try to become all things to all people, they risk becoming no one thing for anyone.

Finally, as a coach, developing a higher sense of service orientation enables you to connect, communicate, position and put things in an order that gets the best out of your clients by working in the way that works best for them. When there is a lack of understanding of service orientation, even the best coaching sessions can flounder and lack results.

Model 43. The sense of service model

The big picture

Individuals, teams and organisations will have a strong service orientation that motivates and drives them to make a positive difference. However, these drives and motivations are not always shared or common, neither do they have a consistent or uniform value or impact. Service orientation is best demonstrated when the drives and motivations presented are indeed those that will make a difference.

This model was created and developed for coaching in response to the many situations where there was a clear mismatch or disconnection from what motivates others, or what had been projected or assumed as being their driver proved not to be. The model's aim is to empower people, teams, coaches and organisations to get the best out of themselves and the best out of others. Fundamentally, there are two senses of service:

- Sense of service to self.
- Sense of service to others.

Although each individual, team and organisation will have both senses, the premise of this model is based upon there being one that leads while the other follows; we are driven more either by a sense of service to self, or by a sense of service to others.

When we communicate, position and order things in a way that works with our driving sense of service, we perform at a higher level as a priority, and deliver better results quicker and more naturally. When things are communicated or positioned in a way that does not work with our driving sense of service, we will get the logic behind it and we will put it onto our 'to-do' list, but it will only remain as something that we might get around to.

This model was created in response to observing why people would be immediately effective in certain circumstances, yet lacklustre in others. You can extend this into teams where members of the same team working on the same projects could have opposite perceptions as to what is of priority, value and highest impact. For organisations also that communicated only one sense of service and not the other, there would be a split in terms of who was fully engaged and who was not.

Figure 15.1 The sense of service model

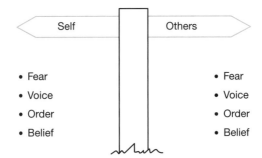

When to use it

- To increase motivation to make things happen
- To understand why people 'do' and why people 'do not'.
- To re-energise projects.
- To get the best out of people.
- To position, communicate and connect better.
- For situations that have stalled or are not getting started.
- To become more influential and effective with self and others.

How to use it

Someone who has more a sense of 'service to self' is not selfish, neither are they self-centred; they do, though, have a set of specific drivers and needs. They are likely to do and say things that they are fine with and positively expect others to feel the same way.

- Their biggest fear: Letting themselves down.
- The voice they listen to most: *Their own* (even when others are speaking to them).
- Their preferred order of things: *What they need to do comes first* (then happy to do what others need of them).
- Their core belief: *If they get to where they want to get to, others will want to follow* (this can mean they find themselves isolated at times).

Someone with more a sense of 'service to others' is neither a soft touch, nor a charitable guardian angel; they also have a set of specific drivers and needs. They are likely to do and say things that they positively expect others to be fine with even when it is not quite to their own preference.

- Their biggest fear: Letting other people down.
- The voice they listen to most: *Other people's voices* (very sensitive to others' feedback or criticism and reliant on the endorsement of others).

- Their preferred order of things: *What others need of them comes first* (they will only then enjoy doing what they want or need to do).
- Their core belief: *If they help other people get to where they want to be, then they themselves will arrive at where they want to be* (this can lead them to become resentful of others' needs and see these as blocks or distractions).

To carry out a quick *personal assessment,* consider which set of characteristics and drivers best describes you. You will have both, but one set of drivers will be stronger for you. You may have a clear strength in one of these, but it may be marginal and more difficult to call. It is a 50:50 call, so, if unsure, try one on for size and see how well it fits.

For the *assessment of others,* remember that their sense of service is not determined by *what* they do, it is about *the reasons why* they do what they do. Good indicators are the words that people choose to describe things ('I' or 'we') and whether they play back what you have said using the words you used ('others') or their own interpretation of your words ('self').

The vital ingredient in this recipe is to *avoid judgement.* Having more a sense of 'service to self' is not a criticism or a flaw, and having more a sense of 'service to others' is not a compliment or strength; it is just the manner in which you are driven. Both drivers have their benefits and drawbacks; your success is in how well you manage and channel this energy.

The key to success is how well things are *positioned for motivation.* If someone has more a sense of 'service to self' then things must be positioned as being to *their direct benefit or detriment* for that task to become a priority for them. However, if they have more a sense of 'service to others', things must be positioned as being to the *benefit or detriment of others* for that task to become a priority.

For *effective communication* it is important, and of benefit, to understand the client's sense of service. If they have more a sense of 'service to self ' then the voice they are listening to most (especially when you are talking) is their own. For them really to hear something, they themselves must say it, and therefore the most effective way to communicate with them is by *asking questions.* With those who have more a sense of 'service to others' the style of communication will have to be more *directive,* as it will be your voice that they are listening to most.

Getting the order right also differs depending on someone's sense of service. For 'service to self' it is best to do what they need to do, or say what they need to say, first so that they are then ready to be more receptive to what others might need or want to say. However, for 'service to others' it is best to understand the other person's needs, and hear what the other person has to say, first before they feel comfortable in putting forward their views or getting on with what they themselves need to do.

The challenge is firstly to accept that the powerful 'sense of service' driver will not change. The 'sense of service' is to be understood and developed, not fought against or changed. Secondly, the development here is to do what can be done to align the supporting driver behind the stronger sense of service.

If they have more a sense of 'service to self' then they will grow to realise than unless they also maintain a level of 'service to others' then they will ultimately create their biggest fear (letting themselves down), but if they have more a sense of 'service to others', then they will start to understand that unless they also do the things that they need to do for themselves then they will eventually manifest their biggest fear (letting other people down).

There are *no limits* to success when the 'sense of service' is fully understood. This awareness is empowering and enabling because it unleashes the strongest driver. Whether sense of service to self or others, it channels the motivation and capability to achieve great success in whatever is desired at any level. The results that can be realised by those who are driven more by service to self or others are exactly the same. What will be different, however, is the reason and drivers behind that success!

Coaching tips

This coaching model is one of the most effective keys to unlock someone's full potential because it works *with* their most powerful drivers. If you listen closely, people will indicate to you whether they are more sense of service to self or to others by the words they choose to describe situations; what they need or what everyone needs are subtle choices of words that will help you gauge. When you feel that you can assess, or when you just need to eliminate one or the other, you should follow the guide below.

Coaching 'sense of service to self'

- For any situation, issue or opportunity to be seen as a priority by your clients, it must be positioned in terms of the direct benefit or detriment to them, otherwise it will only make it on to their 'to-do' list and remain there.

- The voices they will be listening to most will be their own, particularly when you are doing the talking. For clients to really hear something they will have to be the ones who say it; you communicate best with this type of client through questions. All that you say to or tell your clients will be translated and interpreted by your clients in their voice.

- Be aware that these clients will create and work to their own interpretation of what has been said, or recommended, and will therefore regularly apply their own version of a coaching model, process or concept that you have presented to them. Although this can be a positive indication that they are making things their own and taking ownership, it can also be that they are now working with a distorted, diluted or partial model. Providing written or drawn documents helps here as these clients will read the illustration in their own voice and so retain it more fully.

Coaching 'sense of service to others'

- For any situation to make it to the top of their 'to-do' list, it must be positioned in terms of the impact it will have, positively or negatively, on those around them for whom they care. When things are seen as being directly for the client's benefit, they will get the logic and quickly agree that it is something that should be done, but the likelihood is that you will still be talking about it weeks and months later.

- As a coach with clients who are more 'sense of service to others' you will have to be more directive in your communication as the voice they will listen to most will be yours. This should also include repeating the answers they have offered to you, and for you to play back what they have been saying as this will give them greater confidence and conviction when hearing it.

- Be aware that these clients will take what you say literally and hear suggestions as directives, therefore they are likely to attribute their progress more to you unless you regularly reinforce your role as the coach and their roles as the main players. They are also more likely to blame themselves for any results that do not work out as planned and see this as their failure; again reinforcement of the ongoing process of learning helps maintain a more balanced perspective.

The five reasons why little things mean a lot

1 **Random acts of kindness are quick, but resonate really well.**
2 **Acts of kindness are increasingly rare!**
3 **Favours and little gestures make a positive difference to everyone.**
4 **A kind thought or act might be just what someone needs.**
5 **Everyone deserves a little kindness.**

Your visions will become clear only when you can look inside your own heart. Who looks outside, dreams; who looks inside, awakes.

C. G. Jung

Model 44. The power of your question model

The big picture

Coaching has always been predominantly more about the question asked than the answer given. The more directive the question, the more you are moving towards, mentoring, training and teaching. The more introspective the question, the more you are moving into counselling and psychotherapy. (See also **Model 55: The development continuum model.**)

The power of your coaching, and the performance of your clients, are highly dependent upon the power of the question being asked, as the quality of the question determines the thoughts, ideas and strategies that we come up with, which then deliver a consequential result. Questions are very much the cause that manifests symptoms that then have consequences. The quality of your questions, and the question that you can get others to ask, is the key cause of all the results that can be produced, and every result has been perfectly designed by the power of the question.

This model was designed in response to the many coaching scenarios with individuals, teams and organisations where the question being asked was clearly not sufficient or relative to the result desired. Typically, when the result being produced is not the result that was desired, the temptation is then to criticise the symptoms of the thoughts, ideas and strategies as being insufficient rather than going to the cause, the current question being asked. The application of this model has turned around the fortunes of teams and organisations that were previously achieving varied results that came from having an inconsistent level of questions being asked, and from having many people who were not aware that there was a question to begin with.

The model illustrates that if you want to improve the result (*the consequence*) you only have to look to improve the question being asked (*the cause*) rather than be critical of what happens in between (*the symptoms*). Good questions, good results.

This is tremendously empowering and enabling for individuals, teams and organisations as a whole, and clearly demonstrates the value of coaching as being able to get clients to ask themselves a better question.

Without this 'better question' approach we are left with the frustration of having a disconnected, unrelated and insufficient approach to achieving our goals. This drives 'frustrated' questions that lead to thoughts and strategies of frustration, and thus we create evermore frustrating results.

The most powerful influence on the result is the question being asked to begin with.

When to use it

- To set and achieve bigger, more audacious goals.
- To improve results, motivation and confidence.
- To have greater influence over groups and teams by setting the right question.
- To galvanise groups and teams for a worthy cause.

How to use it

The questions that individuals, teams or organisations ask are key to their success in everything that they do, as these questions are the *cause* of the strategies that follow, which will then determine the size and scale of their results.

The *symptoms* that are created by the quality of these questions are their thoughts, motivation, ideas, emotions, plans and actions.

Every *result* they then produce has been perfectly designed by the size and scale of the question they have asked: big questions lead to big ideas and plans and

Figure 15.2 The power of your question model

therefore bigger results; smaller questions lead to lesser thoughts and strategies which will deliver that level of result.

If these individuals, teams or organisations really want to achieve *better outcomes* then they should not allow themselves to be disappointed with the level of their ideas or thoughts, and avoid being critical of their strategies or actions. If they want to achieve better results, then they just need to develop and ask themselves a better question!

To improve on existing results, *assess* the current question being asked. This will be known or stated, or be indicated by knowing the current results and working back to the question that was the cause.

By understanding what the current question is, or is likely to be, they can then *introduce a better question* that is more capable of leading to the desired outcome.

Coaching tips

- Introducing this model helps make sense of how current results are the way they are. This model also helps to ensure that big, audacious goals can be aimed for with confidence when starting off with a question that is sufficiently powerful to get you there.

- This model is also a powerful tool to use with teams and organisations, because, by setting the question, you set the tone for the approaches, strategies, thinking and input. To influence people in the way you want them to go, just set and communicate the question you want everyone to be asking.

- Be aware, however, that the question you may wish to ask or set, which you believe has the power to drive towards the desired result, may currently be a bit too much of a leap for your client from where they are and therefore they may struggle, disengage or lose confidence. If you believe that is the case then you should offer a 'handrail' approach in which you invite your client to ask a better question, then the next better question, and so on, rather than forcing the ultimate question too soon.

The seven reasons to do good deeds

1 **You can always make a difference.**
2 **Good karma.**
3 **It feels good.**
4 **It brightens everyone's day.**
5 **It is a nice thing to do.**
6 **The law of reciprocation.**
7 **You are improving the world.**

The scent of the rose lasts longest on the hand that has cast it.

Anon.

Courage doesn't happen when you have all the answers. It happens when you are ready to face the questions you have been avoiding your whole life.

Shannon L. Alder

Model 45. The core success questions model

The big picture

A large part of the value in a coaching relationship is being able to help clients reconnect with when they were at their best. From there, psychologically and emotionally clients can then explore and apply more powerful questions with greater confidence and expectation of success. (See also **Model 44: The power of your question model.**) The successful results they produced were ultimately the consequence of the successful questions they were asking. Out of all the successful questions they will have asked, there will be a 'core success question' from which all others derived.

This model was developed in response to the coaching scenarios where individuals, teams and organisations were able to produce amazing results in certain situations, yet seemed to struggle or under-achieve in others. When individuals, teams and organisations connect and engage with the questions that were core to them in generating the thoughts, ideas and strategies that delivered their greatest successes to date, they can define their 'core success question' for whatever situation they want to achieve their finest results in.

When to use it

- Ideally for coaching sessions, presentations, meetings, events, pitches and proposals.
- In high-performance scenarios (public speaking, media work, interviews, sports, etc.).

Figure 15.3 The core success questions model

- Your best ideas
- Your best focus
- Your strongest intention
- Your best strategies
- Focused execution
- Strategic planning
- Strongest connections

Your core success question

Your finest results

- In difficult relations, arguments, personal conflict.
- For criticism and feedback (positive or negative).
- For unexpected opportunities and unexpected outcomes (positive or negative).

How to use it

Help to *identify* an individual's, team's or organisation's 'core success question' by considering challenging situations, complicated situations and complex issues through which they were able to produce fantastic results: What was the question they were asking of themselves at that moment? *How can they help? How can they make this better? How can they make this work? How can they turn this into something good? And so on.* If they are not sure, then ask them to try one on for size for now and allow their minds to 'percolate' it.

Once they are clear and settle on their 'core success question' (or the one that they are going to start with for now), invite them to *apply* this question to the next situation they face to test it out. If this is the right question for them it will generate the thoughts, ideas, approaches and actions that will deliver successful results. If not, then invite them to try another question that will!

Going with this 'core success question', help them to begin to *prepare* for important situations by connecting with this question so that it becomes their base and starting point. The question will ensure that they have a starting position for any situation that enables them to drive successful results. It is always best to connect to this question in advance, because it can be hard to find when they are already in the middle of a situation.

These steps also apply if the individual, team or organisation wants to help others connect with their core success question. It can be a very gradual process for some people, so it is best not to force or push it, but to encourage people to be patient and to 'percolate' what they believe the core question may be for now and progress from there. It is worth getting there, so it is always best not to try and rush.

Coaching tips

- This is a very powerful coaching model, but it does require a level of self-awareness that has yet to be developed in an individual, team or organisation. (See **Model 7: The confidence v self-confidence model.**) Be careful and considerate therefore with whom and when you would decide to introduce this model.

- It can be the case, for individuals, teams and organisations that have achieved great results before, that they are unaware of why they were successful, or what question they were asking at that time that led to such results. If so, there should not be any pressure or perception of disappointment; this is a common situation. It is best then to explore what the question could have been and how it could be applied now to begin a constructive process of 'trying on for size' to ultimately find the best 'fit'. (See **Model 25: The egg-timer model.**)

- For sure, as a coach, being best prepared for every coaching session, conversation or event should include being connected to your own 'core success question' before you walk into the room, go on the call or step onto the stage, because it can sometimes be difficult to connect with or find it once you are live. When you are connected you will find that your brain works extremely well in terms of instantly finding, connecting and discovering the very best content, examples and models for your client.

- The identity of your 'core success question' is best found when considering the most difficult situations you have faced where you have still been able to achieve optimal outcomes. That is, those traumatic, high-energy, highly stressed, emotional, hugely challenging or vital situations where, in spite of all the pressures, you were able to hold it all together, stay focused and deliver amazing outcomes, solutions or results. In those moments, you will have had a core question in your mind that brought all the strength, clarity and determination you needed to succeed.

- If you have the luxury of choice, then the best time to connect with your core success question is prior to an event or situation that requires your very best thoughts, ideas and strategies to deliver a successful and defined outcome. (See also **Model 1: The EI model.**) There are of course many situations that arrive without a great deal of warning, and as such will rely upon your ability to pause mentally and emotionally, gather your thoughts and reconnect with your core success question. (See **Model 10: The five steps to manage emotions model.**)

The 10 core behaviours for making a positive impact

1 Dedicate yourself to what gives your life meaning and purpose.
2 Commit to continual personal growth and development.
3 Engage with people in open, mutually beneficial ways.
4 Invest your time and energy in what can be.
5 Embrace feedback, critique and constructive criticism.

6   Share what you know.
7   Support and uplift others as they start to fly.
8   View your journey as your goal.
9   Use all of your power and influence well.
10 When you have the option to be 'right' or 'kind', choose 'kind'.

The art and science of asking questions is the source of all knowledge.

Thomas Berger

16

Achieving high performance (leveraging diversity)

[
Leveraging diversity: Fostering an inclusive approach that values individual differences and leverages these towards achieving specific outcomes.
]

One of the most significant areas of social awareness in terms of achieving great things is the ability to utilise, engage and get the very best out of those around you. Coaching individuals, teams and organisations to foster an appreciation of what can be achieved collaboratively and to develop the capability from this to deliver far greater results is of more value today than it ever has been.

With the ability to leverage diversity successfully, individuals can aim big in what they do with the confidence and assurance that their ambitions need not be limited by their own individual limitations, natural skill set or level of competency. If individuals are aiming for something that they know they can achieve on their own, then they either are not thinking big enough, or have a very limited strategy that is unlikely to succeed.

For teams to be successful and realise their full potential, it seems obvious that they have to embrace, engage and put to best use all the resources they have available to them throughout the group. Yet, so often it is the case that the team's achievement sits only on the shoulders of the few rather than in the hearts of the many. High-performing teams have a collective dynamic that is greater than the sum of its parts; they know how to leverage diversity.

For an organisation of any size or scale to be genuinely successful, it has to have an inclusive strategy so that it gets full return from all the resources that it has invested. Too narrow an approach and its success will be overly dependent upon certain market or product conditions and so any success would be limited or short-lived.

For a coach, therefore, being aware of the value and impact that 'leveraging diversity' can have in enabling clients is a must if it is to be of real positive benefit. For their own development also it is imperative that coaches foster an inclusive approach when working towards achieving their own goals and in support of their clients, such as remaining open to the many approaches, techniques, tools and models that are available.

Model 46. The client box model

The big picture

The concept of being client focused is based upon the cognitive framework that what looks great immediately in a client relationship is often less clear or automatic in others. Although we conclude very quickly on the standard of approach, response, delivery and level of consideration that should be applied to, and expected by, a client, we are often reluctant or conditional with others such as family, friends or colleagues.

This model was developed in response to the many coaching scenarios that involve issues with relationships and unspecified service levels where what was expected feels unfair, unclear or unreasonable. For this model, the definition of 'client' is a relationship with formal and stated service levels that clearly must be met. When a relationship is then placed in 'the client box', however, the parameters of what is acceptable and expected become clear. The premise of this model is that when we place other people and relationships – family, friends, suppliers or others – in this box, our perception of the situation changes, our emotional perspective changes and our level of clarity and service increases.

By choosing to place relationships with others in their 'client box' individuals are presented with an opportunity to elevate these relationships to the level of service experienced and enjoyed by their clients. For example, a practical application could be committing to a specific time to be home for dinner with the same determination applied to turning up for a meeting on time, regardless of the traffic, calls or emails, regardless of the alternative requests for your time, just making sure you are there, on time, ready, prepared and in a positive mood. Imagine the client response should you find it difficult to commit to a time to meet, or turn up late, tired or harassed, or be in a negative mood. Yet what we would understand to be unacceptable for a client can sometimes be what our friends, family or loved ones are left with.

Figure 16.1 The client box model

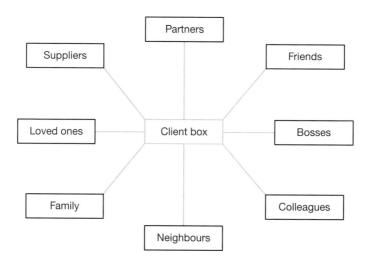

Teams can also be guilty of treating each other in a manner that their client would deem unacceptable in terms of the level of thought, preparation, motivation and even professionalism applied. Yet these same teams get so much more out of each other when they put each other in their 'client box' and put up with others' different approaches, personalities, preferences, flaws and moods and remain focused on creating a 'win–win' solution. The same challenge can be set for organisations that fail to treat their employees, suppliers or industry bodies with the same level of disciplined professionalism, compassion and eagerness to please as they do when they see someone as being in their 'client box'.

For coaches, this model opens up the possibility to help the client go beyond the emotional barriers that get in the way of obtaining the most from all the available relationships they have or could create. To be able to develop this capability with credibility, however, coaches should be clearly demonstrating their ability to place others in 'the client box'. Thus, how you treat those around your coaching client becomes vitally important.

When to use it

- To refresh, redefine and improve existing relationships.
- To establish and clarify your 'client box' strategies.
- To attract and create valuable relationships.
- To communicate the value and importance of a non-client relationship.

How to use it

Being *world class* is when an individual, team or organisation no longer needs to think about what they should do; it is the highest standard that they consistently deliver. World class is when it all just seems natural, obvious and logical to perform to a standard that for others would be exceptional. Individuals, teams and organisations are 'world class' when they do not consider anything less than this standard to be acceptable: always on time, always there when needed, always caring and concerned, always positive and constructive.

The *client box* is the box where world class individuals, teams and organisations place people with whom they perform to this highest standard, the people with whom they know exactly how they need to do, say and react to things because they hold them as being clearly important and are committed to satisfying and making happy.

Their *others box* is the box in which they will have placed everyone else, those who are not always clear or consistent in how they say, do or react to things because they do not see them as clients. They will decide on what they do or say based upon what they feel they are able to do rather than focusing on what these people need most from them. Most of the time they will offer something that will do the job for now, but it will often lack that personal focus, care and attention that make such a difference from time to time.

To ensure that they satisfy and make happy some of the others when they really need to, or just want to, they must *transfer them into the client box* by asking, 'What if they were clients?' This may not be on every occasion, in every situation; however, everyone deserves to experience being treated as a client every now and again, at least so that they can appreciate what world class looks like.

Coaching tips

- 'The client box' can be a powerful model when getting clients to look differently at their other relationships and from a more objective perspective, but the power will be diluted if it is seen as being a 'for ever' and 'for all' solution.

- This model is for improving relationships when they need an 'upgrade'. It should be applied to specific relationships at specific times on a specific aspect, such as getting home on time. The idea is not to treat your loved ones as a client at all times; your loved ones would not feel loved if you only saw them as a client.

- The model is best used by applying the same level of thought, discipline and energy to certain other relationships at certain times on a certain aspect, as you would do with a client.

- To assess your credibility as a coach with this model, your clients will look not only at how well you deal with them, but also at how well you deal with their others and your own. Having your own examples of how you have consciously done this will give your clients more confidence in you.

The three common decencies

1 **Turn up on time.**
2 **Do what you said you would do.**
3 **Remember to say 'please' and 'thank you'.**

Successful people are always looking for opportunities to help others. Unsuccessful people are always asking 'What's in it for me?'.

Brian Tracy

Model 47. The interdependence model

The big picture

The success of coaching and development is measured in terms of the changes and improvements in behaviour that the clients and those around them are aware of or experience. Great successes for individuals, teams and organisations will require hearts, minds, beliefs and behaviours to work together to produce more than the sum of their parts. The most powerful dynamic to bring diverse people and approaches together positively is a culture of interdependence: the combined trust, openness, synergy and appreciation of dependent and independent behaviours.

The concept of interdependence became widely popular in the 1990s thanks to the hugely successful book *7 Habits of Highly Effective People* written by Steven Covey and credited for influencing most of the management models that have appeared since. Steven Covey was a renowned educator, businessman, author and keynote speaker. Coaching greater interdependence within individuals, teams and across organisations has since become one of the most relevant approaches to improving personal, professional and business performance.

The *interdependence* model was developed for coaching in response to the many sub-optimal results and outcomes that appear in coaching sessions and conversations driven by either a purely independent or dependent approach. No one individual, team or organisation can be accurately defined as being either wholly independent or dependent; these are choices of behaviour that are open to all when there is an awareness of choice. This model illustrates that there are choices to be made, options to be explored and opportunities to be realised.

The premise of the model is to be able to take all the positive aspects of both dependent and independent behaviour, without taking on the negative aspects, to create the powerful combination that results in interdependence.

The practical application of interdependence results in individuals being able to lead and have strong opinions (independent) but also being able to include others and ensure that they are listened to and feel involved (dependent).

When teams become interdependent they are able to focus on making sure that everyone has a voice and a contribution to make (dependent) but that they also make decisions and focus on what needs to be delivered, even when it could be unpopular (independent).

When organisations develop a culture of interdependence, they acknowledge and respect those who are dependable and stick to the plan, so long as they do not

Figure 16.2 The interdependence model

Dependent attitudes	Independent attitudes
(+) Good listener	(+) Shows initiative
(+) Follows instruction	(+) Willing to take risks
(+) Consistent	(+) Self-managed
(+) Good team player	(+) Self-motivated
(+) Asks questions	(+) Takes responsibility
(+) Sticks to the plan	(+) Doesn't need to be asked
(−) High maintenance	(−) Not a good team player
(−) Appears compliant	(−) High-risk maverick

become high maintenance or disingenuous (dependent). They also look to reward and promote those with initiative and those who are motivated and want to take responsibility, so long as they are not lone mavericks putting everyone at risk by doing their own thing (independent).

In terms of enhancing social awareness, the model of interdependence can be extended across all relationships, situations, scenarios and opportunities as a way of enhancing the trust, openness and mutual respect required to create optimal outcomes.

When to use it

For teams and organisations:

- When forming a team, group or unit.
- When dealing with conflict or sub-optimal performance.
- To encourage inclusion and delegation.
- To increase effectiveness, delivery and utilisation of all available resources.
- To develop a culture of trust, value, appreciation and respect.

For individuals:

- To get beyond the labels and definitions of being dependent or independent and see it as a choice and approach.
- To develop a broader and empowering portfolio of options and choices.
- To foster optimal relationships and dynamics with self and others.
- To develop a greater sense of self-awareness and identity. (See also **Model 14: The identity decisions model.**)

How to use it

Being interdependent is an *approach* to take rather than a general description of an individual, team or organisation. Their approach will then drive their attitude and behaviour to a particular task, project, relationship, issue, opportunity or situation. They are not wholly interdependent individuals, teams or organisations, but they can foster an interdependent approach.

Dependent behaviour can be positive in that it leads to good listening, following instructions, team consideration, being manageable and consistency. It is an approach and attitude that can, however, drift into becoming high maintenance, low on initiative and a refusal to take risk, create improvement or take responsibility. Individuals, teams and organisations are not wholly dependent but they can adopt a dependent approach.

Independent behaviour can also be positive in that it can lead to showing initiative, taking leadership, willingness to take risks, being self-managed and self-motivated, not waiting or needing to be asked, and taking responsibility. However, this approach and attitude can also lead to being seen as a maverick and not a team player, appearing not to listen to instructions and becoming a liability with a personal agenda or self-interest. Individuals, teams and organisations are not wholly independent but they can adopt an independent approach.

Interdependence is about creating *positive combinations* that can be achieved by following instructions but still taking the initiative when the opportunity needs or demands it; to be considerate of the team but still step up and lead when there is a need or opportunity to do so; to be great to manage but to take responsibility for actions and outcomes. This combined approach and attitude to build on the positives of each is one of the most powerful influences in creating a success culture within a person, a relationship, a group, a team or across a whole organisation.

Coaching or developing *interdependent teams* involves identifying and acknowledging the specific roles and attributes that are required to ensure high performance and excellent results. There will be roles that require a more independent approach to be successful, while other roles will benefit from a more dependent approach. It is important to ensure that these are communicated equally in terms of importance, value and contribution so that there can be the same trust, value, appreciation and mutual respect between roles that are very different.

Coaching or developing *interdependent individuals* involves being able to identify and acknowledge the choices, attributes and approaches that are available to the individuals at any time. There will be situations where they have been independent in their approach in order to succeed, and other scenarios where they have had to be more dependent to get things done. This appreciation and acknowledgement that individuals can be as dependent or independent as they believe they need to be empowers them to go beyond the label or distinction of being only one or the other; they are capable of making a choice. On accepting that all their dependent and independent approaches are equally important, you can start to focus on making the right combination of choices for the given situation. When individuals develop the ability to combine all the positives of the dependent and independent choices without allowing these approaches to drift into the negative range they will become personally interdependent: self-respecting, self-trusting, self-appreciating and self-confident. (See also **Model 7: The confidence v self-confidence model.**)

Coaching tips

- As an early intervention for groups and organisations, coaching for greater interdependence tends to revolve around the creation of teams, either in the recruitment or set-up phase, or with a team at the early stage of its development as a group. In these cases, the topic of interdependence is very helpful in enabling team members to identify and accept better the attitudes and approaches of others, especially those that are different to their own. This enables them to begin to develop a respect and appreciation for what others can do, and to be better placed to anticipate the approach they are likely to take when they have the choice. (See also **Model 13: The intelligent trust model.**)

- The model in itself, however, needs to be coached if it is to do more than highlight and identify current attitudes and the positive and negative impacts that will follow. This requires you to develop ways of providing feedback that positively encourage change. (See also **Model 62: The constructive criticism model.**)

- Working with individuals requires you to identify the dependent and independent attitudes and choices and provide feedback that positively encourages change. (See also **Model 16: The habits model.**)

The three types of interdependence

1 Pooled: The cumulative impact of separate functions or individuals.
2 Sequential: The process impact that each function or individual has.
3 Reciprocal: The cyclical impact that each function or individual has to create continual change.

Our attitude towards others determines their attitude towards us.

Earl Nightingale

Model 48. The rhino and cattle model

The big picture

Leveraging diversity is fostering an environment where diversity and individual differences are valued and leveraged together to achieve desired goals and outcomes. The 'rhino and cattle' concept illustrates the range of characteristics that, when understood, valued and anticipated, can enhance the level of social awareness significantly.

This model was inspired by the book *Rhinoceros Success,* written by Scott Robert Alexander in 1980, and was developed for coaching in response to the many scenarios arising in coaching sessions that involved clashes of personality, person criticism and destroyed relationships that were based upon individual characteristics that could not be connected or reconciled. These differences, when not properly understood or appreciated, would often lead to behaviour designed to judge, label or even disregard others, thus damaging the trust, value, respect and self-worth in the relationship.

Applying the concept of 'rhino and cattle' allows individuals to protect their self-confidence, identity and values; it is OK to be them. In return, this allows them to have greater confidence, trust and value in others; they appreciate that it is also OK for others to be themselves too. Knowing where you stand in terms of being rhino or cattle enables you to develop a 'scope of appreciation' beyond just where you are and then further along the range to connect with those who are more rhino and more cattle than you are.

Figure 16.3 The rhino and cattle model

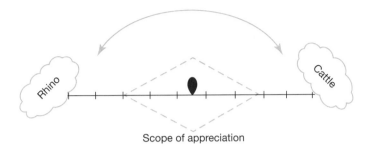

Scope of appreciation

The most successful individuals have high social awareness and develop their ability to connect and therefore influence others positively, whether they are 'rhinos' or 'cattle'. The most successful teams have high social awareness and develop their ability to ensure that they include and get the most out of all the full range of characteristics on offer. (See also **Model 47: The interdependence model.**)

For coaches, the model offers a framework with which to connect with clients, increase their self-awareness and support them to engage and become more influential with others.

When to use it

- To increase self-awareness.
- To explain objectively the characteristics of others.
- To become more connected and influential.
- To create inclusive and optimal strategies.

How to use it

Rhinos have some defining characteristics: they are strong individuals who live in a jungle habitat. They are placid until riled or threatened and then they can get really aggressive. They are very paternal and will fight to protect their own. They are hunted and considered valuable, but sadly their numbers are in decline. They are thick-skinned and robust, they are also partially blind and so rely on scent and imagination. They have a strong sense of adventure and stick their nose in the air to sniff out an opportunity. When they pick up the scent of something they do not meander or stroll, they charge! This does mean that they can often leave a lot of disruption and chaos in their wake. Rhinos are also very resilient and determined, so even when they batter through the jungle only to miss out on the opportunity they imagined, they pick themselves up, search for the scent of the next opportunity and go off again. Rhinos bounce off other rhinos really well for a short time before going back to their own adventures, but if they bounce off each other for too long they will begin to clash.

Cattle by contrast have different characteristics: they are herd animals that are highly productive and typically reside in the more controlled environment of farms and fields. They are docile and timid by nature and work best within set routines and consistent processes. They like to know the clear parameters in which they will operate and are stressed by change and disruption. They follow instructions really well and believe in safety in numbers. When the storm clouds gather they will hunker down and wait for them to pass. Cattle are apathetic in their approach, accepting that their destiny is pretty much mapped out for them.

For a quick *personal assessment* of whether an individual, team or organisation is more 'rhino' or 'cattle', consider what they are most like in terms of their approach and preferences: if they are comfortable with process, or need freedom to explore; if they are comfortable in their own skin or need the support and companionship of others; if they deal better with specifics and consistency or need the sense of adventure to express their creativity; if they like taking risks for rewards or prefer a steadier, more established approach; and so on. They can then begin to consider who around them are more 'cattle' and those who may be more 'rhino'.

Wherever individuals are plotted on the range of 'rhino' and 'cattle' they will be able to access and develop a *scope of appreciation* equally in both directions. This enables them to connect with those who are more 'rhino' or more 'cattle' than they are naturally.

These are not labels of praise or criticism, so *avoid judgement* when assessing; they are more a profile of how to get the best out of them and how they can get the best out of others by understanding and communicating better.

World class 'rhinos' and 'cattle' have extremely *positive relationships* because they develop a trust, value and mutual respect for what each can contribute. World class 'rhinos' appreciate that, without the structure, process and consistency of the world class 'cattle', there would only be chaos, disruption and isolation. World class 'cattle' appreciate that without the courage, ingenuity and creative force of the world class 'rhinos', there would only be monotony, decline and apathy.

Although 'cattle' will often frustrate 'rhinos', and it is fair to say that 'rhinos' can scare 'cattle', there is always the potential to create a *powerful combination* of all the best attributes from both sources, leaving behind, or at least reducing the impact of, the more extreme behaviours of each. With a strong bridge between these two characters that is built upon trust, value and mutual respect, innovations and ideas can become something that is practically delivered; new ways of living can become the solid foundations for what comes next.

Whether more naturally 'cattle' or 'rhino' in their approach, individuals, teams and organisations still have *decisions* to make and choices in front of them, and they always have the option to be either 'rhino' or 'cattle'. Their 'cattle' decisions will be more predictable, steady, safer, considered and, to begin with, feel more comfortable but also a little vulnerable. 'Rhino' decisions by contrast will be more volatile, less predictable, of higher risk, more reactive and, to begin with, feel more exciting but also a little exposed. They can choose either approach in the extreme or they can also create combinations and blends that work best for them. If they are looking for a more predictable path then their decisions should have more of a 'cattle' feel to them. However, if they are looking to explore then they will need at least a sprinkling of 'rhino' to bring out that flavour of adventure!

Coaching tips

- This model can be a fun and light-hearted framework for objectively categorising characteristics. The characteristics of rhino and cattle offer a clear and valuable contrast that then sets out a range of options.

- Be aware, though, that when used to establish self-awareness in terms of 'Are your approaches more cattle or rhino?', there can be an emotional perception that rhinos are in some way better, stronger or more valuable than cattle. This can result in people either being offended and disengaging as a result, or pretending to be more of a rhino. Typically, people think that when they are clearly a 'rhino' then they are either superior or cool. The purpose of this model is to highlight characteristics and strengths, not to define or judge people.

- Wherever people plot their position on this spectrum, the value of their coaching is how better they can develop a scope of appreciation that gets the best out of all the levels of the cattle and rhinos around them.

- Highly successful people surround themselves with the rhinos and cattle that they anticipate they will need. Highly successful teams and organisations have a healthy range of rhinos and cattle working to their strengths; rhinos are not great at cattle activities, and vice versa. They also appreciate that too many rhinos can create more chaos than can be managed, while too many cattle and not enough rhinos will reduce the level of chaos necessary for healthy growth and progress.

The six steps to leverage diversity

1 **Set a clear and inclusive vision.**
2 **Increase the quality and quantity of conversations.**
3 **Walk the talk.**
4 **Approach as a partner; forget hierarchy.**
5 **Deal with the whole person.**
6 **Increase involvement and engage.**

The five tips to deal with different personalities

1 **Assess an individual's personality type.**
2 **Connect to build a relationship**
3 **Set the bar high in your conversations.**
4 **Understand clearly what is important to the other person.**
5 **Do not take things personally.**

Diversity: the art of thinking independently together.

Malcolm Forbes

PART FIVE

Leadership coaching

Relationship management: A strategy to manage, engage and influence key relationships and networks.

Relationship management is the fifth of the six key areas of coaching development. Individuals who are strong in the management of relationships are able to connect better with others who can then contribute towards shared goals and outcomes. Teams that benefit from stronger relationships internally and externally are able to engage others with effective communication strategies. Organisations that develop strategies to manage relationships are able to share their vision and achieve sustained success through the development of strong succession.

This part focuses on how to develop relationships that contribute to successful outcomes: the strategies that create and communicate value between individuals, teams and across organisations. Parts Five and Six are where most people expect to see the impact and value from coaching being demonstrated.

In this part we present relationship management as the combination of these four elements:

This selection of coaching models has been specifically designed to develop higher levels of relationship management.

Influential leadership (influence)

17

[
**Influence: Being a compelling force to affect
the actions, behaviour, opinions and
performance of others or a situation.**
]

While management may be considered as maintaining or containing situations to remain optimal in the box that they are currently in, leadership is regarded more as a disruptive approach to create a whole new box in which situations can flourish to new levels. A leader aiming to be successful in transforming this chaos into sustained success will need to be positively influential.

Influence is defined as the effect that someone or something has on someone or something else. Influence happens even when it is not deliberate or planned; it is an energy that remains even after the 'someone' or 'something' has left the room. Influence is a powerful force, positive or negative, and it is an essential attribute for any individual, team or organisation to develop that aspires to be successful.

Individuals who understand how to be influential are able to connect and build relationships of value that provide direction, confidence and increased capability. Influential teams appreciate that how they approach situations and scenarios will determine whether they keep secure what they are trying to achieve or whether they are going to end up in a compromising position. Organisations that know how to develop greater influence appreciate how the dynamic of their perceived power can affect their level of influence and so manage this with consideration.

Coaches are in a fantastic and privileged position to become positively influential with those that they get to work with; it is important that this responsibility is understood and treated with care.

Model 49. The creating value model

The big picture

The most successful relationships on an individual, team or organisation level are those interactions that are able to create genuine value – where there is something more added each time there is a connection. The ability to manage and influence relationships so that there is always added value is a key component of successful leadership.

This model was designed and developed for coaching in response to the many situations where relationships have become difficult, strained or lack connection. The model provides a simple and practical illustration of what it takes to create relationships that provide genuine value.

Individuals who are able to create such value in their relationships will benefit from stronger connections and longer lasting bonds, with friends, family, colleagues and clients. Teams that develop valued relationships understand the difference they can make and the influence they can have. Organisations with strategies to forge influential relationships internally and externally are able to communicate where their unique value lies and why they are confident in the capability of those involved. Overall, being able to create, communicate and demonstrate the value in a relationship achieves a high level of influence in where that relationship goes next.

All coaching relationships should create value that can be quantified, communicated and demonstrated clearly.

When to use it

- As a framework for creating and communicating value in a relationship.
- To identify specific areas of strength or weakness in a relationship.
- To bring clearer direction, greater confidence and enhance the capabilities of a relationship.
- To ensure that a relationship has ongoing and evolving value to avoid complacency, being taken for granted or feeling commoditised.

How to use it

To influence the appreciation of value in a relationship, leadership must be shown in order to provide clear *direction*. This is achieved by communicating an understanding of the key dangers and risks that are most current and relevant, and the biggest ideas

Figure 17.1 The creating value model

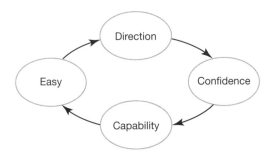

and opportunities that would be desired. If a relationship is not heading anywhere, if it is not able to eliminate danger or realise opportunities, it is of no great value.

Next, to establish a relationship of value, it must be used to build *confidence* in both parties. This is achieved by listing all the things that can be regarded as strengths or achievements, making clear the relevant successful track record or previous examples that exist, and assuring that this is a consistent approach to protect and build confidence.

The next step in creating value is about showing creativity that will enhance the *capability* of the relationship. To do this, explain what is unique, special or individual about what each party can bring and why this fits comfortably and complementarily. Finally, the focus needs to be clear that there is a commitment to work beyond the present and that the value is ongoing in the longer term.

The final step is crucial: it must be *easy to get started.* Having established the direction and increased the confidence and capability, there should be a quick and easy, low-barrier-to-entry method of getting things started, ideally no more than a three-step process. Thus, the biggest hurdle will be overcome and a great starting result influenced and achieved.

Coaching tips

- Valued relationships have the combination of leadership so that it is heading somewhere; confidence so that both parties can feel assured; the capability to do more together than could be achieved apart; and finally a good, easy and quick connection so that the experience is always positive.

- Good relationships are when people get on well together; valuable relationships are when people achieve something together that makes a difference.

- All valuable relationships will retain their value when these four steps are reviewed and revisited regularly. As people evolve, each of these steps will require assessment to remain relevant and current.

- Without leadership, confidence, increased capability and ease of dealing with, relationships lose value, become a commodity and eventually wither away.

The five measures of influence

1 Voice: Does what you say do you justice?
2 Audience: Do you connect with the people you really want to?
3 Relevance: Is what you are focused on your highest priority?
4 Context: Does what you communicate paint the bigger picture?
5 Reach: Are you getting your message across consistently enough to the people who can make things happen?

Try not to become a person of success, but rather try to become a person of value.

Anon.

Model 50. The what, why and how model

The big picture

Individuals, teams and organisations that achieve what they want to, say what they want to, do what they want to, for all the reasons why they want to achieve, say or do what they do, understand that to remain this free from compromise, they must challenge themselves on how best to approach and influence each situation or scenario. With a clear sense of direction for where they want to go, and with many motivating reasons for getting there, successful leaders appreciate that to protect these elements as non-negotiable they will have to remain negotiable in order to influence positively. (See also **Model 19: The negotiable and non-negotiable model.**)

This model was created and designed in response to the many coaching scenarios where there was a lack of clarity on the direction, motivation or influence in a situation, or where clients were not aware of asking all three questions. This simple process of defining each component and understanding what each part brings to the equation has been highly effective in locating the specific issue or missing element. The model also illustrates the choices available in terms of what needs to be protected and what needs to remain flexible.

With a strong sense of direction, a high level of motivation and a range of strategies to influence the desired outcome, individuals, teams, coaches and organisations are better equipped to influence the results and outcomes they desire.

When to use it

- To illustrate clearly the three components of any scenario or situation.
- To clarify the role and value of influence.
- To explain the need for a broad and flexible range of influence strategies and options.

Figure 17.2 The what, why and how model

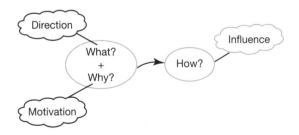

- To identify and isolate the specific issue in any given situation.
- To protect the 'what' and 'why' by being open to challenge on the 'how'.

How to use it

Being clear and specific on the 'what' that is wanted (to have, be, or to get to), provides *the value of direction.* This enables a focus on the outcome desired with confidence and conviction, and identifies what success will look like.

Having a compelling reason why something is wanted (to have, be, or to get to), energises *the power of motivation.* When the reasons for doing something are many and of meaning then there can be commitment to doing whatever it takes to make it happen. (See also **Model 41: The power of 'why?' model.**)

Consistent success comes with developing *the art of influence:* knowing how to make things happen. This includes not just the 'how' but also the 'where', the 'when' and 'with whom' things are done.

Measuring influence is not just about the result or outcome achieved, it is measured in the value of the part in the result or outcome that the choice of 'how' had. Influencing is not about being there for the ride, it is about participating in a way that made things happen that were aligned to the 'what' and 'why' which may not have otherwise occurred.

Individuals, teams and organisations, and their environments, are *always influential;* awareness and acceptance of this principle should act as a reminder that, one way or another, all people and the environment play a part, and even by contributing nothing they are still influencing what is going on. It comes down to choosing what influence someone wants to have, and whether it helps or gets in the way of achieving the desired outcome.

Being *negotiable on the 'how'* presents two key advantages. Firstly, it keeps the mind open to options and opportunities; secondly, it reduces many of the conditional preferences that can block the path to success. Broadening the 'how' options increases the confidence to remain negotiable.

To *live without compromise* is to stay true to the 'what' and 'why' by keeping both of these as non-negotiable. To do this, the 'how' has to be made flexible and open to change. As soon as the 'how' is held as non-negotiable, it should be understood that the 'what' and 'why' will be compromised. (See also **Model 20: The result v process model.**)

The missing link for most people in terms of their mastering the art of influence is having a big enough 'why?'. When they have this it is amazing what they are then willing and able to do, to consider or make happen. Consequently they will work out 'how' to influence extraordinary outcomes and results. If they really had to, they would!

Coaching tips

- Begin with the 'what' and take enough time to clarify this specifically.
- Expand the 'why' as much as possible; with great motivation, all options will be considered.

- Explore all current options for 'how' and then challenge and create further options so that there is a choice of influence strategy.
- Most people have issues that are not clarified by these three components; there is immediate value in being able to present the issues back in these terms and in this order.

The five influence styles

1 **Asserting.**
2 **Convincing.**
3 **Negotiating.**
4 **Connecting.**
5 **Inspiring.**

I am too positive to be doubtful, too optimistic to be fearful, and way too determined to be defeated.

Anon.

Model 51. The power v influence model

The big picture

As the perceived power of an individual, team or organisation increases, it is more difficult for them to become influential. Those who can expertly manage relationships appreciate the impact that their perceived power has on their ability to influence others positively. Understanding how to manage the perception of power rather than denying or ignoring it is their first advantage; their second is their ability to develop strategies of influence that exceed their perceived power.

This model was designed and developed for coaching in response to the many situations and scenarios where the importance of becoming more influential was clear. The practical illustration makes clear the relationship between the perceived power of an individual, team or organisation and what this is made up of. The model also provides insight into what makes up the influence potential that can be achieved by developing direct and indirect strategies of influence. The choice, and consequences of, being considered as either 'powerful' or 'influential' are also explored.

When individuals are aware of how much perceived 'power' they bring to a situation, they can then appreciate the level of influence they will need to develop to be more influential than powerful, or they can decide to remain as powerful and keep driving.

A team that wants or needs to become more influential so that its initiatives can be in 'the hearts of the many' rather than 'on the shoulders of the few' can manage its current level of power while developing direct and indirect strategies of influence.

An organisation that wants or needs higher engagement and ownership across its business has to develop consistent strategies and approaches to increase its influence. Without influence, the organisation can only concede or resort to the use of power to dictate and mandate its wishes, creating a 'them' and 'us' relationship. With direct and indirect influence strategies in place, an organisation can reap the rewards of high engagement, participation, ownership and commitment.

Coaches often bring a significant level of perceived power to each session: they understand the process better; they know the questions better; they are likely to have many coaching hours and experience behind them; they have many other sessions and clients to compare with; they are likely to be more relaxed and confident; they have had more practice and gained more coaching qualifications – all of which can seem powerful to a client, particularly in the early sessions. It is important for coaches to be aware of their power so that they can manage the perception and build appropriate levels of influence quickly.

When to use it

- To appreciate the relationship between power and influence and their consequences.
- To develop awareness and assess the formal and informal levels of perceived power.
- To consider how to manage and mitigate the perceived power so as not to hinder the ability to become influential.
- To define and create direct and indirect strategies of influence.
- To become more influential than powerful to get more people to achieve more things.

How to use it

To assess whether an individual, a team or an organisation is more *powerful or influential,* consider how many things they have to do directly, and how many things they can get others to do. When perceived as more powerful than influential they will always have to drive the things that they want to happen; however, when perceived

Figure 17.3 The power v influence model

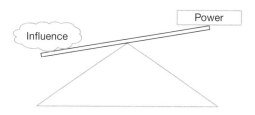

as more influential than powerful they significantly increase their capacity to make things happen with, and through, others. To be successful using power, they will always have to be the driving force. Being influential allows individuals, teams and organisations to delegate, appoint and facilitate others to be the driving force on their behalf so that they can enjoy greater and multiple successes and so increase their capacity.

Power is 20 per cent formal and 80 per cent informal. Formal power includes things such as position, level of authority, seniority, age or length of service, track record, reputation, etc. Informal power, however, is made up of things such as personality, character, energy, ambition, enthusiasm, mood, sense of humour, resilience, vision, imagination, determination, willingness to learn, ability to listen or speak, etc. When listing formal and informal power it will become clear as to how much power an individual, team or organisation can bring to a situation, and then what level of influence they will need to develop in order to be considered more influential than powerful.

Influence is 20 per cent direct and 80 per cent indirect. Direct influence is what they can make happen by what they say and do directly, while indirect influence is about what they can get others to say and do on their behalf to make things happen. This is why references, endorsements, referrals and the personal opinions and recommendations of others can be so impactful.

The more powerful an individual, team or organisation are considered to be, the more difficult it can be for them to exert influence. Success comes not from pretending to be less powerful than they are, or denying how powerful others perceive them to be, but from understanding the perception that others have of their power and making sure that they have even greater strategies of influence. *Relative perceptions* are a key factor. If an individual is considered to be funnier than another person, they will see this sense of humour as being powerful, so it will be more difficult to be influential with that person when humour is used too often. However, if the other person feels that they are just as funny as the individual concerned, they will not be intimidated by this sense of humour and it may actually help the individual to be more influential as a result.

Increasing direct influence can be done in three ways: by improving what is said or done to get other people to want to do things; by improving the context and understanding of why something has been said or done; and by improving how messages are delivered so that the words and actions encourage others to engage and participate.

Increasing indirect influence can also be done in three ways: by engaging regularly with those who are quick to grasp what is being said or what is happening; by asking these people for introductions, recommendations, endorsements, referrals and for them to share their personal opinions and experiences with others; and by creating platforms, forums and environments for advocates to become influential with their peer groups. As peers, there will be far fewer barriers of power to overcome, so influence can happen quickly and smoothly.

Coaching tips

- Most people are unaware of the power they are perceived to have and generally under-estimate this or believe that they are powerless. This is often why people are not able to influence successfully.
- Power is not a good or bad thing, it is a strong energy and a perception that needs to be considered, factored in and managed in order to have influence. Many people fear being seen as powerful for a number of personal reasons, but we all have power, and good things can come from it.
- Denying power is a reaction not a strategy, and, as with all reactions, it does not have long-lasting impact. Power can be managed so that it does not become unnecessarily difficult, but it should not be denied.
- Developing strong strategies of influence (direct and indirect) enables individuals, teams and organisations to become more powerful with the confidence that in doing so they will not be compromising their ability to influence.

The five levels of influence

1 Position: Influential because of who you are.
2 Permission: Influential because others want you to be.
3 Production: Influential because of your high performance.
4 People: Influential because you have earned respect and loyalty.
5 Pinnacle: Influential because you inspire others.

The key to successful leadership today is influence, not authority.

Kenneth Blanchard

18 Strategic leadership (vision)

[**Vision: Inspiring, guiding or directing others towards a compelling picture of what could be.**]

Strategic leadership is about having the vision and ability to influence others to make voluntary decisions that enhance the prospects of long-term success and stability. Strategic leaders apply different approaches to inspire the vision, growth and success potential of individuals, teams and organisations by formulating and implementing strategies that provide direction, alignment and ownership.

Success as a strategic leader is heavily reliant upon getting the starting position right so that the leader can choose the approach that is best suited to what happens next. This ability to understand when to lead, when to manage and when to be operational in approach largely determines the capacity available for delivering excellent results.

Teams that are able to create a compelling picture of the future understand that the purpose of having a vision is to provide direction, guidance and inspiration, while its value is to generate the momentum required for achieving amazing outcomes of high impact and high emotion. Those organisations that are able consistently to influence others to focus on outcomes and overcome uncertainty ensure that they avoid the trap of ambiguity by concentrating on what they do know for sure.

Coaches can lead by example in the approach that they take, by the scale of their own vision, the strength of their goals, and how they manage to build upwards and away from the traps of ambiguity they face.

Model 52. The leader–manager–operator model

The big picture

Strategic leaders have the ability to look towards the longer term outcomes they want to achieve and from there make a decision on how best to approach the situations and scenarios they currently face. This is so that their approach can be strategically aligned to where they want to go, rather than off in another direction. In any situation they will be aware that they can choose to lead, to manage, or to be operational.

This model was designed and developed for coaching in response to the many situations where choices were being made that were not equipped to deliver what an individual, team or organisation wanted to happen next. The model defines the three valid options that are available and what happens as a consequence of each choice. The model also illustrates the importance of getting the starting position right so that all options remain available.

When individuals are clear on what they want to happen next, to own the situation, to oversee it, or to be clear about it, they will know what choice is best to make that happen. They can then develop the approach with confidence and conviction rather than taking an instinctive approach that is not aligned to the outcome they desire or restricted by their formal position.

Teams that are more aware of the three options and the consequences of each choice are able to take decisions based upon what they are best equipped to deal with as a result. That is, they are able to play to their strengths rather than managing through their weaknesses.

Organisations that wish to develop stronger strategies of succession and progression will see in this model the necessity to start from the right level so that their approach can deliver the outcome that they want to achieve. Coaches also appreciate that their strongest starting position needs to be as a leader in order for all three options to remain available.

When to use it

- Be aware that there are always three options of approach available for every situation or scenario.
- To understand the consequence of choosing 'leader', 'manager' or 'operator' as an approach.
- To anticipate the consequence of the choice made and ensure alignment with the desired outcome.
- To ensure that the starting position is optimal and not restrictive.
- To develop a strategy for what you want to keep doing, for what you want to keep on top of, and for what you want to be free from.

Figure 18.1 The leader–manager–operator model

This model looks at the *choices of approach* available to individuals, teams and organisations. It does not define people, tasks, meetings or roles as being leaders, managers or operators but is about the choice of *approach* available to all individuals, teams and organisations in any situation or scenario.

It is a *choice* whether to take the approach of a leader, manager or operator. This approach is not determined by the situation, it is down to the decision on how best to deal with the situation, and there should always be three options to select from:

- An *operational* approach is defined as doing something in a way that means that the individual, team or organisation will be responsible for doing the same thing again next time.

- A *management* approach is defined as making sure that something is done by others to a required standard, in a way that means the individual, team or organisation will have to ensure that it has been done by others to the standard required.

- A *leading* approach is defined as getting something managed by others in such a way that the individual, team or organisation no longer has to deal with it.

Best decisions in terms of approach are defined by when the choice results in what the individual, team or organisation want to happen next. For example, if they want to keep doing something, they choose 'operational', but if they want not to have to do something again, they will need to choose 'leading'. Poor decisions are when the approach taken does not lead to what they want to happen next.

To ensure that there is always a healthy awareness of the three available options, the *home base* and starting position has to be 'leading'. From this starting position, individuals, teams and organisations can still choose to visit the approach of 'management' or have a vacation in 'operational' but must always remember where their home base and starting point is.

Strategic decisions are of value to consider, but these are only available when the starting position is the 'leader' approach. These decisions can be considered as 'strategic' when individuals, teams or organisations take an 'operator' approach, but for strategic reasons. An example would be a CEO of a fast-food chain deciding to flip burgers and serve customers so that the CEO can redefine what the customer strategy needs to be going forward.

Coaching tips

- Most individuals, teams and organisations naturally start from an 'operator' point of view because the emotional drive to be doing something is always strong. Remember that this approach is a valid choice as long as they are happy to continue doing so, but it is important to encourage the development of a 'manager' or 'leader' approach so that they have a genuine choice to make.

- 'Operator' is a very popular choice of starting position because of the belief that they can start there and work their way up to a 'manager' approach, and then eventually up to a 'leader' approach over time. Unfortunately, the nature of having an 'operator' approach means that this is where they will stay and really struggle to ever get beyond this.

- It is important to reinforce that the 'best decision' is not always to take a 'leader' approach; the best approach is the one that takes the individual, team or organisation to what they want to happen next. If they want to keep doing something that they love and enjoy, they should develop an 'operator' approach.

- Some believe that taking a 'leader' approach excludes them from the 'manager–operator' options. On the contrary, from the 'leader' approach, both the 'manager' and 'operator' approaches remain available, but an immediate 'operator' approach is likely to be restrictive in terms of other approaches.

- It is a common perception initially that only leaders can choose the 'leader' approach, that only managers can select the 'manager' approach, and that if someone is an 'operator' then all that they can consider is an 'operator' approach. All three approaches remain available for all levels of individual, team and organisation. Going over the definitions of an approach, and the natural consequences of each, helps clarify the value of this model.

The five levels of leader

1 **Strong individual contributor.**
2 **Contributes to the team.**
3 **Manages strong team performance.**
4 **Leads strong teams towards ambitious results.**
5 **A genuine, authentic, inspiring leader.**

Strategy is just a fancy word for coming up with a long-term plan and putting it into action.

Ellie Pidoy

Model 53. The momentum model

The big picture

Momentum, derived from Latin and meaning 'movement', is defined in physics as the property that a moving object has due to its mass and motion; the strength and

Figure 18.2 The momentum model

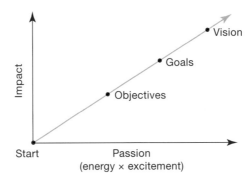

force that something has when it is moving in a line that allows it to continue to grow stronger or faster as time passes. Momentum is measured as the product of mass and velocity.

Adapted as a component of strategic leadership, momentum is the product of the scale of impact projected and the level of energy and emotion created. The most successful strategic leaders understand the value of creating a compelling vision that has aligned goals and then objectives to support it.

This model was created and designed for coaching in response to the many scenarios and situations where a lack of vision had led to a lack of passion and impact, causing everything to slow down and go flat. A graph of this plots clearly what is involved in creating momentum: the ability to generate a compelling energy that drives individuals, teams and organisations to achieve meaningful and impactful outcomes.

Individuals with a clear sense of a vision that is high on impact and high on energy and emotion are able then to set goals that are strategically aligned with the vision they aspire to. Teams with such a vision will be able to channel this high level of impact and passion into the smallest of operational objectives because they are of strategic importance in reaching the vision. Organisations with the high level of momentum that comes from having a genuine vision are able to travel faster, further and to greater heights as all their efforts are strategically aligned.

Coaches who apply this model clearly benefit from seeing each question they ask and each session they conduct as being part of a bigger vision that is of high impact, energy and emotion. In doing so, they generate a level of momentum in each coaching intervention that can drive amazing results and achievement.

When to use it

- To illustrate the purpose, value and role of momentum in leadership.
- To make clear why it is so important to create and develop a compelling vision.
- To provide a visual representation of what strategy looks like (the blue line).

- To create a strategic vision, set strategic goals and agree strategic objectives.
- To explain why 'burnout' happens.

How to use it

Momentum in this context is measured as the amplification of *impact x passion.* The highest level of momentum is generated by a connection to something that is high on impact and high on energy and emotion (passion).

- A *vision* is at the highest end of momentum. A vision is something that is huge on *impact* and *emotion* as it is so far reaching and exciting. This is because a genuine vision is when it is not yet known what it actually looks like, and there is no knowledge yet as to how to get there.

- *Goals* are also high on momentum, but less so than a vision. Goals are there to support the vision; they are specific things, so it should be known what they look like, but importantly it should still not yet be known how to achieve them. This is important as it leaves enough room for energy and emotion to be attached to the possibilities.

- *Objectives* are lower again in terms of momentum. Objectives are the components that lead to the achievement of the goals; it should be known exactly what these look like, and it should also be known exactly what is going to be needed for them to be completed. This level of clarity and certainty on what they look like, and what needs to be done, replaces all other possibilities, which is why there is less passion generated by, or associated with, objectives.

- At the bottom, in terms of momentum, is the *starting point* where it is known where something is, and it is known how it got to this point. There is no momentum to be had here as this is a stage defined by the past and has no associated or generated forward motion.

The *highest momentum* is achieved when there is a strong connection to the vision as it gives the strongest sense of purpose in what is being done and provides greater value to all the goals and objectives.

Lower momentum occurs when there is only a level of connection further down the graph of impact and passion, when the level of drive comes from either the goals or the objectives, or, even worse, the starting point.

In terms of momentum, the bottom is *not* a good starting point for individuals, teams or organisations because from here they will firstly aim for an objective, yet as soon as they have achieved this, it only becomes their new starting point and so they spiral at the lowest end of energy, emotion and impact, commonly known as the *burnout area.*

Being strategic is defined here as *being on the blue line.* For a goal to be considered strategic, it must be on this line, connected and aligned to the vision; for an objective to be considered strategic, it must also be on the line, connected and aligned to the goals that support the vision. Individuals, teams and organisations can have goals or objectives that are high on energy or emotion, or that are high on impact, but unless they are on the line, they are not considered to be strategic.

Coaching tips

- Most individuals, teams and organisations lack momentum because they do not actually have a genuine vision (something that they are aiming for that is massive on impact and passion, yet they do not know what it looks like or how to get there), although many are convinced that they do. Once they articulate their perceived vision it will become clear whether they are actually working towards a big goal (e.g. to be number 1) or objectives (e.g. to win awards), and why they then have a lower level of momentum than they could have.

- Although it is not necessary to have a genuine vision (e.g. to change lives) in order to succeed, the highest levels of momentum are only generated by having a connection to something that is not yet defined, but has immense impact and powerful meaning.

- Many people are working with an 'objectives' level of momentum, which is why they eventually run dry or burn out. By connecting with bigger reasons for doing what they do, they will experience an immediate increase in their level of momentum.

- Ask the question to encourage setting strategic goals and objectives: 'Does that sit on the blue line?'

The eight essential leadership skills

1 **Inspires and motivates others.**
2 **Displays high integrity and honesty.**
3 **Solves problems and analyses issues.**
4 **Continually drives for results.**
5 **Communicates powerfully and prolifically.**
6 **Collaborates and promotes teamwork.**
7 **Builds strong, lasting relationships.**
8 **Consistently takes the strategic perspective.**

People who succeed have momentum. The more they succeed, the more they want to succeed, and the more they find a way to succeed.

Tony Robbins

Model 54. The spiral of ambiguity model

The big picture

Strategic leaders create a vision for the future that others can then connect with and commit to. Often far reaching and lacking in specific detail, the ability to deal with ambiguity is one of the key components of strategic leadership.

Ambiguity is described as an uncertainty of meaning regarding situations and scenarios where several interpretations and misinterpretations all appear plausible, so the intended meaning cannot be definitely resolved or assured with certainty. When in 'ambiguity', questions do not lead to answers, they only lead to more questions.

This model was designed and developed for coaching in response to the issues and scenarios that were caused by varying levels of uncertainty and ambiguity. The model clearly illustrates how individuals, teams and organisations can find themselves on a downward spiral towards ambiguity when their questions create only further questions, and all imagined scenarios get mentally played out as if they were real.

The model also explains how individuals, teams and organisations can set about climbing out of their comfort zone and further away from a place of ambiguity by asking questions that they are sure of. Crucially, the major deterrent that causes many not to climb is also covered here, so that the fear of uncertainty is put into context and perspective.

Due to the live nature of the work that coaches are involved with, that is individual sessions, group sessions or events where the issues of individuals, teams and organisations are presented there and then, dealing with uncertainty and avoiding the spiral of ambiguity are key attributes for a coach to develop and value.

When to use it

- To avoid asking the questions that can only lead to more questions.
- To move away from the anxiety, concerns and worries that come from the many plausible conclusions from ambiguity.

Figure 18.3 The spiral of ambiguity model

- To learn to be comfortable as an option to avoid ambiguity.
- To develop a strategy for climbing out of the comfort zone and leading towards a vision.
- To communicate a compelling and inspiring message as regards vision, big ideas and ambitious outcomes.

How to use it

The *comfort zone* is where an individual, team or organisation can sit to understand and make sense of what is going on around them.

From there, the *downward spiral* occurs when they continue to ask questions that cannot have specific or defined answers; these are the questions that just lead to more and more questions as more and more plausible possibilities, interpretations and misinterpretations come to mind. This spiral will ultimately drop them into the trap of total ambiguity, feeling helpless and becoming disconnected from all that they do know for sure.

The *upward spiral* takes them out of their comfort zone towards a higher level of understanding and appreciation. This is done by reconfirming all the things that they already know for sure, all the things they already understand, all the things they have already learned and experienced; all the things they believe are safe to assume or settle on in their minds. These steps on the ladder allow individuals, teams and organisations to reach higher than before with confidence.

While the downward spiral leads to a place of *ambiguity,* the upward spiral unfortunately does not lead to *certainty.* It leads ultimately to uncertainty, which puts a lot of people off climbing up in the first place. However, the value of building upon all the things that are already known for sure allows people to see that, ultimately, there may only be *4 per cent uncertainty* as to whether all that they already know will prove to be enough on this occasion. The only way to find out for sure then is to climb the ladder! By building and communicating the approach of having *96 per cent certainty* there is then a strong and compelling case for others to climb the ladder confidently to discover what the 4 per cent of uncertainty might be.

Coaching tips

- Many individuals, teams and organisations can sometimes be found hiding among the ambiguity as a way of avoiding anything uncertain. By helping them climb the ladder from what they can be certain of, their confidence and courage to face those ambiguous fears will grow. (See also **Model 12: The spectrum of fear model.**)
- Many will focus so much on the percentage that is uncertain that it starts to feel like 100 per cent uncertainty in their minds and hearts. By helping them focus on what is known for sure, the perspective, balance and context for what is certain and uncertain will improve.
- Some will be reluctant to climb without guarantees in certain situations, yet they will do so freely in many other scenarios where there is clearly an element of uncertainty (e.g. crossing the road). By relating to scenarios

where they already climb the ladder without any guarantees, they will acquire the confidence and perspective to move away from ambiguity.

- The comfort zone is a good holding place within which to breathe, take stock and decide where to move next. However, it is not a place to stay too long.

The 10 characteristics of successful leaders

1 They value overall success more than personal acclaim.
2 They have fierce will, and personal humility.
3 They are stubborn and ruthless, yet humble and pragmatic.
4 They retain high ambitions and do not let their ego get in the way.
5 They expect great things to be achieved.
6 They appreciate the effort of others.
7 They are decisive with an unwavering resolve.
8 They are highly determined and disciplined.
9 They ask a lot of questions to develop greater understanding.
10 They measure performance, holding themselves and others to account.

Ambiguity: what happens in vagueness, stays in vagueness.

Anon

19

Leadership development (succession)

[
Succession: Seeking and creating opportunities for others to increase their skills, abilities and capacity that will add value when applied.
]

Leadership development is defined as any activity that enhances the leadership capability and capacity in an individual, team or organisation. This is likely to involve the development of abilities and attitudes that deliver successful outcomes using a combination of approaches from classroom-based courses to more experiential learning.

Succession is mainly considered to be the development of 'high potentials' to take over eventually from the current leadership when the time comes, or for the broadening of scope and authority. However, succession can also be considered as a leadership approach in terms of creating and developing strategies to ensure that successful outcomes are achieved not just once, but consistently – a succession of successes.

Effective leadership development for an individual may require a specific approach, or a range of approaches, to ensure that the learning is successfully understood. Appreciating the many valid options opens up opportunities and potential solutions for the successful delivery of development.

Successful teams develop an environment and approach for development that enables them to grow together constructively. Coaching plays an ever-increasing role in the successful development of teams, and well-developed teams of leaders understand and appreciate the process of coaching at an executive level. Organisations that are able to develop successful succession understand the need and value of creating a consistent culture of learning. (See also 'Level 5 Leaders' on *Succession Planning* from Jim Collins' bestselling book, *Good to Great*.)

Coaches have a central role to play in leadership development as the approach of coaching fully supports all the principles of succession; the coach is measured by the performance of those who have been coached. Good coaches know where coaching sits on the development continuum, and what else they are qualified to offer or provide to the individuals, teams and organisations they work with. Great coaches appreciate the depth required as an executive coach and the impact that accelerated learning techniques can have.

Model 55. The development continuum model

The big picture

There are seven widely recognised methods of development for individuals, teams and organisations that range from being directive in their approach to being more introspective. Each initiative has a definite and distinctive process and learning experience associated with it. Over many years it has been appreciated that the choice of how to deliver a development initiative has become a major factor in engagement, retention and long-term value.

This model offers a clear illustration of these seven recognised methods and approaches to development, and where they sit in relation to each other in terms of being more or less directive or introspective.

This model was applied to coaching to explain where coaching sits on the continuum, making clear what it is and, importantly, what it is not. The model provides context for why coaching is more questions based than mentoring or training or teaching, but that it is more outcome focused than counselling or psychotherapy. The model also shows each intervention and approach as being equally effective, rather than as a hierarchy, to ensure that all options are assessed on their own merits.

Individuals who are aware of the full spectrum of the development continuum appreciate that they have seven possible approaches to developing leaders and successful succession; otherwise, they would be restricted to a narrow view based upon whether they believe a subject should be taught or coached. Teams that understand the range of options available can then make more considered choices that reflect not just the topic, but also the optimal learning experience or style that will produce greater outcomes and results. Without this, teams are more likely to consider the 'one way' of developing people across the board, resulting in what is termed 'the sheep dip approach', where everyone goes through the same process, but the output is varied and inconsistent. (This also causes development to be perceived as something to get through rather than a personal opportunity to grow.)

Organisations that extend their options across the full spectrum of the development continuum are able to create and offer combined strategies and solutions that best match a topic, style or situation. This leads to greater long-term benefits of getting the best response from those whom they wish to develop as succession.

Coaches, as part of this continuum, can use this model to great effect. Firstly, to ensure that they develop the discipline of coaching, by not unconsciously straying into mentoring or counselling by becoming too directive or losing focus on the desired outcome. Secondly, to have the confidence to extend consciously beyond coaching into other areas, in which they are qualified, whenever the situation

Figure 19.1 The development continuum model

demands or requires a positive outcome, but always to enter and exit the process from a coaching position.

When to use it

- To be aware and explore all options for development.
- To assess and select the best approach based upon the direction, style and experiences that come with that approach.
- To avoid forcing every situation into the same approach.
- To develop a deeper understanding of and discipline in the selected approach.
- To establish the entry and exit points for development, so as to be flexible in between.
- To create a strategy of development that combines complementary approaches.

How to use it

The spectrum of development spans the most *directive to introspective* approaches to learning and growth:

- At the most directive end, there is *teaching,* which is very focused on what the 'right answers' are.
- A little less directive is *on the job training,* where the focus is on the practical application of the 'right answers'.
- Lower again in direction is *training,* where there is exploring and learning how best to extend the application of the 'right answers' to additional situations or levels.
- At the centre of the spectrum, there is a balance between direction and introspection in *mentoring,* where there are equal parts of answers and questions. This is where some direction is given based upon previous experience, but still having to decide upon how best to apply or implement the advice.
- Moving one level towards the introspective end, where there are more questions and fewer answers, is *coaching.* The structured questioning process of a coaching session is designed to develop the thinking and take it into action to achieve a desired outcome.

- *Counselling* goes deeper into questions than coaching, and there are fewer definitive or conclusive answers, more realisations from within.
- The introspective end of the spectrum is at *psychotherapy,* where there are no answers, just deep and insightful questions from within.

Decide on the preferred *entry point* based upon the style and method that is best suited for the individual, team or organisation to begin with, as this is where the immediate gains are to be found.

From this point of preference *expand, explore and discover* the range of methods and approaches across the development spectrum as there will be amazing insights and learning to be gained and experienced. This allows for a broader approach to development that will have a far-reaching and long-lasting impact.

Coaching tips

- Always remember where coaching sits so that there is no unconscious drift into other areas.
- Explaining the development continuum is one of the best ways to illustrate to individuals, teams and organisations what coaching actually is, and what it is not.
- Expand your awareness, knowledge and expertise (and maybe your qualifications) into as many areas on the continuum as you can so that you can professionally and competently adapt to the people and situations that you work with; but remember that you are a coach.
- As long as you clearly have coaching as your starting and exit points, you will be able to counsel, mentor, train or teach during a coaching session, and as long as you are clear that you are a coach who is able to adapt rather than a generalist.
- Not every situation you are faced with is a coaching situation; if you can adapt along this spectrum, you will be of value more consistently across a wider range of scenarios.
- If you ever find that you are being asked or would have to become something that you are not confident or qualified to do, then bring the session graciously to a halt, explain where coaching sits on the continuum and offer some guidance for seeking more appropriate support.

The five keys to developing others

1 **Make the time.**
2 **Look beyond the visible skills.**
3 **Create opportunities for development.**
4 **Encourage, acknowledge and appreciate.**
5 **Regularly review progress and learning.**

Only the people who take learning, growth and skills development into their own hands will be tomorrow's leaders.

Alli Worthington

Model 56. The executive coaching model

The big picture

There are various levels of coaching, from personal to business, speaker coaching to boardroom coaching, but the most powerful and effective coaching for developing leaders and a successful succession for individuals, teams and organisations is executive coaching. Where other levels of coaching are focused on delivering successful outcomes, and where people know what to do to make things happen, executive coaching is driven to deliver a succession of successes through greater *understanding* of why something works rather than just *knowing* that it does.

This model was designed and developed as a coaching tool in response to the need for clarity in what this level of coaching is about and why it differs from other coaching options. The model clearly illustrates the steps of the executive coaching process, where the breadth of knowledge is combined with the depth of understanding that can deliver a succession of successes.

When individuals, teams and organisations appreciate the executive coaching process they can quickly engage with, participate in and contribute to the success of each session. They also learn to value the role of their awareness as the catalyst for development, the importance of connecting this with experience to validate, and the capability that extends because of knowing something that was not known before; they can see that this is a level of success in itself. In terms of developing leaders, they will see that they are required to get beyond just knowing what to do so that they understand why to do something in order that they can, as leaders, communicate, influence and develop greater succession.

For coaches, this model represents the process of executive-level development through coaching and so provides a way of clarifying what executive coaching is about in comparison to other coaching options. This model also offers a framework for executive coaches to work from consistently.

Figure 19.2 The executive coaching model

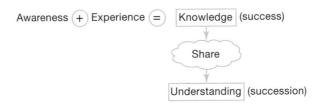

- To illustrate what executive coaching and succession look like.
- To explain the executive coaching process.
- To pinpoint the value and role of each component in the process: awareness, experience, knowledge, sharing and understanding.

How to use it

The first stage of this development is to increase *awareness* by taking the time to reflect upon what has gone well and what will need to go better next time.

Build on this increased awareness by connecting it to the specific *experience* of it: when it has happened before, when it happens now, and when it can be made to happen in the future.

When combined, the awareness and experience of something automatically increases *knowledge* of it; it is known for sure that it happens.

Successful solutions can be found here that are known to have worked, known to work, or known to be a good option to work in the future. (See also **Model 25: The egg-timer model.**)

To make valuable progress beyond just knowing that something happens or works is to develop a deeper *understanding* of why it happens or why it has, does or will work. This is best achieved by sharing and applying what there is an awareness of, has been experienced and is now known.

When *developing solutions,* first become aware of the options. Connect by applying them to previous or current experiences; it will be known if this is a worthy solution. That is, to apply and implement the solution to develop greater understanding of why it works, rather than just knowing that it would work now or that it did work before.

Coaching tips

- Some individuals, teams and organisations are satisfied with extending their knowledge, confident that they have a solution or answer to a specific issue or problem. However, until they understand why that solution or answer works, they have only been coached for success and will need to revisit this situation again as other issues and problems arise. Coaching for succession helps to create a strategy for dealing with such situations rather than just a reaction to something.
- When the waves of emotion roll large, people will forget what they know, and only as the waves withdraw will they remember; but no matter how high the waves of emotion, people will still connect with what they understand.
- Executive coaching is about coaching for succession: coaching individuals, teams and organisations to coach.
- One of the most common traps in coaching is when the people being coached either pretend to be their coach, or, at the other extreme, put the

success solely down to the coach. Executive coaching is about developing the individual, team or organisation to be the coach that they can genuinely become: developing their methods; communicating their messages; being the coach they can be. Providing this context helps avoid this pitfall.

The six levels of coaching

1 Witness.
2 Tell, be an expert.
3 Follow the client's explicit interest.
4 Offer feedback.
5 Follow the client's implicit interest.
6 Share wisdom, speak the truth.

Speak in such a way that others love to listen to you.
Listen in such a way that others love to speak to you.

Anon.

Model 57. The accelerated learning model

The big picture

As the desire and demand to develop have increased, so has the pace in which learning is required to be absorbed, understood and implemented. There are a number of recognised processes for increasing the speed of development and learning, but by far the most recognised and applied is accelerated learning.

Accelerated development is a method of learning that has been based upon more than 25 years of research into how the brain works. This approach to learning involves three basic principles:

1. The realisation that individuals, teams and organisations each have a preferred style, a way of learning that suits them best. When the techniques adopted match the preferred style of learning, it becomes more natural, easier and, therefore, quicker.

2. The realisation that individuals, teams and organisations learn better and faster when they are encouraged to make connections to what they already know and understand.

3. That accelerated learning is a total system involved in the design and delivery of the learning process by involving the thoughts, emotions,

Figure 19.3 The accelerated learning model

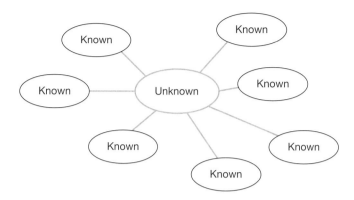

experience, knowledge and physical activity of the individual, team or organisation.

This model was designed and developed for coaching to illustrate the simplicity and encourage the use of accelerated learning techniques as part of the coaching process. The model makes clear the power of connecting 'knowns' to 'unknowns', which is of great value when looking to extend the range of options, approaches and strategies that could be considered or created.

When individuals are connected to what they already know, they feel confident and assured in their ability to apply this to something related that they did not know before. When teams connect to what they know, they look at what they have yet to know with courage and ambition rather than trepidation. When organisations look at what they do not yet understand in terms of what is already understood, they are able then to embrace new ways of working, new markets, new technologies and new conditions for success with a greater sense of composure and positive expectation.

When coaches use accelerated learning techniques for their own development, they will be more aware of the opportunities to apply these in their coaching sessions with individuals, teams and organisations.

When to use it

- To look at new approaches or ways of working that are considered as yet unknown.
- To enhance and speed up significantly the learning and development process.
- To reframe an unknown quickly so that the individual, team or organisation has confidence and assurance.
- To help quickly make sense of and calm the emotions that come with unknowns.

- To develop a strategy for enhancing and accelerating development for successful succession.

Accelerated learning consists of connecting a *known to an unknown* using a basic known example, analogy or metaphor to illustrate or explain something not yet understood.

The art of accelerated learning is *keeping it simple,* such as slices of cake to explain complex fractions or the importance of a steering wheel in a car to describe the value of providing leadership and direction.

Not yet knowing something (particularly when it is expected to be known) can generate emotions that get in the way of intelligence and logic in that moment and slow down the ability to learn. Using analogies and examples to illustrate and relate to provides the platform for *objective learning* by reducing the level of emotion and stress.

Coaching tips

- Some people would rather avoid saying 'I don't know' by saying that they do, just in case they come across as being inadequate or lacking in some way. It is sometimes easier to admit not having done something than not knowing what to do. If you sense a degree of denial or avoidance, reframe the question to make it easier. From there, you can offer an analogy to relate to.

- Practise building up a portfolio of analogies, examples, simplified models, etc., so that you are best prepared for accelerating the learning and development through new or created issues and opportunities.

- The value of a coach in many circumstances is the ability to make the complex simple, the unknown known and the misunderstood understood.

- One of the most positive and powerful applications of accelerated learning is to relate the unknown to a time, situation or scenario where the individual, team or organisation has achieved a successful outcome. This provides even more belief, confidence and positive expectation than an analogy or example that may be considered theory.

The accelerated learning cycle

1 Engage with the learners.
2 Connect with what they already know.
3 Introduce their current unknown.
4 Relate what they already know to this unknown.
5 Apply the principles of their known to this unknown.

Anyone who stops learning is old, whether at twenty or eighty. Anyone who keeps learning stays young.

Henry Ford

20 Compelling leadership (communication)

[
Communication: Expressing opinions, desires, needs and fears verbally and non-verbally in ways that are appropriate and effective to the situation.
]

Compelling leadership is defined as being able to engender loyalty, attract followers and use risk as a technique to grow and learn. These leaders drive growth and achievement for individuals, teams and the organisation. Central to this is their ability to communicate with power, clarity, influence and a clear context.

Compelling leaders are powerful and influential; they can lead from any position and understand what they do and do not yet know. They take and drive action, are willing and able to take risks, and are always open to learning; they inspire and give confidence to others through the power of communication, explanation and leading by example.

Individuals with these attributes understand the value of communicating to create relationships that have an optimal balance of formality and informality so that trust, confidence and certainty can be achieved. Teams that become successful leaders communicate and engage others expertly by telling compelling stories that generate emotion, empathy and objectivity. Organisations that provide compelling leadership communicate consistently the big, bigger and biggest pictures; they share the thinking behind their decisions, and they are then clear on what has been decided.

Effective coaches make influential connections with the individuals, teams and organisations they work with so that the content, stories and examples they share can be considered objectively and trusted to reach optimal conclusions.

Model 58. The formal v informal model

The big picture

There are two main categories of communication that define the relationship between individuals, teams and organisations. When the communication is considered to be entirely 'formal' this then defines the relationship as being formal: one that might be formally required, but one that is not considered as being wanted or informally valued. When the communication is considered to be entirely 'informal' this then defines the relationship as being informal: one that is wanted and appreciated informally as friends would be, but not a relationship that is considered to hold any formal value or purpose.

Many relationships, though, develop degrees of formality and informality, and this combination then defines the levels of trust, confidence, doubts and questions that make up the relationship.

This model was developed for coaching as a way to illustrate the complexities of communication and how this defines relationships. The model also illustrates the simplicity of developing formal and informal communication to achieve optimal relationships.

When individuals are engaged mainly in formal communication, they will always have a relationship that has doubts, questions and uncertainty surrounding it. Only when they engage in some communication that is considered to be informal can any trust, confidence or certainty develop. When teams lack any structure for their communication and it becomes completely informal, they may bond well together, but are likely to fail to deliver anything of formal value. When organisations learn to communicate more informally, and not just when they feel required to do so formally, they can create a culture that is built on confidence, trust and certainty, even when the message is not popular or positive.

Coaches who retain an overly formal approach to their communication and relationships with individuals, teams and organisations will always find it difficult to influence no matter how well or how hard they work. With a winning combination of protecting the formal coaching process, allied to an appreciation of building trust, confidence and certainty through informal choices and approaches, coaches can then build and maintain an optimal relationship.

When to use it

- To appreciate the current status of communication and why this impacts on relationships.

Figure 20.1 The formal v informal model

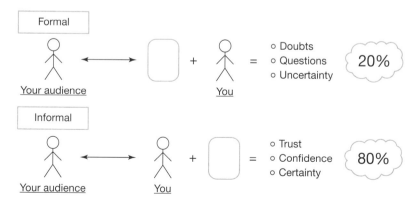

- To manage, and expand if necessary, the communication styles and strategies.
- To improve relationships through the combination of formal and informal communication.
- To define what formal and informal communication look like.
- To create a strategy for optimal relationships.

How to use it

Formal communication is important as it provides focus and direction, and confirms what is required to be said and informed in a way that is expected from the formal element of the relationship. This also includes formal announcements and declarations.

Informal communication is important as it develops understanding by offering insight into what an individual, team or organisation chooses to share, and the context and consideration beyond what is formally required (want to, rather than have to). This is about choosing to communicate and share beyond that which is formally required or expected. This includes informal conversations and the sharing of the context and consideration behind a conclusion or decision.

No matter how clear the formal communication is, or how the formal conclusion or decision is defined, when delivered in isolation it still results in creating *doubts, questions and uncertainty.*

Informal communication, however, drives *trust, confidence and certainty* in the relationship because it offers greater context and consideration behind the conclusion and demonstrates that the sharing is a *want* to, rather than *have* to.

Optimal communication is achieved through the *80:20 balance*: 80 per cent of communication is informal and the remaining 20 per cent formal. This ensures that there is still a clear sense of direction and purpose to the communication (formal), but in a way that engages the audience rather than just being notified. This also ensures that even the most informal chats still have a defined purpose and value.

Coaching tips

- There are areas of communication that are considered to be mainly formal: letters, announcements, long emails, meetings, appraisals, disciplinary sessions, interviews, etc.
- There are areas of communication that are considered to be mainly informal: chats, sharing of thoughts and ideas, short emails, catch-ups, discussions, etc.
- There are areas of communication that will be defined as either formal or informal by how they have been delivered; there can be informal discussions and there can be formal discussions.
- A birthday card will be considered or judged as being more formal because of its recognition of a formal date. A 'keep up the good work' card will be considered or judged as being more informal.

- Informal does not mean 'social'; informal communication that develops trust, confidence and certainty is about sharing something that is being chosen to share for a positive reason, even though there is no formal need to do so.
- Great coaching relationships are created when there is an optimal balance of the formal process not exceeding 20 per cent so that the other 80 per cent can be more intuitive, creative and personal.

The five levels of communication

1 **Acquaintance.**
2 **Sharing of information.**
3 **Sharing of ideas.**
4 **Sharing of emotions.**
5 **Gut-level sharing of insights.**

You can have brilliant ideas, but if you can't get them across, your ideas won't get you anywhere.

Lee Lacocca

Model 59. The power of the story model

The big picture

Compelling leaders, whether as an individual, a team or across an organisation, may have different styles and approaches that suit them best, but what they will all have in common if they are going to be able to drive towards and influence great outcomes is their ability to tell inspiring, compelling and empowering stories.

This model was developed as a tool for coaching in response to the many situations where individuals, teams or organisations struggled to communicate sufficiently to achieve their desired outcomes, often when utilising one or two of the three components that make a story inspiring, compelling and empowering. The model illustrates the components involved and the process of pulling together the full power of the story.

When the value and purpose of each component of the story is understood, individuals, teams and organisations are able to build the full story that delivers the level of emotion, empathy and objectivity required to drive extraordinary results. Without this balance, the story could be too emotional for the audience to be able to fully listen or understand the key message or points. With too much empathy, the story is unlikely to be engaging for the audience, and with too much objectivity, the story risks becoming a story of theory only.

From a coaching perspective, this model offers the coach an insightful framework for each coaching session using the analogy of a 'story' to assess, manage or create optimal coaching sessions that have the powerful combination of emotion, empathy and objectivity.

When to use it

- To appreciate the components required for compelling communication.
- To develop awareness of how to combine these components for the full power of the story.
- To respond to, manage or complement the existing energy of the message.
- To develop a strategic framework for all communication.
- To act as a framework for all coaching sessions.

How to use it

The first component of a powerful story is the part that focuses directly on the audience as this will generate and stimulate their *emotion*. This ensures a personal connection for the audience to the message and increases their level of emotional engagement. These parts of the story will start with the wording of 'you' and be focused on the perspective of the audience: things that are about them, involve them or say something about them. These things will increase their level of emotion, positive or negative.

The second component of a powerful story is focused on the individual, team or organisation delivering the message; this serves to generate a feeling of *empathy* with the audience. This gives both the storyteller and the audience something to share and connect on, something they can have in common, relate to and understand. These will be things that are about the storyteller ('me') that involve or say something about the storyteller, but also have relevance or relate to the audience. These things will increase the level of empathy between the storyteller and the audience, positive or negative.

Figure 20.2 The power of the story model

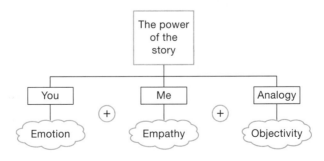

The third component involves the use of an analogy or analogies to ensure that there is a high degree of *objectivity*. This gives both the audience and the storyteller something to consider that sits outside of them both, something that they can both observe or consider from a detached and objective point of view. These things may be examples, stories about other people, case studies, models, concepts, theories or articles that are separate to them both, but have some relevance or meaning, positive or negative.

The aim of maximising the power of the story is to create the *powerful combination* of emotion, empathy and objectivity, by having the story cover bits about the audience, bits about the storyteller, and by adding relevant analogies or examples that have meaning to both.

The storyteller must show *considerate balance* by assessing how much emotion, empathy or objectivity the audience have already brought with them so that this can be complemented rather than the story becoming overloaded on just one or two components and suffering from a lack of emotion, empathy or objectivity. To increase the level of emotional engagement in an audience, bring in more about them. To increase the level of empathy with an audience, share a bit more about the storyteller. To increase or introduce more objectivity, use an analogy that offers explanation through examples, concepts or models.

Coaching tips

- The most effective and impactful coaching sessions always have the optimal combination of emotion, empathy and objectivity. The sessions that do not quite work tend to have had too much emotion in them, not enough empathy, or too much, or too little objectivity.

- Be aware as the coach (storyteller) that you are accountable for making sure that the optimal combination of emotion, empathy and objectivity is reached and maintained.

- It is crucial that you quickly appreciate how much emotion, empathy and objectivity the individual, team or organisation is bringing to the session so that you can then bring more of the other component or components to create the optimal combination.

- It is important to be aware and to manage what you as the coach (storyteller) may be bringing to the session in terms of your levels of emotion, empathy and objectivity as these will have an impact. When you as the coach (storyteller) can enter the session with an equal level of emotion, empathy and objectivity you can then focus on the levels brought in by the individual, team or organisation you are working with. Ensuring you are in balance before each session is advisable.

- You will know when the session is out of balance and has become too emotional and too directed at the person you are working with when they feel judged or criticised and become either defensive or aggressive. Time then to offer an analogy or share something about you that is relevant and can be related to so that the conversation can open up and be better balanced.

- You will know when the session is out of balance and has too much empathy when there is a higher degree of interest in what you are doing, or what you think, than the person you are coaching. Time then to ask about the person you are coaching to increase their emotional engagement, or offer an analogy or share something about you that is relevant and they can relate to.

- You will know when the session is out of balance and has become too objective when the session is wrapped up in theory, case studies, the stories of others. Time then to ask some direct questions as to how the person you are working with could apply the concepts covered, or share how you have done so in a way that is relevant.

The five communication styles

1 **Assertive.**
2 **Aggressive.**
3 **Passive.**
4 **Submissive.**
5 **Manipulative.**

Tell me and I'll forget. Show me and I might remember. Involve me and I will understand.

Benjamin Franklin

Model 60. The context–consideration–conclusion model

The big picture

The third element involved in becoming a compelling leader is the ability and discipline to communicate more than just the decision or conclusion reached. Compelling leaders know the value and effectiveness in communicating first the big picture, then the thoughts, structures and points that need to be taken into consideration to get to the decision and conclusion. This approach ensures that the leader is not left exposed or isolated, or to justify, or to battle with the emotional reaction of the audience around the decision.

This model was designed and developed as a coaching tool in response to the many decisions, conclusions or answers that were either lost or compromised due to the lack of context or consideration communicated. Too often, strong decisions and conclusions have floundered or failed because they created an emotional response that was not helpful, and these emotional responses are more often than not a reaction to not understanding fully the context for the conclusion, or the considerations that lie behind the decision. This simple and effective model illustrates the optimal process for protecting the value of the conclusion.

Understanding this process enables individuals to communicate and engage others with the conclusion they have come to by helping others appreciate the journey and process involved in getting to this end point. Without the context and consideration, there can only be an emotional reaction based upon whether the decision is liked or disliked. From this point there is now an emotional barrier that moves the conversation into justification rather than implementation.

Teams that do not communicate the context and consideration behind a conclusion can often find themselves looking for a conclusion that will hopefully receive a positive emotional response rather than looking for the best decision. When teams appreciate this process fully, they are able to generate positive and objective responses to the best conclusions because their audience understand where this sits within the bigger picture and the quality of consideration that has been involved. This approach allows the audience to appreciate the value and quality of the decision.

Organisations that fail to communicate the bigger picture context, and those who do not share the level or volume of considerations that have gone into coming to a conclusion, tend to split their audience into three groups: those who think they understand and agree; those who think they understand and disagree; and those who do not understand, so they do not know how to engage. By applying this process consistently, organisations are able to foster trust, transparency, engagement and following because their audience can all understand and appreciate how a decision has been made, even if it is not a conclusion that they would have wanted.

It is important for coaches to develop the good habit of providing context and consideration behind what they have decided to ask or share with those that they work with, otherwise the latter will make their own assumptions; if they are being asked a lot of questions, they may assume that they are expected to know the answer; if they are not given answers or suggestions, they may assume that there are no answers; if they are being asked for alternative answers to those that they have given, they may assume that they are getting it wrong. Yet with the bigger picture context, and the sharing of what a coach has to consider, the person being coached can appreciate that there are often questions that are designed to stimulate thought rather than just an answer; that it is their answers that count most and it can be

Figure 20.3 The context–consideration–conclusion model

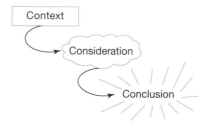

unhelpful to lead with suggestions; that looking for alternative answers broadens their thinking and increases their conviction.

Whether with individuals, teams, organisations or coaches, the main cause for the context and considerations not to be communicated is that the conclusion is believed to be right or obvious, so it should not need either context or consideration. However, if it is the right conclusion, it deserves to be protected and communicated effectively by sharing the context and considerations behind it.

When to use it

- To appreciate the process of optimal communication of a conclusion or decision.
- To understand the role and value of the context and considerations behind a conclusion or decision.
- To ensure that the conclusion or decision receives a positive and objective response rather than an emotional reaction.
- To develop an inclusive strategy of communication rather than being exclusive only to those who will emotionally agree.
- To protect the best ideas, decisions and conclusions by providing big picture context and sharing the considerations that lie behind it.

How to use it

Successful communication is built upon being able to *avoid the conclusion habit*. This is the habit of communicating only, or firstly, the conclusion without sharing any insight into how it was arrived at, or where it fits within a grander scheme of things. Without context and consideration, there can only be an emotional reaction to a conclusion: whether it is liked, or not.

Providing *big picture context* helps explain the biggest reason and purpose for the conclusion in a way that puts the decision into a healthy perspective. This will consist of the longer term view, the ultimate outcome or destination that is being aimed for.

Explaining then the *thoughtful consideration* that is required in relation to the 'bigger picture' helps to provide a clear framework of the thoughts and questions that need or had to be considered in order to support the ultimate outcome.

With an appreciation of the 'big picture' that is then combined with an insight into what needs or had to be considered, this will deliver a *compelling conclusion* that has clear context and thoughtful consideration behind it.

Receptive audiences are those that have been respected and valued enough, and considered important enough to communicate in a way where they feel involved and are offered insight into the process of how decisions are made.

- The power of the context is related to the size and scale of the big picture used: 'over the next 5–10 years . . . ' provides greater context than 'by Wednesday of next week . . . '.

- The greater the scale of the context, the more the considerations will be received with perspective and objectivity.

- The considerations should be all the important pillars, building blocks, framework, strategic measures or components that support or play a part in the bigger picture and are relevant in coming to the conclusion or decision.

- If the context and considerations have been clearly communicated, it is likely that the audience will have anticipated and be ready to arrive at the conclusion.

- This process does not eliminate resistance to the conclusion; it reduces the unnecessary emotional rejections and barriers to the conclusion caused by a lack of context or understanding.

- You demonstrate the value you hold in your audience by taking the time and thought to communicate with them the expansive context, insightful consideration and clear conclusions.

The 10 steps to effective communication

1 Clarify the whole idea before you communicate.
2 Focus your communication on the needs and interests of your audience.
3 Consult before you communicate.
4 Give consideration to the tone, language and content.
5 Communicate the value to your audience specifically.
6 Invite, accommodate and encourage feedback.
7 Be consistent in your message.
8 Follow up; always have a clear 'call to action'.
9 Listen to your audience.
10 Make clear that the message is now theirs.

Effective communication is 20 per cent what you know and 80 per cent how you feel about what you know.

Jim Rohn

PART SIX

High-performance coaching

Value delivery: Everything necessary to ensure that promises are delivered, a reputation for delivery is established, and a strong referral network is built.

Value delivery is the sixth of the key areas of coaching development. Individuals who are known to perform at a level where they consistently deliver value are considered to be the high performers in teams and across an organisation as they do what it takes and change what needs to be changed in order to keep their promises. Teams that rate highly on value delivery create a collaborative environment internally and externally to avoid compromise and focus on optimal outcomes. Organisations that are considered to be high performing consistently deliver on their promises and create additional value for their employees and customers. These organisations are driven to ask questions to challenge the creation of experiences that lead to higher engagement and loyalty.

This part focuses on how best to develop high-performance strategies of delivery; to make sure that everything is done to keep promises and build a reputation of trust and high value. This part is where the results and value from coaching are most clearly demonstrated.

In this part we present value delivery as the combination of these four elements:

This selection of coaching models has been specifically designed to develop higher levels of value delivery.

Managing issues (conflict management)

[
Conflict management: Dealing with, resolving and negotiating to create optimal solutions in situations of conflict.
]

High-performance individuals, teams and organisations have to deal with as many issues as those who perform at lower levels; high performers, however, develop strategies to manage those issues in a way that leads to even better outcomes and results.

Conflict management is described as the process of limiting the negative aspects of conflict while increasing the positive aspects. The aim of conflict management is to enhance learning and group outcomes in effectiveness and performance.

Individuals who manage issues successfully see conflict as a process rather than a personal battle; they develop a range of approaches so that they can get the best return from any situation. High-performing teams appreciate that there is great value in being able to challenge each other constructively so that they can raise their level of performance and deliver even greater value. Organisations that consistently deliver great value and keep their promises to their employees and customers develop strategies and approaches that enable them to channel the learning from issues towards even higher levels of performance.

For coaches, managing issues and driving high performance are key indicators of their value and impact. Successful coaches build a reputation on which they can be referred and recommended with confidence and trust. Dealing with issues of conflict, criticism and being able to build optimal solutions is the cornerstone of a high-performing coach.

Model 61. The conflict options model

The big picture

Conflict has a broader context than most people imagine because it can take on a variety of guises: it can be a disagreement over issues such as cost, performance or aims, or issues being avoided; it can be a clash of personalities, styles or expectations; it can be driven by an environment that is competitive, being compromised or going in a different direction.

Conflict can pull people together or rip them apart; however, conflict is neither a good nor bad thing, it depends on how well it is managed. There are many breakthroughs, inventions, ideas and solutions that arise from being in conflict with how things currently are. There are many relationships that reach higher levels because of a period of conflict rather than in spite of it. There are many developments made by individuals, teams and organisations because they decided that more could be achieved, and in doing so put themselves into conflict with how things had been or were now. Conflict may not feel pleasant, but it can be the vital catalyst for change and improvement when managed optimally.

This model was adapted from the Thomas–Kilmann Conflict Mode Instrument (TKI) tool, created by Kenneth W. Thomas and Ralph H. Kilmann, and considered to be the leader in conflict resolution assessment since 1974. The concepts were applied to coaching in response to the many situations and scenarios where individuals, teams and organisations were holding onto only one or two approaches when faced with conflict and experiencing limited results as a consequence. The model illustrates clearly that there are five valid options to consider and have available when dealing with a situation or scenario of conflict. With all five options available, individuals, teams and organisations are empowered with a greater range of options to choose from that may suit the situation best.

With an understanding of the five approaches available, and an appreciation of the conditions, environment or situation, so that the most appropriate selection or approach can be made, individuals, teams and organisations are in a far better position to manage conflict towards an optimal result.

For coaches also, this model sets out the range of approaches that can be taken so that they keep all options available to make a considered choice, which may be to let something go rather than always pick up on every word; stay strong on a point rather than be ambivalent; concede a point rather than force a compromise; find some middle ground rather than hold a position; extending a point into a far larger context rather than sticking to the current issue.

This model also applies to the inner conflict that individuals, teams, organisations and coaches experience: their strengths and weaknesses; their ambitions and anxieties; their imagination and sense of reality. Keeping all five options available at all times (situations can change) is the base on which to manage issues and conflict, the success of which is determined by choosing the best approach in relation to the situation and environment.

When to use it

- To define the power and value of conflict so that the fear of conflict does not overshadow the potential that conflict can be a positive catalyst when managed optimally.
- To develop and maintain awareness of the five options available when dealing with any situation or scenario involving conflict.

- To understand and appreciate the value of each of the five options available when dealing with conflict.
- To be aware of the options that you rely on too much, and those that you tend not to go to often enough, so that you can give more balanced consideration to all five.
- To consider what scenarios, circumstances and environments suit each of the five available options.
- To understand and manage the approaches of others that you are in conflict with.
- To develop a more objective strategy for dealing with conflict by viewing it as a process in which you have a range of valid approaches to choose from.

How to use it

The first consideration when dealing with conflict is the ability of the individual, team or organisation to be *assertive* to the degree that is most constructive. Their level of assertiveness should reflect the level of value they hold in the specific point of conflict compared to the other party involved: when it matters a lot more to them, be highly assertive; when it does not matter as much to them, be less assertive; when it is of equal value to both, a moderate level of assertiveness is required.

The second consideration is how *co-operative* to be, and this should reflect the level of value that the other party involved holds in the specific point of conflict com-pared to the individual, team or organisation: when it matters a lot more to the other party involved, the individual, team or organisation should be highly co-operative; when it matters little to the other party, but means a lot to the individual, team or organisation, then they may be less co-operative on this point; when it is of equal value to both, a moderate level of co-operation is required.

In any situation of conflict there are five options available to the individual, team or organisation, the first one being to *avoid.* This approach is low on 'assertive' and low on 'co-operative', and is therefore a 'lose–lose' approach for both parties, for the time being.

Figure 21.1 The conflict options model

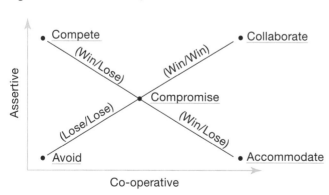

Avoiding is a good option when . . .

- There is no real value to either person and so it is not worth fighting over.
- There is a high level of emotion and stress, so stepping back for a bit allows everyone to calm down and think more clearly.
- There is a low level of trust between those involved at that moment, so there is no base on which to build constructively.
- There is time available when it is not urgent, so it can be dealt with at a more relevant time.
- There is a low level of complexity involved, so this specific point of conflict can be avoided in isolation without directly affecting or restricting other things.

Avoiding can allow time and space for people to gather their thoughts, to calm down, to gain perspective, to consider more urgent things and to consider how to build bridges of trust.

There is also the choice to *compete* when in a situation of conflict. This approach is high on 'assertive' but low on 'co-operation' where the individual, team or organisation is prepared to stand firm on exactly what they want or need, even disregarding the other involved party's needs or wants. This choice puts the conflict on the 'win–lose' line where the individual, team or organisation is out to win and the other party involved does not get anything. The level of assertiveness determines how much is won or lost: the more assertive, the greater the margin.

Competing is a good option when . . .

- There is high value to you in getting what you need, but it is of low or no value to the other person.
- There is only a moderate to low level of emotion and stress involved so that both parties can communicate effectively.
- There is at least a moderate level of trust established between those involved so that winning and losing can be discussed, agreed and understood fairly.
- There is no or little time left, so a decision has to be made, and when the cost of no decision is too high.
- There is a moderate level of complexity involved, which is seen and treated as an individual point that may be connected to one or two other points that could be accommodated to bring about balance and build trust. Competing should not be perceived as setting a precedent or norm, or an isolated victory, but as being connected to other points on which there could be compromise or accommodation.

Competing is an important and valuable approach on a situation-by-situation basis because it helps keep things moving, avoids stalling and can lead to important break-throughs. However, it remains low on co-operation and so will require to be brought into more balance at some point soon. It is likely that an individual, team or organisation will have to accommodate or compromise on other points to build trust.

The direct alternative to competing is to choose to *accommodate,* where the individual, team or organisation is happy to forgo their own needs in concession to the other party's needs or wants. This choice also puts the conflict on the 'win–lose' line where the individual, team or organisation give up what they need to allow the other party involved to gain. The more co-operative they are here, the greater the margin between what they lose and what the other party gains.

Accommodating is a good option when . . .

- There is low or no value to you, but it is of high value to the other person.
- There is only a moderate to low level of emotion and stress involved so that both parties can communicate effectively.
- There is no or little time left, so a decision has to be made, and when the cost of no decision is too high.
- There is at least a moderate level of trust established between those involved so that winning and losing can be discussed, agreed and understood fairly.
- There is a moderate level of complexity involved, which is seen and treated as an individual point that may be connected to one or two other points that could be competed for or compromised on to bring about balance and build trust. Accommodating should not be perceived as setting a precedent or norm, or an isolated defeat, but understood as being connected to other points on which there could be compromise or competition.

Accommodating is an important and valuable approach on a situation-by-situation basis because it helps keep things moving, avoids stalling and can lead to important breakthroughs. However, it remains low on 'assertive' and so will require to be brought into more balance at some point. It is likely that an individual, team or organisation will need to compete or compromise on other points to feel that there is trust building.

The 'middle ground' option is to choose *compromise* where both parties involved forgo some of their own needs in concession to some of the other person's needs or wants. This choice keeps the conflict on the 'win–lose' line where both parties are giving up part of what they need to allow the other to get part of what they want. Be aware that the result of compromise is that neither party is getting what they want, but they are both getting something.

Compromising is a good option when . . .

- There is equal value to you both: equally high, or equally low.
- There is only a moderate to low level of emotion and stress involved so that both parties can communicate effectively.

- There is no or little time left, so a decision has to be made, and when the cost of no decision is too high.
- There is at least a moderate level of trust established between those involved so that partial 'winning' and partial 'losing' for both parties can be discussed, agreed and understood fairly.
- There is a moderate level of complexity involved so that it is seen and treated as an individual point and not perceived as setting a precedent or norm, but understood as being connected to a bigger picture.

Compromising can be an important and valuable approach on a situation-by-situation basis because it helps keep things moving, avoids stalling and can lead to important breakthroughs; it is a balanced and moderate approach in terms of being assertive and co-operative. It can be a good holding position and a platform for other choices.

The optimal approach is when the environment and relationship allow the individual, team or organisation to choose *collaboration* when dealing with conflict. This is when both parties are able to create powerful solutions because of points of conflict. Here both parties are able to gain all the points that are available to them without compromise or concession and achieve even greater benefits together. Collaboration is an approach that has to be taken together; it will not be sufficient for just one party to decide to take a collaborative approach without the other party joining in fully.

Collaborating is a good option when . . .

- There is high value to both parties.
- There is a low level of emotion and stress involved so that both parties can be innovative and creative.
- There is a generous amount of time to work with so that imaginative and big picture options can be considered and thought through properly.
- There is a high level of trust established between those involved so that winning for all parties can be discussed, agreed and understood fairly.
- There is a high level of complexity involved, a level that takes into consideration all the needs and wants of all parties, consistently taking a 'bigger picture' view.

Collaborating is a highly valuable approach when the right environment is established or created. Being high on both 'assertive' and 'co-operative', collaboration puts conflict on the 'win–win' line where solutions can be created that meet or exceed the needs and wants of all parties.

The current *environment* of a conflict situation informs the best available option at that time. The five components of the environment are:

- Value.
- Emotion and stress.

- Time.
- Trust.
- Complexity.

By assessing whether each of these environmental factors is currently high, low or moderate, it will be clear as to the best approach. This assessment will also indicate the area or areas that need to be developed or improved if looking to adopt a different or preferred approach.

Coaching tips

- Everyone will have their own two or three approaches that they naturally revert to in situations of conflict, either out of habit, comfort or because they believe this is how they are expected to deal with conflict in the role that they have or perceive.
- Over-reliance on one, two or three approaches to conflict can be down to a lack of awareness that there are other options available that are indeed viable, because people often disregard options as not being a real option for them. All five remain valid at all times.
- Explaining what each of the options means immediately opens up people to having five valid options, as often their perception of avoid, compete, accommodate, compromise and collaborate is neither clear nor accurate in terms of managing conflict.
- Communication of the approach taken is important; if you choose to accommodate but do not make this clear, it can be perceived that you are compromising, so there will be misunderstanding as to whether you are owed something to bring about balance.
- Compromise is a very popular focus for individuals, teams and organisations to reach as it appears to mean that no party has lost. Compromise, however, means that neither party are getting what they want, but at least both get something. When compromise is seen more as a secondary or equal objective rather than primary, then all five options and outcomes remain available and achievable.
- There are three levels of development with this model:
  1. *Operational*: Be aware that there are always five valid options available.
  2. *Management*: Select the best approach based upon the assessment of the conflict situation and environment in terms of value, emotion, time, trust and complexity.
  3. *Strategic*: Look to create the environment that is optimal or preferred by influencing, building or improving the communication of value, emotion, time, trust and complexity.

The five stages of conflict management

1 **Latent.**
2 **Perceived.**
3 **Felt.**
4 **Manifest.**
5 **Aftermath.**

Co-operation is not the absence of conflict, but a means of managing conflict.

Deborah Tannen

Model 62. The constructive criticism model

The big picture

Constructive criticism is defined as the process of offering valid and well-reasoned opinions about others, involving both positive and negative comments in a non-confrontational manner with the aim of raising performance standards. High-performing individuals, teams and organisations appreciate the value of constructive criticism as a powerful tool to create bonds, strengthen relationships, set high standards and drive even greater performance. For those who manage issues optimally, they recognise the opportunity to provide constructive criticism for their highest performers and not just situations around under-performance or under-achievement.

This model was developed for coaching in response to the many situations and opportunities where issues and concerns could be managed in a manner that is positive, productive and drives high performance. The model sets out a proven, step-by-step guide to driving high performance through constructive criticism to empower individuals, teams and organisations to overcome the biggest barrier: the fear of making an issue worse.

It should be considered acceptable for individuals, teams or organisations to make a mistake or to fall short of what was expected; however, it should not be considered acceptable for this to continue to occur. This is where the value of being able to deliver constructive criticism to a high standard consistently and frequently ensures that issues are well managed in order to establish standards and performance that deliver the desired results and outcomes, while communicating the value and importance of those receiving the criticism.

Many coaching sessions follow the structure and format of this model and process. The principles of driving higher performance through greater awareness and understanding are closely aligned to the coaching framework. Developing the ability and expertise to deliver constructive criticism to the highest standards enables coaches to deliver greater value for their clients by directing them constructively to specific areas that would have a big impact if developed further. This level of insight and connection enhances the coaching relationship to higher levels as the role of the coach is seen to be less passive and more participative.

When to use it

- To give individuals, teams and organisations valuable feedback and insight into how they could achieve higher levels of performance.

- To observe criticism as a constructive and positive process rather than something to avoid for as long as possible.

- To build a strong and participative relationship by demonstrating the value, care and respect held.

- To be able to set and maintain, or to reset and stretch, the levels and standards of what is expected to be delivered on promises.

- To develop a strategy of continuous improvement through constructive criticism.

How to use it

When an individual, team or organisation are providing constructive criticism it must be done *quickly, face to face and in private.* It is best not to hold onto a criticism, best not to use an email or phone call if at all possible, and best not to criticise in public!

Next, they should *agree the facts* so that both parties can understand the full picture. This is about agreeing the facts, not just presenting the evidence to back up

Figure 21.2 The constructive criticism model

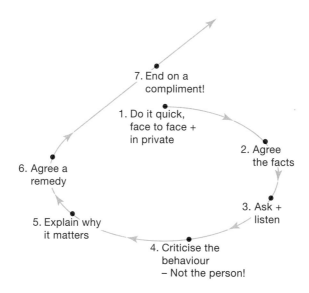

either side of an argument and expecting a positive response. If emotions run high, leading to either defence or aggression, then the facts have not been 'agreed'. They should be investigated: seek to understand so that there is a connection that remains.

It is important for the individual, team or organisation to *ask and listen* clearly to the other party so that there remains a connection and level of engagement; this is not about taking sides or sitting in judgement, but about being positively influential. This part of the process is to help identify the specific behaviour that will be criticised. Only when the specific behaviour has been identified can the process progress to the next stage.

The key principle of constructive criticism is to ensure that *it is the behaviour that is criticised, not the person,* so the person does not become over-emotional or overly defensive or feel personally attacked. This separation of behaviour and the person enables both parties to view, observe and consider objectively the specific behaviour. This keeps both parties connected and together rather than becoming the prosecutor and the accused. (See also **Model 39: The connect 2 understand model.**)

Taking the time to *explain why it matters* provides context for why this was a criticism worth making, why it was worth taking the risk to make a point of it, why the other party is worthy of dealing with it, why this is important, why this then affects and leads to other things, why this is a great opportunity to reach higher levels of performance. (See also **Model 41: The power of 'why?' model.**)

Agree a remedy that is owned by the other party, their strategy or solution for ensuring that they avoid a repeat of the events or the conversation. This is not about giving solutions or providing leading suggestions, but about the other party owning a solution that the individual, team or organisation are confident in as a remedy that can make enough of a difference, and then seeing how they can support it if necessary.

End on a compliment to reinforce the positive and constructive intent behind having the conversation, and why this person gives the individual, team or organisation the confidence that there will be a constructive, positive and considered response in order to drive performance to higher and more consistent levels. The compliment, or compliments, should be genuine, heartfelt and ideally involve examples and evidence that are relevant to the issue or behaviour being criticised in terms of when there was positive performance previously. This explanation of any compliment is key to validate the sincerity behind it so that it cannot be perceived, conveniently or otherwise, as a shallow or manipulative comment. It is best for the individual, team or organisation to have the compliments clear in their mind before the process is started so that they are easy to find when needed.

Coaching tips

- The process is best followed in the order presented. Each step may require more or less time depending on the issue or person being managed; it is best to complete each step thoroughly before moving on to the next one.

- Having a strong belief in a positive outcome helps set the tone and mindset for success.

- Explaining that there are steps to follow can help the other person see this as an objective process rather than an emotional discussion or debate.

- The best preparation is to have the compliments ready before you start the process, as it can sometimes be difficult to find them once you are in the middle of it.

- Remember never to criticise the person as this would only disconnect and disengage you from them. Criticising the behaviour allows you both to remain connected, both doing the same thing, both observing the behaviour objectively. This allows the conversation to explore and expand on the impact of that specific behaviour and the possible consequences that follow.

- The issue being managed does not have to be proven to be true or beyond doubt before it can be constructively criticised, as this can often work against the first step in the process: *quick, face to face and in private.* The perception of an issue is sufficient to act upon, as both parties can then proceed on the basis of 'even if this is just a perception . . . ', which can sometimes be easier to deal with as the defence barriers are less likely to rise.

The five tips for communicating through conflict

1 Make clear the value for your relationship.
2 Communicate slowly and deliberately.
3 Seek to understand the position of others.
4 Actively listen to what others are trying to communicate.
5 Confront the situation, not the person!

Criticism may not be agreeable, but it is necessary. It fulfils the same function as pain in the human body. It calls attention to an unhealthy state of things.

Winston Churchill

Model 63. The three-boxes model

The big picture

Managing issues to achieve optimal results has a lot to do with where the issue is placed, as this will determine whether a situation is going to work against, work for or be a continual battle to stay on top of. Individuals, teams and organisations that drive high performance understand how to manage issues and conflict in a way that does not just avoid, mitigate or nullify; they develop strategies that channel those same issues and conflicts in a way that drives them to ever-greater outcomes and results.

This model was created and developed as a tool for coaching in response to the many situations and issues that were clearly holding individuals, teams and organisations back, draining their energy and reducing their confidence while producing ever-decreasing results and returns. The model clearly illustrates the three options available in which to place these situations and issues, and what then happens as a consequence.

While individuals, teams, organisations and coaches will all have situations and issues in each of these boxes, by understanding this model and the process that occurs, they can make more informed and considered choices in terms of the self-confidence and the returns they get from all that they invest in those situations.

When to use it

- To understand how issues affect self-confidence and the returns achieved from all that is invested in situations, and how to improve these.
- To appreciate that there are three boxes in the process to choose from and that situations can be moved.
- To adjust the mindset and approach to current and historical issues and situations for greater results.
- To develop strategies that channel issues and situations towards greater self-confidence and higher returns.

How to use it

The vertical axis of *return on investment (ROI)* measures what is obtained from a given situation relative to how much has been put in. What has been put in may

Figure 21.3 The three-boxes model

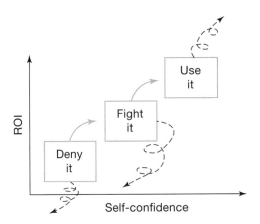

be measured in terms of time, energy, money, thought, planning, anxiety, worry, effort, etc.

The horizontal axis of *self-confidence* measures how an individual, team or organisation feel about themselves, a very important component in dealing with all situations and opportunities.

The first box in which to place something that has happened, or is happening now, is the *deny it* box. In this box, the aim is to pretend that what has happened or is happening has no impact or value in terms of self-confidence or achieving success. It takes a lot of energy to stay in denial, yet it gives nothing back. This quickly undermines the level of self-confidence as it maintains a constant state of pretence, denial, allowing the situation to become a perpetual bully.

The next box is the *fight it* box, where the aim is to succeed *in spite of* what has happened, or is happening. Although this approach initially does provide a positive return for all the energy that it takes, this return starts to diminish as the constant battling and refusal to be beaten become exhausting. In terms of self-confidence too, the initial boost that comes from facing up to what has happened gradually reduces over time because it does not lead to forward movement.

The top box in which to place whatever has happened, or is happening, is the *use it* box. This is where what has happened, or is happening, has been considered and the decision is then taken to be even more successful *because of* what has happened or is happening. In this box there is a significant and sustainable gain of far more energy than has been put in and the ability to turn issues into a platform rather than a burden ensures that the level of self-confidence builds and builds.

All this is a process for *continual progress* rather than a concept of perfection. There will be things that have happened, or are happening, that sit in each of these boxes; this is natural and to be expected. It is always good to know, though, that for a greater return on all that is being invested, and for greater levels of self-confidence, the work can be put in ultimately to place these issues in the 'use it' box to be successful *because of,* rather than in spite of, or being left in denial.

Coaching tips

- Always provide the healthy context that everyone will have things in each box as there are some issues that are being denied, fought against and used to increase returns and build self-confidence. To be in denial or to be fighting against something is not a failure; it is a process.

- It is not recommended to try and jump boxes; if in the 'deny it' box, best then to move to the 'fight it' box before reaching for the 'use it' box. This process can take some time, but not always; however, it remains a process where the steps and stages are best followed.

- The 'use it' box is the place where a collaborative approach is taken on issues, situations, perceived weaknesses, tendencies or preferences. (See also **Model 67: The conditions for collaboration model.**)

- Some people do not want to move certain issues, even though it would be beneficial for them to do so. These feelings should always be respected. When these people are ready to do so, and once they have moved some other issues up a box and have more confidence, that will be the right time.

The six steps to conflict resolution

1 Identify the source of the conflict.
2 Look beyond the point of conflict.
3 Ask for suggested solutions.
4 Clarify solutions that everyone can support.
5 Help to create and connect to the common ground for everyone.
6 Ask for commitment beyond just agreement; actions, not just words.

Conflict is the beginning of consciousness.

Esther Harding

Value creation
(building bonds
and connections)

[**Building bonds and connections: Working with others towards a shared vision by creating a collective energy, added value and a sense of loyalty to pursue meaningful goals.**]

High-performance individuals, teams and organisations build connections and bonds internally and externally that create immense value through even the toughest of times. These connections are made to happen, they are not just waited for, or taken for granted; they are the result of clear intention and disciplined habits that communicate their current and future value.

Value creation is being able to imagine and deliver more than can be currently seen. These bigger value outcomes are rarely achieved without understanding how to best connect, influence and drive others towards a shared vision for what could be possible. High performers appreciate the importance of communicating their level of interest in others to build bonds of real value; high performers know how to ask questions that encourage and establish powerful connections; high performers understand the key components to drive satisfaction and loyalty in those relationships.

It is essential for coaches to be able to create value from each session they deliver. To do so, they must be able to build bonds and connections with the individuals, teams and organisations they work with so that they can influence and support approaches that lead to high performance. This section is one of the most fundamental for coaches as it is covers the quality and impact of asking questions, and the ability to define the components that drive satisfaction and loyalty.

Model 64. The value of asking questions model

The big picture

It is widely accepted that proper and effective questioning has become a lost art and this has been put down largely to the way individuals, teams and organisations incentivise, and are incentivised, to provide correct answers rather than to ask great questions. Asking questions can even carry the risk of the questioner becoming isolated, ignored, or being perceived as troublesome. Another factor in the lack of questions asked is the way that decision making has gone from 'soon' to 'now' to 'yesterday', causing people to jump to conclusions that can often be defunct of context or credible consideration. (See also **Model 60: The context–considera-tion–conclusion model.**)

This model was created and developed for coaching in response to the many situations where, with just a few more questions asked, far better outcomes and relationships could have been created. This simple and effective illustration maps out the barriers to be overcome, and then the levels that can be reached by asking more questions of value to communicate and demonstrate the value you hold in that connection.

High performers who know how to create bonds and valuable connections appreciate that the barriers to asking questions are mainly associated with the answers or potential answers, and they also appreciate that the value in asking questions is what they are communicating and demonstrating by asking in the first place. While others miss out on building those bonds and making those connections by not asking questions – in case they do not get the answer they want, or they get the answer they do not want, or they may seem foolish by not knowing the answer – high performers ask the questions to demonstrate their interest, care and value in those being asked. (See also **Model 30: The motivation to move model.**)

For coaches, for whom there is a formal expectation that questions will be asked, it is valuable to remember the value and importance that your questions demonstrate and communicate. For coaches, asking questions can become the job or the habit that comes with the role; however, the question should be assessed on its value and impact rather than its difficulty or complexity. Great bonds and connections are built by coaches with the individuals, teams and organisations they work with, largely because of the level of interest, thoughtfulness, care and consideration they communicate by asking questions.

Figure 22.1 The value of asking questions model

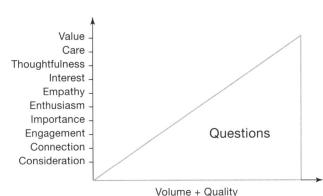

- To make clear the value and impact of asking questions in order to overcome the fear and perceived risk of asking.
- To communicate that there is, or there could be, a stronger connection and bond to be built.
- To demonstrate that the connection is seen as one of importance and interest and that to develop it further would be looked upon positively.
- To ensure that questions are asked so that better decisions can be made.
- To get beyond 'knowing' and move to 'understanding'. (See also **Model 56: The executive coaching model.**)
- To develop a strategy for building stronger bonds and connections.

How to use it

It is important first of all to appreciate the *barriers* to individuals, teams and organisations asking questions. These barriers can range from fear of what the answer may be to fear of what the answer is known to be; fear of looking stupid for not knowing the answer; fear that the other person may not be able to answer the question and feel stupid; fear that the answer may not be liked, or assuming that everyone already knows the answer, etc. All the main barriers to asking questions revolve around the answer.

On the *wedge of value,* the answer to a question is at the low end; the high end is what is being *communicated* by asking the question. If the focus is on avoiding the risk of asking questions, then these risks will be many, and asking questions will be difficult. If the focus is on establishing the higher value benefits of asking questions, then these benefits will be many, and asking questions becomes easier. (See also **Model 30: The motivation to move model.**)

With an appreciation of *what asking questions demonstrates* there will be more reasons, more confidence for individuals, teams and organisations to look for more opportunities to ask those questions. Asking questions can demonstrate many things: that there is interest, value in the other person or the conversation, enthusiasm, care, a level of importance held in the person or the conversation, appreciation, a level of empathy, thoughtfulness, a high level of engagement, consideration, a connection there, focus, and that they are really being listened to.

Individuals, teams and organisations should always consider *what happens when the questions are not asked.* In some cases, it may be a sharp contrast that implies that there is no interest or care, or that they are not being listened to. In some cases, however, it may not be such a sharp contrast, but it will still put a question mark against how much they are being listened to, or just how much they are cared for, or to what level there is of genuine interest. Whether a sharp contrast, or just a degree of doubt, it is costly not to make the effort to ask questions – even when it can be predicted what the answer will be!

- When in any doubt, ask the question.

- The main emotional barrier to asking questions is the fear of then losing control, yet the person who is asking the questions is the one who is in control, the one who is being influential, the one who is setting the direction and the agenda.

- Some individuals, teams and organisations have become unaccustomed to being asked questions, such has been the drive for answers. For some, being asked questions is a refreshing change of approach which they welcome and enjoy, while for others this can be initially uncomfortable. Providing context as to the reason, intent and value for asking questions is helpful in encouraging them to trust in the coaching process.

- Some of the most valuable questions will not immediately or easily be answered by those with whom you work. It is important for both the coach and the client to be clear with each other that it is fine not to have an immediate answer, as some of the most valuable questions are designed to stimulate thought before reaching a considered conclusion or answer. Sharing this context helps the client avoid feeling stupid, or that they are failing, or letting you down. This context also allows the coach to ask some of the most valuable questions without the fear that the client might not have an answer.

- When asking clients what appears to be a big question, it is important not to hold them too much to their initial answer, as they should be encouraged to take time to give these questions more thought and consideration. This approach also creates and protects the longer term value of the question.

The nine ways to bond with someone

1 **Ask for their story.**

2 **Find out their personal interests and passions.**

3 **Give small, informal tokens or gifts.**

4 **Give tokens or gifts that are of personal value.**

5 **Get involved in shared projects.**

6 **Ask searching questions, and listen.**

7 **Always start with a positive introduction.**

8 **Be authentic; be genuine; be you.**

9 **Engage with their wider network.**

Judge a person more by the questions they ask than the answers they give.

Voltaire

Model 65. The questions to be impressed model

The big picture

Building the bonds and connections that create additional value relies heavily not just on the questions that are asked, or the reasons behind asking those questions, but the manner in which those questions are asked. (See also **Model 50: The what, why and how model.**)

This model was created and developed for coaching in response to the many scenarios where individuals, teams and organisations were setting great questions, but asking them in a way that generated unhelpful, unwanted or negative responses that could pull apart the bonds and connections they wanted to build. This simple and effective model clearly illustrates the two main approaches involved when asking questions: to impress, or to be impressed.

High-performing individuals, teams, organisations and coaches appreciate the importance of asking questions in a manner that helps to bring them closer together, to move their relationship forward, to build stronger bonds and warmer connections. While others may believe that asking the right questions is sufficient for their part, high performers take the time to ask their questions in a way that opens up even greater possibilities, with both parties feeling recognised, respected and confident.

This is very important for coaches to grasp, because even the right question asked in a way that is perceived to be making a point or to impress will immediately put off a client or at least put a little distance between you. (This is not always intentional, so good practice and discipline of approach will make this sub-optimal outcome less likely.) However, even a lesser question that is asked in such a way as to enable the client to impress will serve to encourage the client to engage further with confidence and trust.

When to use it

- To ensure that the positive meaning, intention and value of the question is protected.

- To avoid unnecessary and unhelpful emotions caused by asking questions that feel like a point is being made, or that a judgement has been cast. In these moments, the question is no longer the issue!

- To develop a strategy of using questions to build strong bonds and connections from which to drive high performance.

- To be able to bring individuals, teams and organisations closer together.

Figure 22.2 The questions to be impressed model

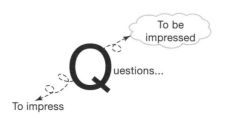

How to use it

There are two *types of questions* that can be asked and each has a *reaction* and an *impact* that naturally follows. There are 'questions to impress' and 'questions to be impressed':

- *Questions to impress* are delivered as statements that are fuelled by judgement but presented as a question, for example: 'What made you think that this would be OK?' This type of question will generate a defensive, passive or aggressive reaction, causing the relationship to become a bit more distant, a bit more difficult than before.

- *Questions to be impressed* are delivered as genuine enquiries that are free from judgement, for example: 'Why did you decide to do this?' This type of question will generate a more open, confident and engaged reaction, causing the relationship to remain as close as it was, or even to bring people that bit closer.

Coaching tips

- To be of influence and value, there must be a strong bond and connection between you and the individual, team or organisation you are working with. Consistently asking questions in a manner to be impressed allows the relationship to develop as it should.

- No matter how unimpressive an answer is, when asking a question to be impressed you can still be impressed by the honesty and frankness of the response.

- You will know instantly if the question you have asked is being perceived as a question to impress: the client will respond as if being challenged, judged or criticised. The client will emotionally, psychologically and even physically move away from the process and you will sense the distance between you expand. Quickly offering to ask the same question in a better manner, to be impressed, will stop the distance growing, and with further questions in this manner the relationship will begin to get closer again, question by question.

- Knowing the answer, or thinking that you know the answer, should never get in the way of asking the question in the right manner. When as a coach you seek to learn and remain fascinated, asking questions to be impressed becomes automatic.

The five habits for building good relationships

1 **Keep building your network; do not go stale.**
2 **Keep communicating; do not go quiet.**

3   Keep sharing your ideas; do not go missing.

4   Keep rewarding your best relationships; do not treat them all the same.

5   Keep introducing and being introduced; do not become an island.

Ignorance is a temporary affliction, remedied only by asking the right questions in the right way.

Colin Wright

Model 66. The satisfaction and loyalty model

The big picture

Considered among the most important indicators of high performance are the combined abilities to generate high levels of both satisfaction and loyalty. When applying this further to the building of bonds and strong connections it can be seen that, without the elements of satisfaction and loyalty, there cannot be bonds built or sustainable connections made.

Satisfaction is defined as an overall attitude or emotional reaction to the difference between what was anticipated and what was received in terms of the delivery of a need, goal or desire. High-performing individuals, teams and organisations do not leave this to chance or wait for satisfaction to grow, or not. High performers ask questions of themselves and their teams that lead to the creation of powerful strategies that drive and measure satisfaction internally and externally.

Loyalty in this context is defined as the likelihood of someone continuing to engage with a specific individual, team, organisation or coach. High performers do not wait to see if others will remain loyal to them; they communicate consistently how important these relationships are in terms of their current and future value, trust and mutual benefit.

This model was designed and developed for coaching in response to the many situations where individuals, teams and organisations were focused on the areas that would not deliver the level of satisfaction and loyalty at the expense of the drivers that could drive the level of satisfaction and loyalty they were aiming for. The model illustrates the three main components and the degree to which they impact on the decision to be satisfied and loyal. This model also identifies the key drivers within the main component that matters most.

Whether focused internally or externally, the model presents the opportunity for individuals, teams and organisations to develop strategies that can drive higher levels of satisfaction and loyalty so that the bonds and connections necessary for great achievement can be created.

For coaches, the aim must be to develop their delivery across the board in terms of quality, innovation and, as a priority, the coaching experience.

Figure 22.3 The satisfaction and loyalty model

When to use it

- To be clear on the components that will contribute to the decision of being satisfied and loyal.
- To ensure that the appropriate level of effort and focus is put into each component, understanding that the overall experience plays such an important part.
- To define and develop a strategy for increasing satisfaction and loyalty.
- To assess the level of quality, innovation and experience that should be aimed for, and what this would look like.
- To ensure that there is focus on each of the five drivers of the experience.

How to use it

There are *three components* that create high levels of satisfaction and loyalty in any relationship: the quality of what is shared or delivered; how innovative what is shared or delivered is; and the overall experience of receiving what has been shared or delivered.

1. The *quality* will be measured in terms of the quality of what has been shared or delivered; this may be the quality of output, of a product, of a service, of the content, of the person involved, etc.

2. The *innovation* will be measured in terms of how different, unique or special what has been shared or delivered is. This may be the spontaneity, how fresh the ideas are, doing new things, going to different places, trying things for the first time, being creative, different offers, being solution focused, etc.

3. The *experience* will be measured in terms of how it feels to receive what is being shared or delivered. Measurement of the experience will be based upon considerations and perceptions of how well they were treated, in terms of reliability and trust, consistency, dependability, convenience and flexibility,

willingness to adapt, personal focus, individual attention, the clear benefits they get, etc.

An *impact assessment* of what makes someone feel satisfied and loyal in a relationship is: quality, less than 25 per cent; innovation, 25 per cent; the experience, greater than 50 per cent. Therefore, unless there is a strategy for developing the experience, it is going to be difficult and unlikely that satisfaction and loyalty will be achieved at any great level, because working purely on being innovative or delivering high quality alone will not be enough.

There are *six drivers of the experience* that need to be developed to complement being of high quality and innovative:

1. **Trust:** Be transparent and deliver promises and commitments.

2. **Consistency:** Always turn up on time and make the experience as relevant and valuable as possible.

3. **Convenience:** Be accessible, flexible and willing to work to the other person's preferences when possible.

4. **Direct benefits:** Personalise and modify the product, service or approach to recognise and create optimal value.

5. **Systematic:** Create and keep to a specific process in terms of frequency and reliability.

6. **Ongoing:** Demonstrate the importance of the relationship by looking at the future value above and beyond any one specific situation, issue or transaction by maintaining regular contact and dialogue.

Coaching tips

- Quality and innovation are important aspects of developing greater satisfaction and loyalty and should not be ignored, neglected or underestimated. However, quality and innovation alone will be disregarded if the experience of receiving what has been shared or delivered is poor.

- If the experience of receiving demonstrates and engenders trust, consistency, convenience, direct benefits, and is systematic and ongoing, then even if the quality is not the best, and not unique, there will still be enough satisfaction and loyalty to be given at least another opportunity.

- Satisfaction and loyalty are such key measures for coaches because the most important indicator will be whether the individual, team or organisation choose to rebook. If clients feel more confident and enabled through the experience of being coached they will be more assured on the quality and level of innovation delivered.

The four quick tips for keeping good relationships

1 Notice what is going on in the client's world.

2 Make time for individual conversations.

3 Find ways to keep in touch regularly.

4 Get organised so that important people remain a priority.

The key is to set realistic expectations, and then not to just meet them, but to exceed them – preferably in unexpected and helpful ways.

Sir Richard Branson

Managing high-performance teams (teamwork and collaboration)

23

[Teamwork and collaboration: Working with others to inspire the achievement of shared goals and win-win solutions.]

Managing high-performance teams is a key attribute of individuals, teams and organisations that achieve successful outcomes and results. They are able to work effectively with others on common tasks that they have created or identified, always taking actions that respect and value the needs and contributions of their teams. Those who deliver value from high-performance teams appreciate the need to create the environment and conditions that inspire and encourage behaviours that support achievement. (See also **Model 26: The conditions for success model.**)

High-performance teams produce their best results when they are empowered to lead; to take the initiative; to own the outcome. Individuals, teams and organisations that manage these teams to an optimal level understand how to inspire and energise them to deliver and take ownership. Communication also plays a large part in the management of high-performing teams because the balance between being directive and consultative needs to be right so that there is a clear outcome, but there is also a high level of involvement and participation involved in the process. Enabling high-performance teams to thrive requires the creation of an environment where there is a clear result to be reached, where trust is always present, where stress and conflict are positively managed, and what they are aiming for is of significant value and meaning now and in the future. These key components ensure that the full capability and capacity of a high-performing team can be realised.

It is often assumed that a coach is only brought in to work with individuals, teams and organisations that are not performing well, are broken, or really need to step up or fix things. Although these can be valid reasons why a coach starts working with people, it is also just as likely to become, or be from the start, a situation where top performers are looking to develop and progress further, and so managing high performers is an important and valuable asset of a coach. Creating an environment for high-performing clients to develop further requires the coach to create the right environment, to ensure that the client leads each session and on each solution, and that the optimal balance of being directive and consultative is maintained throughout.

Model 67. The conditions for collaboration model

The big picture

Collaboration is defined as an approach to working with others to deliver on a task or to achieve shared goals of a scale and complexity that would not be achieved by any other approach or individual endeavours. A collaborative result is defined as all parties achieving their desired outcome without compromise, that is win–win solutions.

This model was applied and developed for coaching in response to the many situations where individuals, teams and organisations were determined to adopt an approach of collaboration, but as the conditions were not aligned, they ended up with a result of compromise or accommodation. This illustration sets out the conditions required for a collaborative approach to succeed because, without these conditions being in place or being developed, lesser outcomes will occur.

Collaboration is considered to be the optimal approach to creating a solution because it can deliver all that an individual, team or organisation seek to achieve, and often more. Success, however, is not just in deciding to be collaborative, it is in being able to create, manage, maintain and protect the conditions by which collaboration remains the most viable approach.

Without these conditions, the alternative options of competing, accommodating, compromising or avoiding become more viable and therefore appropriate.

For coaches to be able to achieve all that they can with the individuals, teams and organisations they work with, it is imperative that they look to develop and maintain

Figure 23.1 The conditions for collaboration model

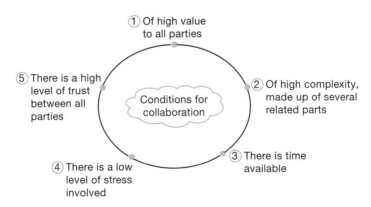

the conditions for collaboration in terms of trust, stress, value, time and scope of complexity.

When to use it

- When setting out the conditions for projects, initiatives or new teams.
- When establishing conditions for success. (See also **Model 26: The conditions for success model.**)
- To create and develop win–win solutions.
- To define and maintain an environment for high-performance teams.
- To get beyond patterns of avoiding, competing, accommodating or compromising.
- To develop a strategy for creating collaborative relationships with willing partners.

How to use it

Firstly, the specific situation and desired outcome must be of *high value* to *all* parties for collaboration to happen. This may require taking single points of the situation or opportunity and projecting them onto a far bigger picture or context.

The situation and desired outcome must be of *high complexity* for it to be of high value to all parties; it must be made up of multiple components and points or seen as the culmination or collective result. When the point of issue or opportunity is seen as being a powerful catalyst for further opportunities in the future, it is easier to foster collaboration.

Collaboration *requires time* due to the necessary level of complexity and value of the desired outcome. Short-term and immediate issues are more likely to result in compromise, accommodation or remain competitive rather than collaborative. This may require projecting some short- or medium-term issues or opportunities onto the longer term view in order to gain the necessary length of view.

Collaboration happens more readily when there is *low emotion and stress* involved in the situation. When there is high stress or emotion, the level of creativity, innovation and the ability to listen are too restricted to enable a collaborative approach. The positive energies of excitement and anticipation, however, are great drivers of collaboration. This may require picking the right time and circumstance to develop a collaborative approach so that a calm and considered decision can be made to collaborate.

It is critical that there is *high trust* between all involved so that a collaborative approach can be successful. If there is a lack of trust between any of the parties involved, it will end up at best in a compromising 'win–lose' outcome or even a 'lose–lose' scenario where the opportunity is being avoided. It can often be the case that more time is needed to build a level of trust before collaboration can be considered, and this can be done by compromising, accommodating or competing considerately for now on individual issues so as to build up a better understanding, a stronger connection and a level of intelligent trust in one another.

- No matter how enthusiastic an individual, team or organisation are to collaborate they still need to have the conditions in place to succeed.

- If one of the parties is not open to one of these conditions, reluctant to look longer term, unwilling to trust, cannot see the other opportunities that could be created, does not see the potential value, etc., then collaboration is not a viable option for now. It is best then to focus on what would be the most effective and appropriate approach. (See also **Model 61: The conflict options model.**)

- Creating the conditions for collaboration may be a simple process for some individuals, teams or organisations because there may only be one or two components that require some work or development. However, creating these conditions can sometimes be a significant project. Be patient and determined; it is always best to break it down into manageable chunks.

- For your credibility, ensure that, as a coach, you practise what you preach and always maintain the conditions for collaboration throughout each session.

The seven habits of high-performing teams

1 **Always view the team as an entity.**

2 **Always be willing to learn from each other.**

3 **Always encourage two-way communication.**

4 **Always avoid unnecessary interference and distraction.**

5 **Always make team members feel valuable.**

6 **Always create ways to recognise and reward achievement.**

7 **Always encourage, support and challenge each other to achieve more.**

Coming together is a beginning; keeping together is progress; working together is success.

Henry Ford

Model 68. The optimal 72 model

The big picture

More than ever before, the issue of managing energy is considered to be the key attribute to maintaining high performance. As many high performers are likely to push themselves and others harder to achieve results and work longer hours, they are also more prone to exhaustion, burnout and breakdowns.

Teams that are pushing too hard and not managing their energy will eventually lose their motivation, be affected by absence and experience higher levels of conflict, blame, cynicism and mistakes. Organisations with high performers that do not manage their energy, in time will suffer from declining levels of engagement, increasing levels of distraction, higher turnover and soaring medical costs.

This model was created and developed as a coaching tool to put into context the desired and sustainable level of energy that delivers optimal results and returns. The model illustrates the range of energy to work from to be optimal as an individual, team or organisation, and the various components that contribute to their energy number, such as their enthusiasm, desire, ideas, motivation or determination. The model also covers the dynamics of how to increase or reduce the energy number to achieve the optimal level.

For a coach, it is vital to appreciate the energy number involved in each coaching session so that it can be managed and influenced towards the optimal level.

When to use it

- To assess the current energy number and mange this to the optimal level.
- To avoid burnout or apathy becoming the expected 'norm' or being seen as acceptable.
- To maintain high-performance energy at all times.
- To ensure that those who are expected to drive have the enthusiasm, desire and energy to lead.
- To help to reduce the energy number of those who risk exhaustion, or to increase the number of those who could do with a bit of a spark or higher engagement.
- To develop a strategy for creating optimal energy across individuals, teams or organisations.

How to use it

Personal energy is made up of the combined emotional, psychological and physical vibrations within:

- The *emotional* number is made up of feelings: anxiety or excitement create a higher vibration than feelings of calmness.

Figure 23.2 The optimal 72 model

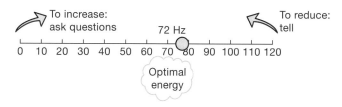

- The *psychological* number is made up of thoughts: ideas and imagination create a higher vibration than meditation.
- The *physical* number is dictated by the current physical condition, namely level of exercise, quality of sleep and diet: physical stress creates a higher vibration than being relaxed.

Being optimal is operating at a level where everything that is put into a situation generates the maximum output and return. This is often referred to as being in 'flow'. On a universal energy level, the optimal number is measured at 72 hertz (Hz) as this is closest to the frequency of vibration for ground-living things and so is in balance with the natural surroundings.

High numbers are hit when this optimal energy level is exceeded. This will be clear when the levels of enthusiasm, ideas and participation are massive in comparison to what is then achieved or delivered. This imbalance and sub-optimal situation where there are lots of input, but low output, is an indication that the energy number is exceeding 72.

Low numbers are hit when the energy number falls significantly below 72. This will be clear when enthusiasm is low, or ideas and participation have to be forced, and even though the output produced may match the level of input, it still achieves and returns less than it could have done if the energy number had been higher.

To *reduce the number* to get to 72 it is important to take some time away from what is being done or discussed: take a break, do something else instead, go for a walk, sleep on it, etc. When there is an awareness of putting so much into something yet getting less in return, it is important also to connect with what is already known and understood rather than get caught up in more and more questions. These approaches allow the energy number to moderate down to 72 where feelings of awareness, calmness and clarity can be found. (See also **Model 54: The spiral of ambiguity model.**)

To *increase the number* to reach 72 it is necessary to introduce fresh energy and input into what is being done or discussed: ask new questions, seek new information, gain a new perspective, utilise fresh ideas from a book, article, magazine or someone else, etc. When there is not enough being contributed to build up a head of steam it is important to adopt an inquisitive and open approach to new perspectives and ideas. These approaches will drive the energy number to increase to an optimal 72 where feelings of being motivated, inspired, alert and clear can be found. (See also **Model 54: The spiral of ambiguity model.**)

For *optimal performance* between two parties, the aim is to reach an energy number of 72 collectively so that both numbers add up to 72 when combined. The person with the 'higher' number in the relationship should be the one who is expected to go and do something next because they will be the most enthusiastic, most committed and have most input. It is important that the person expected to lead does actually end up with the higher number, otherwise there is likely to be little achieved.

The measure of *influence* between two parties is the difference between their two numbers. If one party has 40 and the other 32 then they are pretty close in terms of their enthusiasm, commitment and wanting to input. If, however, one party has 68 and the other 4 then there is clearly one party who is driving this almost completely and with very little input from the other. It is important to decide how much influence is desired or required so that the appropriate numbers can be reached.

To *manage* someone else's number, you either ask questions or provide information. To *increase* someone's number, ask questions; this will invite their ideas, thoughts, participation and contribution, which increases their energy number. To *reduce* someone's number, provide information or tell them things; this will halt their ideas, thoughts, participation and contribution for the moment, which in turn reduces their energy number.

Coaching tips

- As a coach, you will operate to an optimal level when your own energy number is 72. Do all you can personally and professionally to ensure that you can be at your best. Researching and creating new content is likely to raise your energy, while deciding to reconnect and go back to basics is likely to moderate your number.

- In a coaching session, you should first assess the number that your clients bring, and adapt your number from there to maintain as close to 72 as possible.
  — If their number is very high, it is best to just listen and let them talk so that they get it off their chest and reach a number that you can then add to.
  — If their number is very low, you will have to raise the energy with questions, new content or case studies as a way to increase their interest and engagement.

- There are many individuals, teams and organisations operating at the intensity of a high number, so there is immediate benefit for them being able to talk things through with the coach and, in doing so, moderate their number.

- There are also individuals, teams and organisations operating in the slump of a low number, and by being asked questions by their coach they become more focused and energised.

- It is important to remember that clients should always leave the session with the higher number, as they need to be the party committed to doing something as a result of the session and determined to take action. When the coach has the higher number, the sessions become theoretical and lack impact.

- Each coach should figure out how much of an influence they ideally need to have with their clients (32:40, for example); in many cases, the clients will adapt to this as the 'norm'.

- Be aware also that the clients will have a preference regarding the coach's level of influence depending on the situation or issue. There will be some scenarios which the clients will want to do on their own with minimal support, and there will be other scenarios where the close support of the coach is highly appreciated. If unsure, ask the clients.

The four key ingredients of teamwork

1 Focus on the strengths of the team (individual and collective).
2 Commitment to teamwork.
3 Alignment to a common goal.
4 Cumulative results that are measured and published.

Teamwork divides the task and multiplies the success.

Anon

Model 69. The directive and consultative model

The big picture

Communication skills are critical for high-performance teamwork and collaboration to be established, as they will determine the level of cohesion and the strength of relationships. Individuals, teams and organisations that manage high-performance teams effectively ensure that the balance of communication between telling and inviting is in place to set the ground rules from which goals can be best achieved.

This model was created and developed for coaching in response to the many situations where the message was so direct that it was lost, diluted or rejected because the balance of communication was not right. The model also deals with the many scenarios where, due to a lack of direction or an over-eagerness to involve everyone, there is no clear message or decision taken.

Individuals, teams and organisations that communicate expertly with high-performing teams appreciate that the value of their message is best delivered with a combination of direction and consultation that engages those involved, but still comes to the point where a decision is made. They are aware of the pitfalls of being too directive and where they could lose the engagement or interest of the team; they are also aware that if they are too consultative, they may end up going round in circles. They understand also that managing their balance of communication is a continual, flexible and 'live' process that reacts and responds to the mood of the room. Although they will plan and prepare, this is not something that can be set rigidly or in advance; the reaction of their high-performing team will indicate when there is too much telling or inviting going on, and they must be ready to respond and react.

This is also a key model for a coach as it illustrates the need and value for creating a combination of being directive and consultative to gain all the positives without risking the negatives. Effective coaches know how to maintain this optimal balance flexibly in each session they deliver. When a coach is too directive, the engagement with the client is likely to reduce and the coach becomes more of a trainer or mentor. When a coach is too consultative, the direction and focus for the client can be lost and the coach becomes more of a therapist or counsellor. When the balance is optimal, the client can rely upon the coach to be fully engaged, and trust that, when required, the coach will offer sound guidance and direction.

When to use it

- To understand the components of direction and consultation in delivering optimal communication.
- To achieve the optimal balance in all communication for clear direction and positive engagement.
- To capture the positives of being directive and consultative without drifting into the negatives.
- To develop an optimal communication strategy for high-performing teams.

How to use it

The *triangle* in communication signifies the *directive* style where someone stands at the front and tells everyone what the message is. This can also represent formal announcements and emails.

The *circle* signifies the *consultative* style of communication where everyone is gathered round to discuss and share the message. This can also represent meetings, gatherings and group forums.

Each communication style has a list of *pluses and minuses,* as follows:

Triangle (directive)

- *Pluses:* Clear, consistent, quick, shows leadership, focused, strong, etc.
- *Minuses:* One-dimensional, dictated, narrow-minded, detached, not engaging, etc.

Figure 23.3 The directive and consultative model

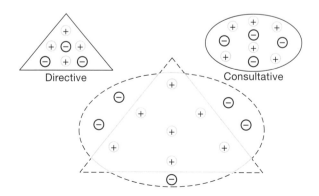

Circle (consultative)

- *Pluses:* Involved, engaging, open to ideas, collaborative, inclusive, etc.
- *Minuses:* Time consuming, lacks direction, open to argument and conflict, lacks decisions, seeks only consensus, etc.

Powerful communication creates the *positive combination* of the pluses of both the *triangle* and *circle* so that there is clear leadership *and* high engagement; that there is an openness to new ideas *and* clear decisions are still made; and that there is a clear and consistent message *built upon* the collective opinion and input from a wider group.

Although all communications should be planned and prepared for whenever possible, there should at least be a degree of a *fluid approach* so that the level of direction and consultation can be adapted based upon the reaction and energy of the audience.

Coaching tips

- As the coach, be aware of the balance in each session you deliver and look for the signals from your clients as to when they need more direction or more consultation to get the balance right for them.

- Some people will have a natural preference or sense of comfort towards being consultative. This will be apparent if they are experiencing too many meetings and conversations without actually making things happen. If they always end up in compromising or seeking consensus before making a decision, this is another sign of being too consultative. (See also **Model 43: The sense of service model.**) By explaining what directive communication looks like, and that this is something to add to their preferred style, not a replacement, they can begin to develop a stronger balance and combination.

- Some people have a natural preference for or a sense of control in being directive. This will be apparent if they are experiencing a lack of engagement or following. If they are having to force issues and decisions, and if they are becoming isolated, having fewer meetings and discussion or creating factions, these are signs of being too directive. (See also **Model 43: The sense of service model.**) By explaining what consultative communication can bring and that it does not mean giving up control, they can begin to develop a stronger balance and combination.

- There are times to be completely directive; if there is a fire in the building, it is best not to gather people round to find out what they think.

- There are also times to be completely consultative, for instance if there are no decisions to be made or if the purpose of the meeting is purely to get people involved and get a sense of the thoughts and feelings of others.

The 10 principles of teamwork

1   Begin with the end in mind; always be clear on where you want to get to.

2   Establish a way of working together as a condition for success.

3   Be clear on, but do not confuse, the results versus the process.

4   Begin with positive assumptions about all team members.

5   Clarify initial roles and responsibilities, then refresh every so often.

6   Ask for opinions and ideas; encourage diversity; listen actively.

7   Keep the ideas process and decision-making process separate.

8   Agree the decision-making process before the decisions are made.

9   Always seek commitment to the decisions made.

10   Learn to deal with each other directly and with positive intent.

Communication is what makes a team strong.

Brian McClennan

24

Leading through change (developing change catalysts)

[
Developing change catalysts: Working with others to initiate, lead or manage change through to a successful outcome.
]

All individuals, teams and organisations have to deal with change. This can be externally driven by a number of factors, such as markets, economic cycles, environmental changes, increased costs, competition issues or new roles. There are also changes that are more internally driven in terms of a desire to improve, a fresh idea, a new outlook or aiming for a new horizon.

Leading through change successfully is dependent upon the ability of individuals, teams and organisations to develop change catalysts so that change can be understood, driven and made to deliver successful outcomes. This involves understanding the drivers of change and having a strategy for overcoming the barriers to that change, mainly fear and resistance. Leaders of change know how to communicate in a way that provides a positive perspective and make sure that they continually provide the context and considerations behind the change. (See also **Model 60: The context–consideration–conclusion model.**)

It is often expected that when an individual, team or organisation work with a coach there will be a visible and measurable change as a result. These anticipated changes may be in the form of new approaches or attitudes, new levels of energy or ambition, improved relationships and effectiveness, and so on. It is important then that coaches understand and accept that a significant part of how they are valued will be determined by their ability to develop change and to develop change catalysts.

Model 70. The overcoming resistance to change model

The big picture

As all individuals, teams and organisations will have to deal with change, and often be expected to develop others to be catalysts of change, being able to overcome the major barrier to change will largely determine their success.

When they are able to identify the drivers to overcome their inner resistance to change, individuals can consistently embrace the changes and improvements that they can make. The main barrier to making change happen is resistance.

This model was adapted for coaching in response to the many situations where change appears necessary and advantageous, yet is being held back or struggling to get started. This effective illustration sets out the straightforward process by which resistance to change can be overcome. Understanding the three components required that, when combined, need to be greater than the level of resistance to change, empowers individuals, teams and organisations to make change happen.

When individuals are dissatisfied enough to become determined to make change happen, rather than just unhappy enough to moan or complain, they can begin to overcome their resistance to that change. When a team has a clear and compelling vision for what change can make happen which is of high value and meaning, rather than the perception of 'change for change's sake', then it can collectively begin to overcome any resistance. And when an organisation is fully committed to doing whatever it takes to make something happen, rather than just having a conditional agreement if need be, then it can begin to eliminate resistance and be free to drive change.

As coaches are often expected to be catalysts of change through their clients, understanding the process to overcome resistance to change is an essential attribute for success.

When to use it

- To understand the key drivers required for change to happen.
- To appreciate the value and power of dissatisfaction, vision and action in making change happen.
- To identify the components that are strong drivers of change, and the components that need to be strengthened and worked on.
- To avoid the moaning, procrastination or inaction that works against making change happen.
- To know that change can be made to happen when the level of resistance is overcome.

How to use it

The first component required to overcome resistance to change is *dissatisfaction* as this is the engine of change. The more powerful the 'engine' of dissatisfaction, the

Figure 24.1 The overcoming resistance to change model

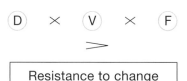

more an individual, team or organisation will be able to drive change. Everything that they have successfully changed first of all started because they were dissatisfied with how things were at that time. But when they have *just* been dissatisfied, they have just been considered to be 'moaners' or 'complainers'.

The second component required is *vision;* this is what 'better' or 'amazing' has to look like for the change to be worthwhile. The clearer and more impactful the desired outcome, the more compelling the reason for change. Everything that individuals, teams or organisations have successfully changed involved their being able to imagine a far better outcome than they currently had. But when they have *just* had a vision but were not yet doing anything to make it happen, they have been considered to be procrastinators.

The final component is the level of commitment to take the *first steps* to make change happen. The more willing and less conditional individuals, teams and organisations are to do what it takes to make the changes they want, the more empowered they will be to drive change. Everything they have successfully changed involved their having to take those initial steps to make things happen. But when they were just keen to do things but lacked the direction of a vision or the motivation of dissatisfaction, they were just considered to be 'busy fools' or 'disruptive', forever running just to stand still.

The level of *resistance* to change will vary depending on the degree and type of change required; there will be some changes that are perceived to be very comfortable and so resistance to these will be low; however, there will be some changes that will challenge the individual, team or organisation's level of comfort, confidence or even what they believe to be true or possible, and in these cases the level of resistance will naturally be high.

To drive the desired changes, the individual, team or organisation must create a *combined solution;* that is, they must be dissatisfied enough *and* have a big enough, compelling enough vision, *and* be determined and committed enough to take those important first steps to overcome their resistance to change. When this combination is greater than the level of resistance, they will create change; when the combination is still less than the level of resistance, change will not happen.

There are occasions when it may be wise to *resist the change* if the level of dissatisfaction, the scale of the vision or the commitment to follow through is insufficient; this may be a sign that this particular change is not worth making for now. The true success of change is measured in the impact and value that it had; it is not measured in how many changes were made.

Coaching tips

- Many clients will have areas that they want to change or improve because they are not happy or satisfied with the current situation. It is likely, though, that they do not yet have enough dissatisfaction actually to make that change. This is one of the most common reasons why individuals, teams and organisations do not make the changes that they could; they learn to live with the situation, or work around it, or accept it. Enhance and expand the level of dissatisfaction by asking what the knock-on effects and consequences are of this issue without diluting with immediate solutions.

- Some clients will have developed a great deal of dissatisfaction but feel trapped in a state of unhappiness or irritation because they cannot yet see what better would look like, or what they can see does not seem to be worth the hassle. Enhance and expand the scale of their vision by asking what their amazing or ideal would look like, and what then would become possible and available to them as a result.

- Most clients engage with a coach because they are keen to take action to make things happen. However, some clients can be very conditional when it comes to doing what they think it will take to make things happen, so they find themselves waiting for things to change, procrastinating, hoping for the ideal moment or an easier time to get started. Encourage and empower by breaking things down into the smallest steps and gain commitment at least to these.

- Always be respectful; when a client does not want to make change happen, then this has to be acceptable, even when you can see what could become possible for the client. This space is likely to allow the client to come to a more positive conclusion in due course. Forcing, even with positive intention, only generates an emotionally negative response. (See also **Model 3: The men v women model.**)

The top three catalysts for change

1 **A performance issue.**
2 **A personal irritation.**
3 **Externally imposed pressure.**

Cause change and lead; accept change and survive; resist change and die.
Ray Norda

Model 71. The 80–16–04 of change model

The big picture

Leading successful change is a continual process for individuals, teams and organisations that seek to improve, develop and grow on an ongoing basis towards great outcomes. Successful leaders of change appreciate that standing still is not an option if they are to make great things happen, so they refuse to rest on the laurels of past performance and results; however, they also respect, appreciate and value the aspects that work well and provide the platform on which successful change and improvement can be built.

This model was created and developed for coaching in response to the many situations where individuals, teams and organisations were forcing through too much change too quickly under the banner of 'transformation', only to end up back where they started, or left with something broken that used to work. The model was also designed to encourage and support those who were resisting and feared making changes because they were looking at everything that needed to be changed.

With an understanding of the successful components of change, where there are parts that will need to stay as they are, parts that may need to be looked at differently and parts that are ready and right for change, individuals, teams and organisations can develop this process into a strategy for successful change. With an appreciation of the relative percentages of each component, change as a process can be viewed in a healthy perspective and context, and then be communicated.

This is a valuable model for coaches to embrace because it serves as a reminder not just to focus on the perceived gaps of a client, but to ensure that what needs to stay the same is also recognised and acknowledged. From this platform, clients will approach change, improvement and growth with greater confidence and security.

When to use it

- To provide context and perspective for the change process.
- To manage successful change.
- To ensure that there is a strong platform on which to build improvement and change.
- To communicate effectively so that change is approached with confidence, belief and security.
- To overcome resistance and manage fear in relation to change.

How to use it

To create successful change, the 80 per cent that must *stay the same* has to be identified: the things that must be protected and kept for now. Identifying all the components that must stay the same (even just for now) provides a solid and established platform upon which change and improvement can built with confidence, belief and security. This important 80 per cent helps to provide perspective for what will be different, and what will be new.

Next, consider the 16 per cent of things involved that must be kept as *the same, but different:* the things that need to be kept, but also need to be looked at in a different way; faster, better, or in another way, etc. These components also help to

Figure 24.2 The 80–16–04 of change model

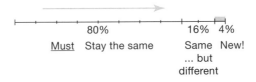

protect confidence and provide assurance while creating a bridge towards what will be new.

The 4 per cent in successful change are the components that will be considered as *new*. These components are the most emotional as they will generate resistance and either fear or excitement (or both), but, in relation to what will remain the same (80 per cent) and what will be the same but a bit different (16 per cent), the dominant emotion will be *confidence*.

This does mean that some things that need to be changed will remain the same for now. Successful change is a *gradual and ongoing* process, so when the 4 per cent 'new' has been achieved it becomes part of the 80 per cent that stays the same and creates capacity for another 4 per cent 'new'. This may create some dissatisfaction in having to put up with something for now that there is a desire to change; this provides a strong engine for change. (See also **Model 70: The overcoming resistance to change model.**)

It is important for individuals, teams and organisations not to confuse 'speed' with 'scale' as this is likely to create resistance to this model. It is a model for *successful transformation,* just 4 per cent at a time. If transformation is required, then by changing 4 per cent each day, there will be 100 per cent changed and consolidated before the end of the month. However, most transformation proves to be sub-optimal, overly disruptive, costly and often even avoided completely because of the fear of spoiling what is good, because it has been approached on a 'full-scale' basis.

Successful change relies heavily on the art and direction of *communication.* The order for successfully communicating change ironically begins with the 80 per cent that must stay the same, then the 16 per cent that will remain the same but looked at differently, and then finally the 4 per cent that will be considered as new. This ensures that the uncertain element (the 4 per cent new) is supported by what is already known and understood (the 80 per cent same and the 16 per cent same, but different). When there is 96 per cent confidence assured and acknowledged, it is easier to deal with the 4 per cent unknown!

Coaching tips

- It is always best to begin with collecting all the attributes, strengths, behaviours, characteristics, approaches and winning strategies that a client already has that must remain and stay the same. This provides the platform for confident change and growth.

- It is then good to explore some of the attributes, strengths, behaviours, strategies and approaches that may need to stay the same for now, but which the client may be asked to look at a bit differently, more strategically, with more consideration or from a different perspective. Having already established the platform for confident change and growth, the client will believe that this can be done successfully.

- With a client who has recognised and acknowledged all that should stay the same and some areas to look at differently, the client will be in a more secure, confident and assured place from which to consider some approaches, models or methods that will be new.

The eight steps to transformation

1. Establish a sense of urgency.
2. Put together a powerful group.
3. Create a compelling vision.
4. Communicate the vision.
5. Engage and empower people to take action.
6. Create, reward and encourage quick wins.
7. Consolidate changes made: create more change and new projects.
8. Embed new ways of 'how things are done'.

Embrace each challenge as an opportunity for transformation.

Bernie S. Siegel

Model 72. The ceiling–floor–furniture model

The big picture

Individuals, teams and organisations that successfully lead through change are able to influence and shape the change they want to happen; they do not just manage changes that are forced upon them, but set their agenda for change and create strategies to accomplish their desired outcomes through change.

This model was created and developed for coaching in response to the many situations where considered strategies, solutions and initiatives for change were challenged or disregarded or rejected because of how they were positioned. The model explains the process and value of building viable options that provide a framework for making choices and decisions easier. This practical illustration has proven to be consistently successful in enabling individuals, teams and organisations to get the decisions and buy-in to the strategies they prefer.

This process provides a framework from which the quality is demonstrated by presenting viable options: an ambitious, a cautious and a considered proposal, giving the confidence and assurance to make an informed and calculated choice. (See also **Model 60: The context–consideration–conclusion model.**)

For coaches, this model helps to provide clients with a framework that puts their preferences into perspective. When they perceive what they want to do, have or be as ambitious, they are always likely either to settle for less, or not to ask or reach for what they want. However, when they see what they want as being a 'considered' option by exploring what ambition really looks like, they approach what they want to have, do or be with a greater sense of confidence, assurance and worthiness.

Figure 24.3 The ceiling–floor–furniture model

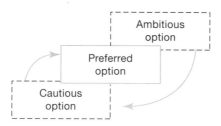

When to use it

- To influence decision making and negotiations.
- To promote or sell a product, service, idea or initiative.
- To reposition aims and desires so as to foster a greater sense of confidence, assurance and worthiness.
- To provide powerful context and perspective to get everyone onto the same page.

How to use it

The most successful approach to influencing change is to *create a framework* so that the context and consideration behind the preferred conclusion is shared, understood and appreciated. Psychologically, the greatest sense of confidence and assurance is found at the centre of the frame, just as there is by aiming for the middle rather than the edge, or landing in the middle of the runway. These steps show how to build this framework.

Firstly, a viable and credible presentation of the *preferred option* must be drawn up. This must be clear on all the things that would need to happen or be committed to by all the parties involved – all investments, assumptions and timescales required to make this option work. This will become the considered option, the 'furniture'.

Next, a viable and credible option that is *seven degrees more ambitious* than the preferred option must be drawn up. Again, this must be clear on all the things that would need to happen or be committed to by all the parties involved – all investments, assumptions and timescales required to make this option work. This will become the ambitious option, the 'ceiling'.

Finally, a viable and credible option that is *seven degrees more cautious* than the preferred option must be drawn up. Again, this must be clear on all the things that would need to happen or be committed to by all the parties involved – all investments, assumptions and timescales required to make this option work. This will become the cautious option, the 'floor'.

To be truly effective and influential in making change happen, the process must be *communicated in order,* that is the 'ceiling', then the 'floor' and finally the 'furni-ture'. By doing so this will create a psychological framework that demonstrates the preferred option in the centre as 'considered' by showing what 'ambitious' and 'cau-tious' look like, and what it would take to make these options work. If started from the 'floor' (cautious), there is a risk that the 'ceiling' option would then look ridiculous and be disregarded. If this were to happen, the framework would be only cautious and considered and the likely choice would be at the centre between these two points. If the 'furniture' is presented first, then there is a risk that this is being put forward as the only viable option, so others will then project their own frame onto it; an ambitious audience will see the proposal as cautious, while a cautious audience will fear that it is too ambitious.

This process is best presented in the order of . . .

1. The ambitious option (people think it is exciting to sit on the 'ceiling', but then feel at risk).
2. The cautious option (people find it easy to sit on the 'floor' but then feel vulnerable).
3. The considered option (people like to sit on the 'furniture' because it feels comfortable and right).

Coaching tips

- When clients are convinced of their preferred option, they can be reluctant to create alternative viable options; however, this is good for their development because it helps secure their preferred option and increases their conviction in what they are asking for as it becomes the considered choice. Be patient and supportive.
- Each option needs to be credible and viable or it is not a genuine option.
- This approach helps people make confident choices because they are given a clear framework and process, and they are then able to make their choice with confidence. (See also **Model 3: The men v women model.**)

The seven habits of a change catalyst

1 **They notice things.**
2 **They notice and explore alternatives.**
3 **They notice in real time.**
4 **They explore different choices in real time.**
5 **They make different choices.**
6 **They enjoy the new change made.**
7 **They notice more opportunities to change.**

What you do makes a difference, and you have to decide what kind of difference you want to make.

Jane Goodall

Index